Chesapeake Bay

EXPLORER'S GUIDE

Chesapeake Bay

EXPLORER'S GUIDE

Natural History, Plants, and Wildlife

DR. DAVID MALMQUIST

Globe
Pequot

Guilford, Connecticut

To a person uninstructed in natural history, his country or seaside
stroll is a walk through a gallery filled with wonderful works of
art, nine-tenths of which have their faces turned to the wall.

—Thomas Henry Huxley

Globe
Pequot

An imprint of The Rowman & Littlefield Publishing Group, Inc.
4501 Forbes Blvd., Ste. 200
Lanham, MD 20706
www.rowman.com

Distributed by NATIONAL BOOK NETWORK

British Library Cataloguing in Publication Information available

Library of Congress Cataloging-in-Publication Data available

Names: Malmquist, David, 1959– author.
Title: Chesapeake Bay explorer's guide : natural history, plants, and wildlife / Dr. David
  Malmquist.
Description: Guilford, Connecticut : Globe Pequot, 2021. | Includes bibliographical references
  and index. | Summary: "A reference guide for visitors to the famous estuary, whether they're
  lying on a beach, walking through marshes, or driving over one of the many bridges that span
  the Bay. This guide provides a concise history of how the Bay was formed, and brief entries
  with full-color images and easy-to-read descriptions on the flora, fauna, and man-made
  artifacts found in the Bay"—Provided by publisher.
Identifiers: LCCN 2020058573 (print) | LCCN 2020058574 (ebook) | ISBN
  9781493051335 (paperback) | ISBN 9781493051342 (epub)
Subjects: LCSH: Chesapeake Bay Region (Md. and Va.)—Description and travel. | Natural
  history—Chesapeake Bay Region (Md. and Va.)—Guidebooks. | Plants—Chesapeake Bay
  Region (Md. and Va.)—Guidebooks. | Animals—Chesapeake Bay Region (Md. and Va.)—
  Guidebooks.
Classification: LCC F187.C5 M34 2021 (print) | LCC F187.C5 (ebook) | DDC
  917.55/1804—dc23
LC record available at https://lccn.loc.gov/2020058573
LC ebook record available at https://lccn.loc.gov/2020058574

♾™ The paper used in this publication meets the minimum requirements of American National
Standard for Information Sciences—Permanence of Paper for Printed Library Materials, ANSI/
NISO Z39.48-1992.

CONTENTS

HOW TO USE THIS GUIDE

"THE CHESAPEAKE BAY." AS WITH A MULTIFACETED JEWEL, its visage depends on your viewpoint. For watermen, the Bay is a briny larder full of crabs and oysters. For beachgoers, it's a refreshing dip from a sandy shore. For mariners, a highway for commerce and military might. For hikers, a tree-framed peek at winding tidal creeks. For anglers, a line cast from a bow or pier. For paddlers, a spreading wake and the croak of startled herons. For travelers, a vista unfolding from a bridge or shoreline parkway. For scientists, one of the world's best-studied estuaries. For history buffs, the home of Powhatan and the cradle of the United States.

This guidebook touches on all these facets of the Chesapeake, but to avoid the heft that might otherwise keep it on a dusty shelf, it focuses on a handful of common Bay experiences:

- A Bridge over Tunneled Waters
- Boating and Fishing on the Bay
- A Day at the Beach
- A Marsh Paddle
- A Walk through Woods and Fields
- Down to the Docks
- Hunting for Fossils

The first section describes where to go and how to get there. Discover how your trip—whether by bridge, tunnel, ferry, or parkway—can be part of your adventure.

The subsequent sections each begin with a map showing selected locations, whether boat ramps, public beaches, marsh launches, hiking trails, urban waterfronts, or fossil-hunting sites. An overview then describes the ecology of the particular landscape or Bay-scape—its "terroir" or "merroir," to borrow from the world of wine and oysters. Consult these before your outing to help choose and appreciate your destination.

Each overview is followed by this guidebook's bread and butter: one- to two-page descriptions of selected plants, animals, and artifacts from the Chesapeake region. Space constraints allow us to highlight only a small fraction of the Bay's almost 4,000 aquatic species; we therefore focus on common ones you're likely to encounter (plus a few rarities just too cool to pass up). For some groups with a number of species that look broadly alike (e.g., cordgrasses, drums and croakers, gulls, sharks) or play similar ecological roles (e.g., butterflies, dragonflies, sea turtles, wading birds), we've combined the entries into a single spread. Consult these single-species and grouped descriptions while afield to help identify organisms and objects.

See an animal or plant that's not described in a particular section, or want to learn more about one that is? Visit its "Deeper Dive" segment. These point to external resources for those seeking a comprehensive taxonomic guide to a specific group of plants or animals, or a more detailed guide to a particular setting.

If you're interested in the Bay's past, visit the Yesterbay sidebars that highlight selected episodes of the Bay's rich history. These are sprinkled throughout the book, like the historical markers that grace roadsides throughout the Bay watershed.

The penultimate chapter—"People of the Chesapeake"—focuses on Native Americans and African Americans, two groups whose contributions to Bay culture have often been overlooked. For each, there's a brief synopsis of past and current contributions, plus a map showing locations of historical and current interest, from Virginia's planned Werowocomoco National Park and Baltimore's American Indian Center to the Harriet Tubman Underground Railroad National Historical Park in Maryland and the Arthur Ashe monument in Richmond.

For those thinking ahead, the book concludes with "The Once and Future Bay," a glimpse at what the Bay might look like in 2050—a future, of course, that all depends on how we treat the Chesapeake and its watershed today.

But first, let's examine the broad forces—the confluence of geology, geography, oceanography, and climate—that conspire to shape and enliven Bay waters and lands.

INTRODUCTION

A Bay Primer

GEOLOGICAL HISTORY

THE MODERN CHESAPEAKE BEGAN to take shape about 12,000 years ago, as the ice sheets blanketing northern North America and Eurasia started to melt. These had frozen so much water on land that sea level was more than 300 feet lower than now, and the mid-Atlantic coastal

Fossil mastodon teeth show that Ice Age creatures roamed what is now the Bay floor.

plain was 50 miles wider. Carving this gently sloping plain was a network of branched valleys. Most prominent were those of the ancestral Susquehanna River and its major tributaries—today's James, York, Rappahannock, Potomac, Pocomoke, Patuxent, Patapsco, Nanticoke, Choptank, Chester, Gunpowder, and Elk Rivers.

As the latest ice age waned and ice sheets poured ever more meltwater into the ocean, rising seas incessantly crept into this coastal landscape. The seawater followed the preexisting watercourses, nosing upstream into the valley of the Susquehanna and its tributaries. Around 8,000 years ago, the water brimmed out of these valleys and quickly flooded across the flatter areas between to fill the rough outline of today's Bay. The ultimate outcome of this geologically rapid flooding is the fractal intricacy of the Chesapeake Bay shoreline, with its countless bays, creeks, coves, havens, inlets, necks, peninsulas, and points.

SIZE AND DEPTH

Chesapeake Bay: It can seem as big as an ocean, but it's as shallow as a lake. This simple statement goes a long way to explaining the Bay's historic bounty—and its modern bane.

YESTERBAY

In Bays of Yore . . .

Remarkably, today's Chesapeake is just the latest in a series of earlier bays, each the result of a peak in the flood and ebb of sea level on geologic time scales. Global geologic evidence points to at least twelve ice ages during the last 2.5 million years, each lasting from 40,000 to 100,000 years and separated by shorter gaps. More localized evidence—from sediment cores and geologic mapping in the Bay watershed—shows that during the three warmest "interglacials," as ice sheets melted, sea levels peaked, and coastlines flooded, a unique "Chesapeake" occupied the mid-Atlantic landscape, each with its own fractal beauty.

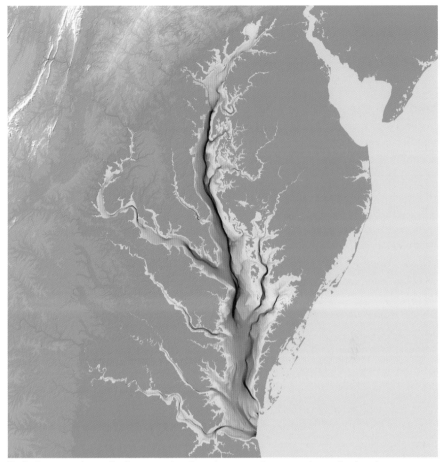

The Bay's origin as a drowned landscape is apparent beneath its waves, where ancestral river valleys form deep-water channels used by modern vessels to reach Baltimore and other harbors.

Areas like Chesapeake Bay where a river meets an indented sea are called estuaries. A good way to appreciate the size of the Bay estuary is from a kayak. If you crossed at its widest point, between the Potomac River mouth and the Saxis Wildlife Management Area on Virginia's Eastern Shore, it would be a 30-mile paddle. If you started near the Bay mouth in Virginia Beach, you'd have to travel almost 200 miles north to reach the Bay's head, where the Susquehanna River enters near Havre de Grace, Maryland.

Look out from many places on the Bay's 14,415-mile shoreline—longer than the US West Coast—and you'll be hard-pressed to see the other side, even on a clear day. All told, the Bay's many-fingered expanse covers 4,480 square miles and holds more than 18 trillion gallons of water. That's enough to fill 27 million Olympic swimming pools and provide every human with 2,500 gallons.

But to some extent, all these superlatives are just surficial bluster, for Chesapeake Bay is remarkably shallow, with an average depth of only 21 feet. A 6-foot beachgoer could wade through more than 1,000 square miles of the Bay—about a quarter of its

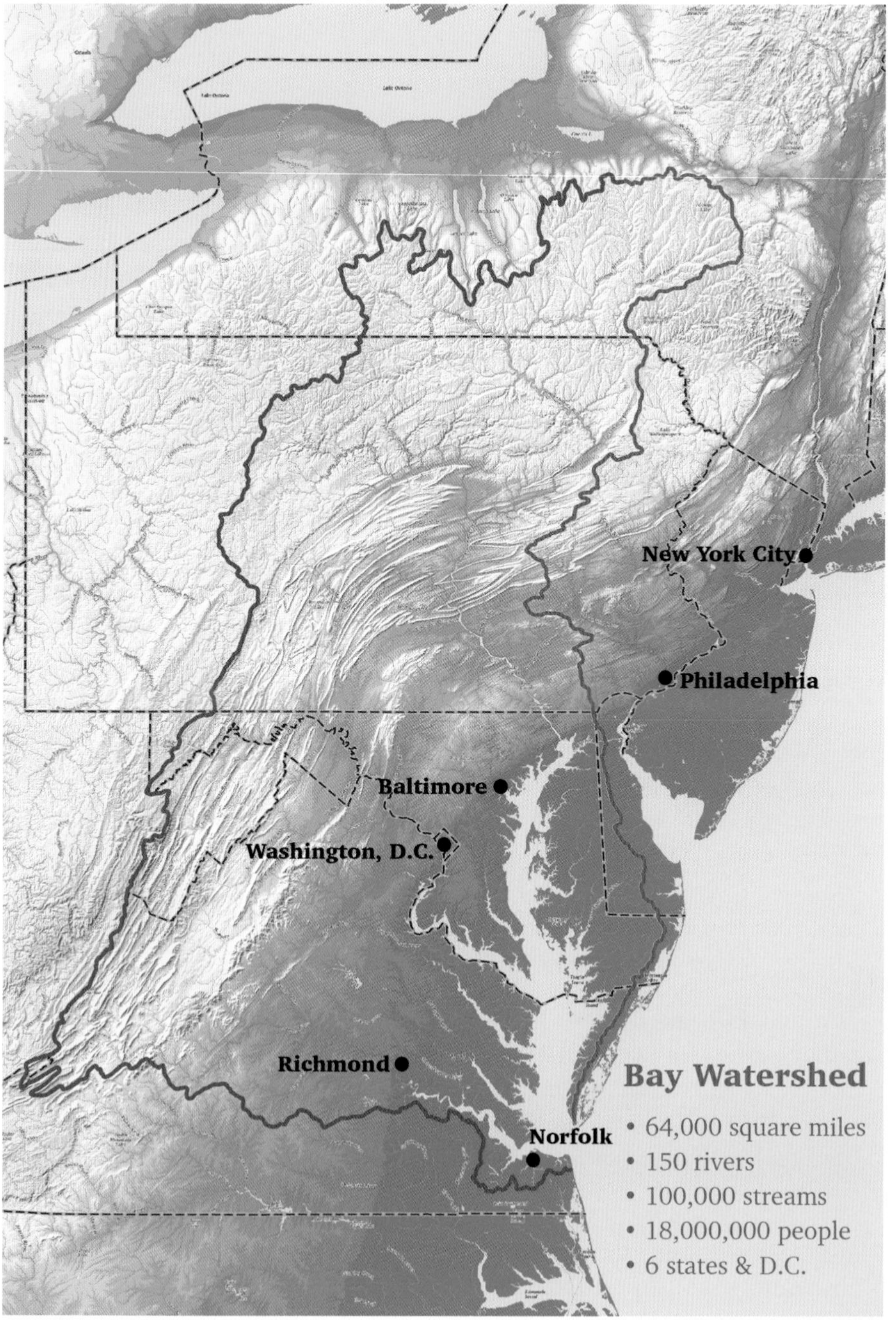

New York City●

●Philadelphia

Baltimore ●

Washington, D.C. ●

Richmond ●

Norfolk
●

Bay Watershed

- 64,000 square miles
- 150 rivers
- 100,000 streams
- 18,000,000 people
- 6 states & D.C.

area—and never wet their sunhat. If we could shrink the Bay to the length of an Olympic pool, it would, on average, be shallower than a dime. At this scale, even its deepest point, the 174-foot "Hole" southeast of Annapolis, would only be as thick as two stacked nickels.

YESTERBAY

It All Started with a Big Bang

To fully understand the birth of the Chesapeake Bay, you'll have to wind your clock back 35 million years. Imagine it's a clear summer morning and you're standing on the mid-Atlantic shore near present-day Richmond. Behind you to the west, a dripping subtropical forest climbs the flanks of the Appalachians; before you, an expanse of rippled blue stretches east across salty waters teeming with corals, clams, and sharks.

As you watch the sun rise over this idyllic scene, a second burst of light appears in the sky. Moments later, your world disappears in an incandescent flash as a 3-mile-wide meteorite slams into the shallow waters of the continental shelf. The impact vaporizes the seawater and crustal rocks, creates a towering tsunami, and sprays tiny droplets of molten rock in all directions. What's left when the chaos subsides is a dimpled rebound crater that quickly fills with water and rubble. As the millennia pass, sediments bury the crater, leaving only a slight depression as evidence of what lies below.

Discovered only in the 1990s, the Chesapeake Bay impact crater takes its name from the bay it ultimately helped shape. First revealed while drilling for water and oil, the belowground crater is about 50 miles across and bounded by a series of concentric faults. Within is a jumble of rocks called breccia and super-salty water that bedevils local communities searching for municipal groundwater supplies.

Not coincidentally, the crater lies directly beneath the bay mouth, where the depression the meteorite left behind drew the waters of the ancestral Susquehanna, York, and James Rivers. The sharp northeastern turn in the lower course of the James and York shows where these rivers met the crater edge and pivoted into its shallow indentation. Following the last ice age, the valleys of these rivers were filled with seawater as rising seas once again flooded the seaward portion of Virginia's continental shelf.

Without this ancient impact, there would be no Chesapeake Bay!

Moreover, like estuaries around the world, the Bay will on a geologic timescale grow ever shallower as river-borne sediments settle out in its relatively still waters. But on the shorter timescale of human habitation, there's an opposite concern. We'll look at sea-level rise and increased coastal flooding in the last chapter, when we envision how the Bay might look in the globally warmed world of 2050.

BOUNTY AND BANE

One benefit of the Bay's shallowness is that sunlight could at least historically reach large areas of its bed, where underwater grasses and seaweeds transformed that solar energy into a cornucopia of vegetable matter. This "primary production"—accompanied by a sprinkling of free-floating algal cells and a serving of detritus from the decay of nearby marsh grasses—supported a rich food web in which energy flowed up through snails, crabs, oysters, and other invertebrates to small fishes, bigger fishes, and sharks; seabirds and fish hawks; dolphins; and even the occasional whale or manatee.

When a snail takes a bite of a seagrass blade—when any animal eats a plant—what it's really eating is an entrée of carbon and hydrogen with a side of nitrogen and phosphorous, all cooked up through photosynthesis. In the shallow, sunlit waters of the pre-colonial Chesapeake, the flow of these elements was in balance as they cycled from the water and bay-floor sediments into plants, then animals, and then through decomposers back into water, sand, and mud.

The Bay's once-clear waters abounded with sun-loving eelgrass.

Today, with more than 18 million people in the Bay watershed, humans have tipped the scales. A flood of nitrogen from fertilizers, wastewater, and car exhaust has overwhelmed the Bay's natural cycles, fueling blooms of single-celled, floating algae that shade sun-loving seagrasses while alive and suck oxygen from bottom waters when they die and decay.

An algal bloom colors Bay waters.

Erosion of soils laid bare by farming and development further shade seagrasses while suspended in Bay waters, and can bury oysters and other bottom-dwellers when they settle to the bay floor. Smothered by silt and stricken by overharvest and introduced diseases, the Chesapeake's once-fabled oyster populations are but a shell of their historical abundance. The masses of algae they once filtered for food now add to the Bay's murkiness, shading seagrasses even further. In a final blow, the loss of seagrasses and their roots allows waves to kick up yet more sediment, in an increasingly cloudy feedback loop.

The Bay's shallowness compounds all the problems that people bring. In coastal areas with deeper, more open waters, nitrogen and other pollutants can sink out or be whisked away by currents. But in the shallow, restricted waters of the Bay, they linger. On average, pollutants suspended in Bay waters stay there for six months before being carried out to sea by the estuary's circulation and tides.

SALINITY

Chesapeake Bay is an estuary, an inlet where a river or rivers meet the sea. One of an estuary's most characteristic features is its wide range of salinity, from the salty seawater near its mouth to the freshwater of its tributaries and the brackish waters between. This salinity gradient provides habitat for a wide variety of plants and animals, one reason estuaries are some of the world's most diverse ecosystems. The Bay alone supports nearly 4,000 species of plants and animals. Salinity's effect on the distribution of organisms is particularly noticeable in Bay marshes, as shown in the "A Marsh Paddle" chapter.

Salinity also changes with weather and seasons. In wet years and during winter and spring, increased runoff pushes freshwater farther downstream and into the Bay. In times of drought and summer's evaporative heat, salt water moves in the opposite direction. Hurricanes can force salt water into normally freshwater habitats through storm surge, or send torrents of freshwater seaward through heavy inland rains. Any and all these scenarios can harm plants and animals adapted to a particular salinity range.

TIDES AND CURRENTS

Tides and currents matter to Bay visitors because they dictate the best times to visit the beach, fish, and safely swim and boat. How water moves into and through the Bay is also an important field of research given efforts to predict and manage the transport and accumulation of pollutants and sediments, the development of low-oxygen "dead zones," and the movement of native and introduced species. Indeed, because of these and other concerns, the Bay is the international poster child for the study of estuarine circulation.

Chesapeake Bay experiences two high tides and two low tides each day. Friction damps Bay tides from about 3 feet near the Bay mouth to about a foot mid-Bay; the tides increase again to about 2 feet at the Bay's head due to its narrowing and rebound of the tidal current. Tides also tend to be more pronounced on the Bay's eastern shore due to its proximity to the Bay's main channel (the drowned course of the ancestral

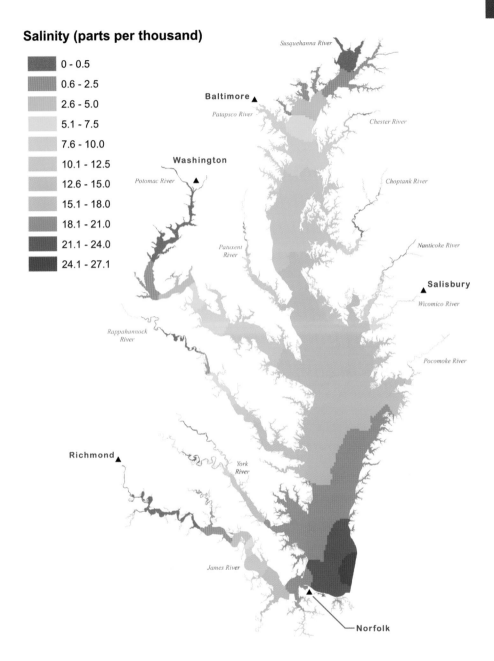

Salinity (parts per thousand)

- 0 - 0.5
- 0.6 - 2.5
- 2.6 - 5.0
- 5.1 - 7.5
- 7.6 - 10.0
- 10.1 - 12.5
- 12.6 - 15.0
- 15.1 - 18.0
- 18.1 - 21.0
- 21.1 - 24.0
- 24.1 - 27.1

Susquehanna River

Baltimore ▲

Patapsco River

Chester River

Washington

Potomac River ▲

Choptank River

Patuxent River

Nanticoke River

Salisbury ▲

Wicomico River

Rappahannock River

Pocomoke River

Richmond ▲

York River

James River

▲

——— Norfolk

Susquehanna River). This allows tidal currents to move with less friction than felt by those in the shallower waters of the western shore.

But the tides don't just move in and out. Tidal currents combine with freshwater input and Earth's rotation to drive the Bay's water in a circular pattern. We can best understand this circulation by starting with the Susquehanna River, which contributes almost half the Bay's freshwater. Because freshwater is less dense than salt, the Susquehanna's inflow

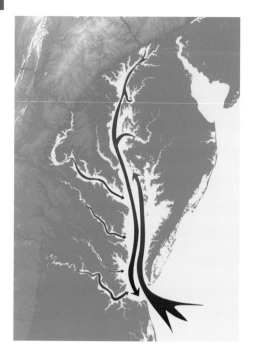

forms a surface layer that floats down-Bay. This is countered by a salty, tidally driven bottom current moving up-Bay. The Earth's rotation—as it does with Northern Hemisphere hurricanes—deflects the northward-flowing bottom current to the right, or east, and the southward-flowing surface current to the left, or west. The end result is a giant, counterclockwise eddy of Bay waters. This eddy is enhanced by freshwater influx from the Bay's other major tributaries—the Potomac, James, Rappahannock, and York Rivers—which all enter along the western shore, adding strength to its southward-flowing current.

Yet nature is never this simple. The Bay's grand, counterclockwise circulation is disrupted by wind, shoals, and friction between its upper and lower layers. These disruptions are key to Bay health, as they promote mixing of oxygen from the air and surface waters into the bottom layer, which can otherwise lose much or all of its oxygen due to the decay of algae that have sunk after blooming at the sunlit surface. Without the vertical mixing brought by winds and turbulence, the Bay's deep waters can quickly develop into low-oxygen dead zones, particularly during summer. These zones stress fish like striped bass by forcing them out of their deep, cold-water refugia and into shallower, warmer waters. Attached and slow-moving animals aren't so lucky—as the name implies, dead-zone conditions can kill them outright.

WEATHER AND CLIMATE

Although we focus here on the temperate, Tidewater climate of the Bay, the Chesapeake is also affected by weather events and climatic conditions throughout its 64,000-square-mile watershed. Events in seemingly far-off places—a cloudburst in the Blue Ridge of Virginia or Maryland, spring snowmelt in the Allegheny Highlands of Pennsylvania and New York—can significantly impact Bay waters.

Stretching 200 miles from north to south, Chesapeake Bay feels significant differences in temperature, particularly during winter. The average annual January high and low temperatures in Aberdeen, Maryland, near the Bay's northern end, are 41°F and 26°F. The values for Norfolk, Virginia, at the Bay's southern end, are 48°F and 33°F. Baltimore, about two-thirds up the Bay, averages 203 days between the last spring frost and the first fall frost; in Norfolk, the frost-free season averages 259 days, eight weeks longer.

The Bay's weather and climate also vary longitudinally, with temperatures along the Bay's east side moderated in both winter and summer by the relatively warm waters of the Atlantic Ocean and Gulf Stream. Average annual highs and lows in Cape Charles, near the Bay mouth on Virginia's Eastern Shore, are 66.9°F and 50.8°F. For Williamsburg, Virginia, at the same latitude near the Bay's western shore, the values are 68.3°F and 48.9°F. Petersburg, which is farther south but inland from the moderating effect of ocean and Bay waters, has average annual highs and lows that are spread even further apart at 70.2°F and 47.1°F.

Precipitation is relatively even throughout the Chesapeake Bay region at between 40 and 45 inches per year, with a slight uptick in summer due to thunderstorms. Boaters and beachgoers should note that these are most likely to occur around 4:00 p.m. Snowfall averages 0–5 inches near the Bay mouth to 20–40 inches at its head.

The Bay's shallow waters heat and cool much more quickly than the deeper waters of the ocean. Indeed, the Chesapeake has one of the widest temperature ranges of any waterbody on Earth, with summer water temperatures as high as 86°F and wintertime lows at or just above freezing. Tributary temperatures can be even higher. In 2019, scientists recorded a high of 93.7°F in the Potomac River following a twelve-day heat wave.

Historically, the Bay's northern reaches iced over fairly regularly, but global warming has made this much less frequent. The Bay's last major ice-over was in the winter of 1976–77, when Maryland's Bay waters were completely ice covered and Smith Island on the Virginia-Maryland border was surrounded by ice for nine straight weeks. Southern portions of the Bay, though typically much milder, have also experienced completely ice-covered tributaries.

We'll peek at predicted changes in Bay weather and climate in the last chapter, when we envision what living in the Chesapeake region might be like in the globally warmed world of 2050.

A Bridge OVER
Tunneled Waters

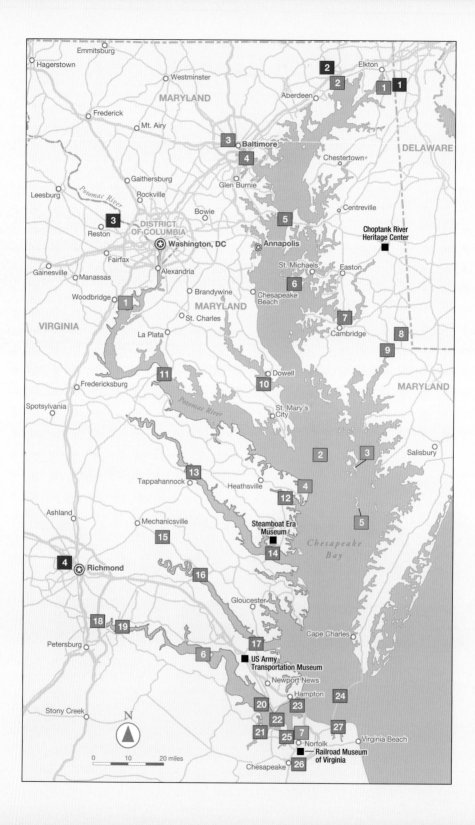

A Bridge over Tunneled Waters

Here we list some of the many bridges and tunnels that enliven driving within the Bay region, along with a number of both historic and active canals and ferries. We also show museums that focus on the fascinating history of transportation across, around, over, and under the Bay.

BRIDGES

1. Chesapeake City Bridge (C&D Canal)
2. Susquehanna River Bridges
   a. Millard E. Tydings Memorial Bridge
   b. Susquehanna River RR Bridge
   c. Thomas J. Hatem Memorial Bridge
3. B&O Railroad Carrolton Viaduct
4. Francis Scott Key Bridge (Patapsco)
5. Chesapeake Bay Bridge
6. Knapps Narrows Draw Bridge
7. Choptank River Bridge
8. Sharptown Bridge (Nanticoke)
9. Nanticoke River Bridge
10. Governor Thomas Johnson Bridge (Patuxent)
11. Harry W. Nice Memorial Bridge (Potomac)
12. Tipers Swing Bridge (Great Wicomico)
13. Downing Bridge (Rappahannock)
14. Robert O. Norris Jr. Bridge (Rappahannock)
15. Walkerton Bridge (Mattaponi)
16. West Point
    a. Pamunkey River Bridge
    b. Mattaponi River Bridge
17. Coleman Memorial Bridge (York)
18. Varina-Enon Bridge (James)
19. Benjamin Harrison Memorial Bridge (James)
20. James River Bridge
21. Nansemond River Bridge
22. Monitor-Merrimac Bridge-Tunnel (James)
23. Hampton Roads Bridge Tunnel
24. Chesapeake Bay Bridge-Tunnel
25. Norfolk Bridges
    a. Berkley Bridge
    b. Downtown Tunnel
    c. Elizabeth River Bridge
    d. Midtown Tunnel
    e. Jordan Bridge
26. High Rise Bridge (Elizabeth)
27. Lesner Bridge (Lynnhaven)

CANALS

1. Chesapeake and Delaware Canal
2. Susquehanna and Tidewater Canal
3. Chesapeake & Ohio Canal National Historical Park
4. James River and Kanawha Canal

FERRIES

1. King's Highway Ferry (Historic)
2. Point Lookout–Smith Island Ferry
3. Smith Island–Crisfield Ferry
4. Sunnybank Ferry
5. Tangier–Onancock Ferry
6. Jamestown–Scotland Ferry
7. Waterside ferries

MUSEUMS

1. Choptank River Heritage Center
2. Steamboat Era Museum
3. US Army Transportation Museum
4. Railroad Museum of Virginia

Dec. 12th, Wednesday. Hard frost. Left Fredericksburg at nine, A.M. Reached . . . Occoguon at half-past five. . . . The five miles beyond Dumfries employed nearly two hours. Roads indescribable.

—John Randolph of Roanoke, 1821

DRIVING ON PAVED ROADS—something we take for granted with more than 100,000 miles in Virginia and Maryland alone—can easily mask the challenges long faced by Chesapeake travelers, and the historic preference for water routes.

YESTERBAY

DOG Street

Duke of Gloucester Street—Colonial Williamsburg's main thoroughfare— provides a striking example of how the Bay landscape has influenced transportation. This 1783 map shows how "DOG" Street closely follows the subtle ridgeline that separates the headwaters of creeks flowing south to the James River or north to the York, thus allowing travelers to avoid ravines. Transportation arteries throughout the Chesapeake watershed, from back roads to interstate highways, likewise follow these relatively level divides along the Bay's many tributary necks.

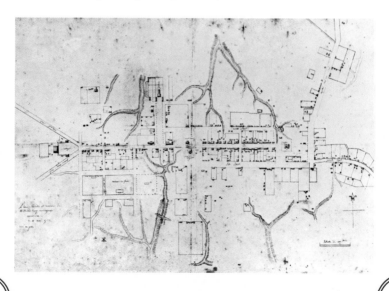

Native Americans traversed the Chesapeake region mostly by paddle, as foot travel was challenged by the forested landscape and the absence of domesticated pack animals (North America's horses and most of its large ruminants had gone extinct at the end of the last ice age). Indeed, their place-names reflect a landscape understood and named from the vantage of a dugout canoe, emphasizing the water's edge, marsh plants, and wetland settings.

They did, however, travel by land. As park and schoolyard paths show, pedestrians habitually take the shortcut while avoiding both steep hills and muddy hollows. Generations of Bay Indians did the same, slowly but surely etching trails that followed the path of least resistance across the landscape. Echoes of these Algonquian footpaths persist across the Bay watershed in routes such as I-64 in Virginia and US 40 in Maryland.

The Jamestown colonists reintroduced horses to the Bay region, allowing land transport of relatively heavy loads. They also introduced oxen, but the scarcity of roads smooth and wide enough for wagons meant that waterways remained the preferred means for transporting goods throughout the 1600s and 1700s. Three of every four seventeenth-century historic sites are within 1,000 feet of the shore.

Likewise, Thomas Jefferson's 1787 *Notes on the State of Virginia* devotes a dozen pages to rivers and transport, but only a single paragraph to roads. As late as the 1930s, a resident of Almondsville on the York River noted that he was more familiar with Baltimore (130 miles away) than Richmond (40 miles distant), as the former was accessible via steamship and the latter only by road.

The amphibious history of transportation in the Chesapeake region—early water travel slowly shifting onto land—remains clearly legible in today's network of ferries, bridges, tunnels, and roads. An observant traveler can thus travel backward in time while moving forward to explore all the beauty and adventure the Bay area continues to offer. Read on to learn more.

ROADS

The King's Highway, a 1,300-mile post road built between 1650 and 1735 to unite the American colonies, was the earliest major land route through the Bay watershed. It had various names along the way, including the Potomac Trail, the Great Coastal Road, and the Virginia Path. Today it lives on in segments of I-95, US 1 in Maryland, and US 17 in Virginia. You can explore the route online, using an interactive map from the National Washington-Rochambeau Revolutionary Route Association, Inc., at w3r-us.org.

Roadbuilding in the Bay region began in earnest only after the War of 1812, when the British blockade of Chesapeake and Delaware Bays exposed the inability of the young American nation to move troops and artillery across the landscape with any speed. With only a meager tax base, early road construction relied on private turnpikes, which travelers financed through tolls collected at occasional barriers. These used a rotating horizontal pole similar to the turnstiles now used in subways. (Showing that human nature has changed little since colonial times, turnpikes quickly gave rise to

YESTERBAY

The Fall Line

The "fall line" marks a natural geographic hiccup in the Bay's transportation networks. Here, where the flat-lying sediments of the Atlantic coastal plain meet the bedrock and rolling hills of the Piedmont, falls and rapids block upstream river travel and require goods to be shifted from cargo vessels to oxcarts and other forms of land transport. This naturally led colonists to establish port cities at the fall line of each of the Bay's major tributaries: Petersburg, Virginia, on the Appomattox River; Richmond on the James; Fredericksburg, Virginia, on the Rappahannock; Washington, DC, on the Potomac; Laurel, Maryland, on the Patuxent; Baltimore on the Patapsco; Havre de Grace, Maryland, on the Susquehanna; and Elkton, Maryland, on the Elk. I-95 closely follows the trail that originally connected these commercial centers. A marker on the grounds of the National Museum of the Marine Corps just off I-95 near Occoquan, Virginia, marks the ruts of the original road.

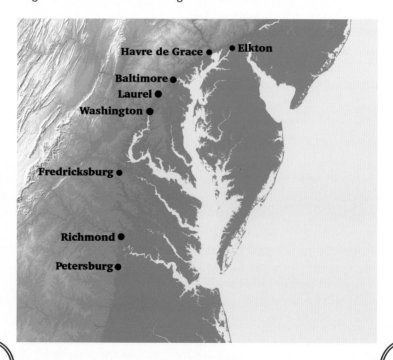

American and French forces traveled the King's Highway to and from the Siege at Yorktown during the Revolutionary War.

"shunpikes," detours built to avoid paying the toll.) Several of today's Bay highways—VA 236, US 50 in Maryland, and US 30 in Pennsylvania—began as turnpikes, and some effectively remain so in the form of E-ZPass gantries.

Today the Chesapeake is completely surrounded by four-lane highways and a dense network of secondary roads, a development that has led to unprecedented mobility (at least outside of rush hour), but also contributes significantly to the urban sprawl and nutrient pollution that bedevils the health of Bay waters. Learn more about these issues in chapters "A Walk through Woods and Fields" and "The Once and Future Bay."

Toll gate on Winchester Pike, Virginia, 1864.

CANALS

By the 1780s, as the new American nation began expanding inland past the fall line, private companies began to "improve" natural waterways via canal building. The ultimate goal was to connect Bay tributaries with the Delaware, Ohio, and Mississippi Rivers, creating inland water highways from the mid-Atlantic to New Orleans.

Though quickly supplanted by railroads, these canals represent remarkable feats of engineering. Several remain at least partly preserved: the Susquehanna and Tidewater Canal between Havre de Grace and Wrightsville, Pennsylvania; the Chesapeake & Ohio Canal National Historical Park along the Potomac River; and Canal Walk in Richmond, the downstream terminus of the James

Fall-line rapids, like these on the James River in Richmond, led to the founding of cargo ports on Bay tributaries.

River and Kanawha Canal pioneered by George Washington. Its towpath now forms the bed for much of the CSX Railway. Still in service is the Chesapeake and Delaware Canal, which significantly shortens the water route between the two bays.

Passenger and cargo boats on the James River and Kanawha Canal in Richmond, Virginia, 1865.

Above: The Susquehanna and Tidewater Canal ran between Havre de Grace, Maryland, and Wrightsville, Pennsylvania. Below: Begun in 1804, the Chesapeake and Delaware Canal shortens the water route between Philadelphia and Baltimore by nearly 300 miles.

STEAMSHIPS AND FERRIES

Steamships provided a popular alternative to overland travel through the 1800s and surprisingly far into the 1900s, until supplanted by bridges. Steamships were faster and more comfortable than the era's poor roads, and they freed sail passengers from the whims of wind. At the height of the steamship era in the early 1900s, more than 20 steamship lines and 500 steamships traveled the Bay, with hubs in Baltimore and Norfolk.

With advances in technology, wooden sidewheel steamships gave way to diesel- and propeller-driven iron and steel ferries for passengers, then cars. Ferries provided the primary connection between eastern and western Maryland until 1952, when the Chesapeake Bay Bridge opened. Ferries were also the main link between Virginia's Hampton Roads and the Eastern Shore until the 1964 opening of the Chesapeake Bay Bridge-Tunnel.

Despite plying Chesapeake waters for nearly 150 years (1813–1962), not a single Bay steamship remains intact. But those looking to enjoy the ferry experience do have options. A passenger ferry runs seasonally to Smith Island, Maryland, from either Crisfield or Point Lookout; another runs seasonally to Tangier Island, Virginia, from either Reedville on the Northern Neck or Onancock on the Eastern Shore.

The Steamboat Era Museum in Irvington, Virginia, offers exhibits, artifacts, ship models, and oral histories. It is also restoring the pilothouse and quarters from the *Potomac*, built in 1894 to transport passengers between Baltimore and Potomac River

The York River ferry at Gloucester Point, Virginia operated until the opening of the Coleman Bridge in 1952.

Steamer Louisiana
Now running between Baltimore & Fort Monroe

This Civil War–era sketch shows the steamer *Louisiana*, which ran between Baltimore and Fort Monroe.

ports. The Choptank River Heritage Center in Denton, Maryland, housed in a replica of an 1883 building at the historic Joppa Wharf, replicates a steamship agent's office and passenger waiting room.

Car ferries carry tourists and commuters across the James River between Jamestown and Suffolk, Virginia.

RAILROADS

Railroads made their first appearance in the United States along the Bay when, in 1828, construction of the Baltimore & Ohio (B&O) Railroad began in Baltimore, then the nation's second-largest city. The Carrollton Viaduct, completed in 1829, still carries B&O trains over Gwynns Falls Creek, a tributary of the Patapsco River. Named for Charles Carroll, the last living signer of the Declaration of Independence, it was the first American stone masonry bridge built for railroad use.

Long Bridge across Antietam Creek was one of the longest on the B&O Railroad, at 400 feet. Built in 1869, it was the only timber trestle bridge in Maryland. It was unfortunately demolished in 1978.

By 1852, the B&O had connected Chesapeake Bay with the Ohio River, and other railways were carrying goods and passengers throughout the Bay watershed, including lines between Richmond and Alexandria, Virginia; Baltimore and Elkton, Maryland; and Portsmouth, Virginia, and Roanoke Rapids, North Carolina.

The Carrollton Viaduct.

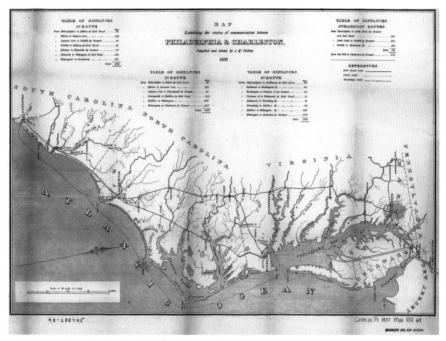

This 1837 map shows the path of railroad lines and steamship routes.

Railroads remained the primary means of passenger transportation throughout the Bay area until the modern interstate era commenced following World War II. Some lines continue to carry passengers today, with Amtrak's Northeast Regional trains an increasingly popular means of exploring the Chesapeake Bay watershed.

The Bay watershed also remains a major freight corridor. The Chesapeake and Ohio (now CSX) Railway is the main route for bringing West Virginia coal to Newport News, as well as Midwestern and Canadian crude oil to terminals in Baltimore (see the "Down to the Docks" chapter).

A CSX train carries coal to the docks at Newport News.

BRIDGES

With scores of major tributaries, more than 100,000 feeder streams, and a highly mobile human population, today's Bay watershed is a land of bridges.

Crossings of smaller streams are typically low, trestle-like structures with pretty views of a marsh or swamp. Some use drawbridges for passage of fishing and pleasure boats. A charming example is the 42-foot-wide Knapps Narrows drawbridge, which connects Tilghman Island to the rest of Maryland. The current structure dates to 1998; the original 1934 bridge now marks the entrance to the Chesapeake Bay Maritime Museum in nearby St. Michaels.

The Bay also features many swing bridges. The Coleman Bridge opens to allow military vessels to sail up the York River to the nearby Naval Weapons Station. It is the largest double-swing-span bridge in the United States and second largest in the world.

The Bay's static bridges are immense, as the need to allow for passage of large commercial and naval vessels requires considerable "headroom." The height and narrowness of these spans give many motorists "white knuckles"; the Bay Bridge between Annapolis and Kent Island is one of the world's scariest according to *Travel and Leisure* magazine, with travelers passing 186 feet above the water. Other daunting spans are shown on the map at the beginning of this chapter.

Knapps Narrows is the busiest drawbridge in the US, with more than 10,000 openings a year.

Top: The Chesapeake Bay Bridge reaches the height of an 18-story building.
Bottom: The Coleman Bridge.

BRIDGE-TUNNELS

Some of today's ships are so tall that constructing a bridge high enough to allow their passage would be too costly. Bridge-tunnels allow for passage of these immense vessels, including the USS *Gerald R. Ford* and other Nimitz-class aircraft carriers homeported at Naval Station Norfolk, which reach almost 250 feet above the water.

One must-do for visitors is a drive across the Bay mouth via the Chesapeake Bay Bridge-Tunnel, named "One of the Seven Engineering Wonders of the Modern World" shortly after its 1964 completion. The 23-mile-long structure features more than 12 miles of trestle, two 1-mile tunnels, two bridges, nearly 2 miles of causeway, and four man-made islands. The 3.5-mile Hampton Roads Bridge Tunnel offers a shorter version. To accommodate both increasing traffic and the deep draft of modern ships—37 feet for aircraft carriers and almost 50 feet for the latest "ultramax" container vessels—these tunnels have to be wide and deep. The newest addition to the CBBT—a parallel two-lane tunnel for northbound cars and trucks scheduled for completion in 2022—will have an outer diameter of 42 feet and a maximum depth of 134 feet below the surface.

Science fiction writer and futurist Arthur C. Clarke famously said, "Any sufficiently advanced technology is indistinguishable from magic." If Native Americans and English colonists were to time-travel 400 years forward and 130 feet below the bay floor into a car moving through a tunnel at 55 miles per hour while a 1,200-foot-long container vessel cruised overhead at 18 knots, they would certainly consider it magic. It's a magical experience for today's traveler as well and shouldn't be missed.

The USS *George Washington* sails by Fort Monroe in lower Chesapeake Bay.

The Chesapeake Bay Bridge Tunnel or CBBT.

A DEEPER DIVE

Dickon, C. *Images of America: Chesapeake Bay Steamers* (Charleston, SC: Arcadia Publishing, 2006). 127 pp.

Guy, C. "Bridge Gets New Home." *Baltimore Sun* (1998). DOI: www.baltimore sun.com/news/bs-xpm-1998-10-08-1998281112-story.html.

Haugen, J. "Exploring the Oldest Road in the USA—The King's Highway." *Explore!* (2017). https://explore.globalcreations.com/theblog/featured/ exploring-the-kings-highway.

Kavanagh, M., et al. "Maryland's Historical Markers" (2014). https://mht .maryland.gov/historicalmarkers/Introduction.aspx.

The National Washington-Rochambeau Revolutionary Route Association, Inc. "Explore the Trail with an Interactive Map" (2020). https://w3r-us.org.

Virginia Department of Historic Resources. "Historical Highway Markers" (2020). www.dhr.virginia.gov/highway-markers.

Voisin, S. L. "A Bridge's Ups and Downs." *Washington Post* (2012). www.washingtonpost.com/local/a-bridges-ups-and-downs/2012/07/26/ gJQAB6hUAX_gallery.html.

Boating AND Fishing
ON THE Bay

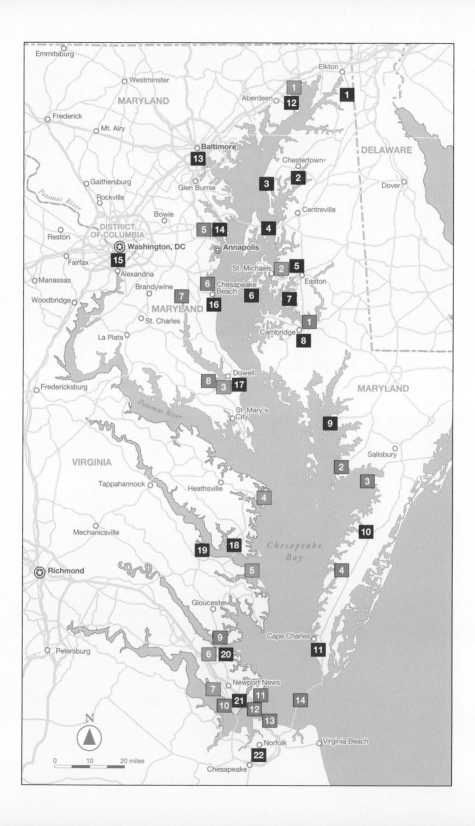

Boating and Fishing on the Bay

The Chesapeake offers a wealth of opportunities to launch and berth your boat, and to fish from a boat or a pier. Smaller marinas are distributed around the Bay shoreline. Here we highlight some sites with a larger marina or several smaller marinas within a relatively concentrated area. We also show museums that focus on the history of Bay boating and fishing.

MARINA DISTRICTS

1. Chesapeake City, Maryland
2. Chestertown, Maryland
3. Rock Hall, Maryland
4. Kent Island, Maryland
5. Saint Michaels, Maryland
6. Tilghman Island, Maryland
7. Oxford, Maryland
8. Cambridge, Maryland
9. Deal Island, Maryland
10. Onancock, Virginia
11. Cape Charles, Virginia
12. Havre de Grace, Maryland
13. Baltimore, Maryland
14. Annapolis, Maryland
15. Washington, DC
16. Chesapeake Beach, Maryland
17. Solomons Island, Maryland
18. Irvington, Virginia
19. Urbanna, Virginia
20. Yorktown, Virginia
21. Hampton, Virginia
22. Norfolk, Virginia

FISHING PIERS (FP)

1. Bill Burton FPs—4,847 feet (N) and 2,860 feet (S)
2. Crisfield Town FP—200 feet
3. Saxis FP—200 feet
4. Morley's Wharf FP—150 feet
5. Jonas & Anne Green Park FP—250 ft
6. North Beach FP—560 feet
7. Kings Landing Park FP—200 feet
8. Pepper Langley FP (Solomons)—400 feet
9. Gloucester Point FP—350 feet
10. James River FP—1,250 feet
11. Buckroe FP—700 feet
12. Engineers FP—190 feet
13. Ocean View FP—200 feet
14. Sea Gull FP—650 feet

MUSEUMS

1. The Havre de Grace Maritime Museum
2. Chesapeake Bay Maritime Museum
3. Calvert Marine Museum
4. Reedville Fishermen's Museum
5. Deltaville Maritime Museum
6. Watermen's Museum
7. The Mariners' Museum and Park

THE CHESAPEAKE BAY HAS LONG been a remarkable place where boats of every imaginable type and size rub gunnels—where watermen aboard a 40-foot "deadrise" workboat hoist their crab pots as a 1,200-foot container ship passes by to harbor, or a family on a 24-foot powerboat bobs in the wake of an aircraft carrier. Here we explore the history and status of the workboats, fishing gear, and recreational vessels used by Chesapeake mariners and describe the animals and plants most likely to be encountered while enjoying the Bay's open waters. To learn about larger commercial and military vessels, see the "Down to the Docks" chapter.

The historical development of Chesapeake Bay watercraft and fishing gear was steered by the types of marine life that inhabit the Bay, as well as the nature of Bay waters—generally shallow, and typically rougher near the Atlantic mouth in Virginia and calmer in Maryland's more protected upstream reaches. What follows thus ebbs and flows between blue crabs and boat types, herring and haul seiners, oysters and oystermen, Virginia "Guineamen," and Kent Islanders of Maryland.

YESTERBAY

Watermen

The term "watermen" might be unfamiliar to those new to the Chesapeake. This collective term describes the men (and growing number of women) who make a living harvesting the Bay's aquatic resources. It includes oystermen, crabbers, fishers, trappers (of beavers and muskrats), and hunters (waterfowl). As working the water requires no ownership of farmland, it was one of the few professions open to African Americans before and after the Civil War, and thus has a rich history of contributions by free and enslaved Blacks. The term dates as far back as the eleventh century in England, where it was originally used to describe ferrymen who carried passengers across the Thames within the city of London. The Company of Watermen and Lightermen still exists as a London City guild. (Lightermen transferred goods between ships and shore aboard flat-bottomed barges called lighters.) The term's use to describe a person who makes their living by harvesting marine life seems to be unique to the Chesapeake Bay.

FROM LOG CANOES TO DEADRISE WORKBOATS

Native Americans were the first to navigate Bay waters, using log canoes to transport goods and harvest the Chesapeake's bounty. English colonists were quick to adopt the fishing techniques and watercraft honed by countless generations of Bay Indians, and later added their own innovations as technology progressed. Echoes of the Algonquian canoe persist in traditional Chesapeake Bay bugeyes, skiffs, and skipjacks. These vessels—along with the modern deadrise workboat—share the shallow draft that made Indian canoes so well suited to Bay travel, but add a wider, more stable beam and other improvements. Examples of these boats can still be seen on the Bay and in exhibits at the Chesapeake Bay Maritime Museum in St. Michaels, Maryland; Calvert Marine Museum in Solomons, Maryland; Havre de Grace Maritime Museum in Maryland; Deltaville Maritime Museum in Virginia; the Mariners' Museum in Newport News, Virginia; and the Reedville Fishermen's Museum in Virginia. Log canoe races take place each summer in and around St. Michaels.

A 1590 engraving by Theodor de Bry offers evidence of Native fishing methods and prey. Based on a 1585 John White painting, it depicts Indians using spears, dip nets, weirs, pound nets, and an onboard fire to attract fish at night. Prey includes fishes (sharks, sturgeon, American eels, shad, catfish, burrfish, skates or rays, jacks), oysters, crustaceans (horseshoe crab, blue crab, ghost crab), and turtles (loggerhead and diamondback terrapin), along with pelicans and waterfowl.

FROM BARQUES TO BYTES

Native Europeans also brought larger, more seaworthy vessels to the Bay. The Jamestown colonists arrived in three barques, with the largest—the *Susan Constant*—stretching 116 feet from tip to stern, a keel length of 55 feet, and carrying seventy-one passengers. Re-creations of this vessel and its sister ships *Godspeed* and *Discovery* are moored at the Jamestown Settlement pier for visitors to board and explore. Another early barque was the 132-foot *Ark*, which together with the smaller *Dove* brought the earliest English colonists to Maryland. A replica of the *Dove* is on display in Historic St. Mary's City, Maryland's colonial capital.

More suited to navigating the Chesapeake's shallow waters was the "shallop," a shallow-drafted vessel with three to four pairs of oars and one or two small, removable masts and sails. Capt. John Smith and crew used this type of boat for their 1608 circumnavigations of the Bay. Modern adventurers can trace these journeys by exploring the Captain John Smith Chesapeake National Historic Trail, a network of water routes along the Bay's mainstem and major tributaries.

As they did with the Indian canoe, watermen and later recreational boaters adapted these European sailing vessels for use in Chesapeake Bay, enhancing them with

The Jamestown Settlement offers tours of replicas of the three barques that brought the first English colonists to Jamestown: the *Susan Constant, Godspeed,* and *Discovery.*

innovations of their own making and features imported from vessels developed in Africa, New England, and elsewhere. This lineage sails on in the schooners, sloops, and rams long used to fish or traverse the Bay; in the oceangoing Baltimore clippers; and in the sleek lines of today's recreational and racing sailboats. Sailing remains a popular Bay activity, with more than 4,000 sail-powered vessels in Virginia in 2012 and more than 30,000 in Maryland.

Emergence of the American leisure class following World War II fueled a new age of recreational boating and fishing on the Chesapeake. Today, the Bay's most common watercraft are fiberglass and aluminum powerboats, from smaller skiffs and V-hulls to larger cabin cruisers and yachts. Statistics from 2019 show 221,629 powerboats in Virginia and 169,891 in Maryland. Almost three-quarters of Maryland's boats are small enough to be trailered, with a similar percentage likely in Virginia. These vessels and related activities are a major economic force, with the same studies estimating total boating-related expenditures of $3.5 billion in both Virginia and Maryland in 2019. Recreational fishing also generates major economic activity, with Bay anglers spending roughly $500 million each year chasing striped bass alone. Kayaking is also of growing popularity (see the chapter "A Marsh Paddle").

Advances in vessel design and materials have been matched by innovations in the technology needed to navigate the Bay's countless bays, creeks, coves, and shoals. Early Europeans relied on compasses, astrolabes, sextants, sounding lines, and paper charts. Today's mariners are blessed with sonar and the Global Positioning System (GPS), which bring the marvels of the digital age directly aboard their vessels. Despite these advancements, the Bay remains a dangerous place for the inexperienced, unprepared, or unlucky, with missing and drowned boaters a continuing, tragic occurrence. The nonprofit BoatUS Foundation offers online and in-person classes in vessel use and safety tailored to both Maryland and Virginia waters.

WORKING WATERFRONTS AND RECREATIONAL MARINAS

The rise of recreational boating also powered the growth of numerous recreational marinas around the Bay—more than 300, according to the latest issue of the *Waterway Guide*. These can be wonderful places to view the rich variety of Bay watercraft and mariners, grab a seafood meal, or hire a fishing charter.

Unfortunately, the rise of these marinas and other high-end waterfront developments has also put a squeeze on working waterfronts, with their noise and often-pungent smells. Efforts are under way in both Maryland and Virginia to sustain these commercial and cultural hubs for current and future generations of Bay residents and seafood lovers. Good spots for visiting Maryland's working waterfronts include Crisfield, Deal Island, Kent Island, Tilghman Island, and West River. Virginia sites include Aberdeen Creek in Gloucester County, the Ampro Shipyard in Weems, the town of Deltaville, L. D. Amory & Company in Hampton, Tangier Island, and the facilities at Willis Wharf.

A working waterfront.

Plants

UNDERWATER GRASSES

They go by many names—submerged (or submersed) aquatic vegetation (SAV), underwater grasses, seagrasses, bay grasses. No matter what they're called, they're incredibly important to Bay health. They provide food and nursery habitat for many marine species, absorb nutrients, reduce erosion, enhance water clarity, and add oxygen to the water. Sadly, many species are also under threat in the Bay and worldwide due to nutrient pollution, propeller scarring, and warming temperatures. What they are not is micro algae (see "Harmful Algal Blooms," p. 31), macroalgae (see "Sea Lettuce," p. 282), or marsh grass (see "Cordgrasses," p. 148). Underwater grasses combine elements of all these groups in an evolutionary masterpiece—complex, rooted plants that grow and flower while fully immersed in water.

All told, the Chesapeake watershed is home to more than twenty SAV species, with the greatest diversity in freshwater. Here are the seven species most common in the Bay's brackish and salty habitats. For full treatment of Bay SAV, consult the references in "A Deeper Dive."

1. Eelgrass (*Zostera marina*)

The Bay's only true seagrass, and most common species in its lower, high-salinity waters. Has strap-like blades that grow to 4 feet long and approximately ¼ inch wide, rising from a stout rhizome at intervals of approximately 1 inch. Provides habitat for blue crabs and seahorses. A cool-water species that dies back during summer's heat, its continued presence in the Bay is threatened by rising temperatures.

2. Widgeon grass (*Ruppia maritima*)

Wide salinity tolerance allows it to grow throughout the Chesapeake; co-occurs with eelgrass in lower Bay waters. Threadlike leaves (1–4 inches long, $^1/_{32}$ inch wide) alternate along thin, branching stems, which grow erect during summer flowering but creep along bottom in other seasons. A key food source for waterfowl.

3. Wild Celery (*Vallisneria americana*)

Prefers the lower-salinity waters of the middle and upper Bay. Blades resemble eelgrass but are wider (to ½ inch), bisected by a light green stripe, and rise from the rhizome in a clump. An important food for waterfowl, including scaups and the canvasback duck, as reflected in the latter's species name: *Aythya valisineria*.

4. Hydrilla (*Hydrilla verticillata*)

A non-native first seen in Bay waters in 1982. Forms dense mats that can impede boat traffic and fishing. Prefers freshwater but tolerates low salinity. Freely branching stems bear whorls of 3 to 5 toothed leaves.

5. Redhead-grass (*Potamogeton perfoliatus*)

Inhabits fresh and brackish Bay waters in calm areas with gentle currents. Easy to recognize by its flat, oval leaves—often wavy like potato chips—but foliage varies greatly with depth. A key food source for waterfowl, including redhead ducks.

6. Sago Pondweed (*Stuckenia pectinata*)

Widespread in the Bay's fresh to brackish waters. Tolerant of waves and currents due to long rhizomes and runners. Slender, highly branched stems bear bushy clusters of threadlike, pointed leaves that fan out at water's surface. A valuable food source for waterfowl and shorebirds. Provides habitat for fish and invertebrates.

7. Eurasian Watermilfoil (*Myriophyllum spicatum*)

An introduced invasive that choked large areas of the Bay from the 1950s to 1970s. Now somewhat under control due to disease and harvesting. Prefers freshwater of sluggish streams and other calm areas. Often the first SAV species to appear in spring. Long stems (to 9 feet) bear feathery leaves arranged in whorls of 4 or 5. May form very dense mats on the surface, with emergent flower spikes developing in late summer. Though non-native, it does provide good cover for crabs, invertebrates, and fish. A favorite haunt of largemouth bass.

HARMFUL ALGAL BLOOMS

"Algae" is an informal term for a diverse group of aquatic, mostly single-celled, plant-like organisms. They underlie almost all marine food webs, transforming the energy of sunlight into sustenance for other sea life. There are two main types: dinoflagellates and diatoms. Dinoflagellates have a whiplike tail, or flagellum, they use to move through the water. Some are armored with flexible shells, while others are "naked." Diatoms have rigid, glassy shells made of silica. Having no flagella, they move with currents.

But sometimes, even good algae go bad. Now often fueled by runoff of excess nutrients from land, they can bloom in numbers great enough to clog gills, abrade the skin of fish and other organisms, and lead to low-oxygen "dead zones" when they die, sink, and decay. Algal blooms were traditionally called "red tides," though they can also stain the water brown, green, and other hues depend-

An algal bloom lights up Bay waters.

ing on the predominant species. Even though composed of microscopic organisms, algal blooms can grow large and dense enough to be visible from space. Some species can also produce their own light, offering spectacular displays of nighttime bioluminescence.

Some algal species release toxins, which can reach levels sufficient to harm filter-feeders such as mussels and oysters, as well as any larger creatures, including people, that eat the toxins concentrated in the shellfish tissues. The number and duration of these "harmful algal blooms," or "HABs," are increasing in many areas around the world, fueled by input from fertilizers, wastewater treatment plants, auto exhaust, and other human sources.

State agencies in both Maryland and Virginia monitor algal activity in Bay waters and post warning signs if toxin concentrations reach worrisome levels. Before heading to the Bay, particularly in late summer, when blooms usually peak, you may want to visit the Department of Health website for Virginia or Maryland for any online warnings or to submit your own observations of discolored or smelly water. For information on safely consuming shellfish, visit the website of Virginia's Division of Shellfish Safety or Maryland's Fish and Shellfish Monitoring program.

Here we briefly describe four of the Bay's most common HAB organisms. For more details on these and other species, consult the references in "A Deeper Dive."

Alexandrium monilatum

An "armored" dinoflagellate that may form chains of up to eighty cells. Easily visible when it produces a red tide or lights up the water at night, this organism produces toxins associated with death of oyster and fish larvae. First conclusively detected in the Bay in 2007, it occurs in moderately salty waters and blooms in late summer or when the water exceeds 77°F.

Chattonella subsalsa

Cell bears two whiplike flagella. Common bloom species that forms "brown tides," which have been associated with fish kills and can produce toxins that threaten human health. Tolerates a wide range of salinities within the Bay. Usually blooms between April and June in water temperatures between 60°F and 77°F.

Margalefidinium polykrikoides

Long known as *Cochlodinium polykrikoides* but renamed in 2017 based on new genetic evidence. An "unarmored" dinoflagellate that forms chains of two to eight cells. Prolonged exposure to this alga can harm larval fish and shellfish. Blooms almost annually during July and August in the lower Bay, in moderate to high salinity waters and when water temperatures reach 80°F to 86°F. Not known to impact human health.

Dinophysis

A group of "armored" dinoflagellates with traits of both plants and animals, harvesting sunlight via photosynthesis but also harpooning prey. Different species produce toxins that can accumulate in oysters and clams to cause diarrhetic shellfish poisoning in people. Long a problem for growers elsewhere in the world, the first closure of a US shellfish harvest due to *Dinophysis* occurred in 2008. Ecology and potential impacts in Chesapeake Bay remain poorly known, with sightings observed in May and June under moderate salinities.

An algal bloom discolors Bay waters.

Wildlife

Bay Anchovy (*Anchoa mitchilli*)

DESCRIPTION

Two to 4 inches long. A silvery, slender fish whose translucent body has a silvery stripe running from gills to tail. Body and fins outlined by numerous tiny black dots. Resembles herring in its single dorsal fin and forked tail, but distinguished by its mouth, which is much larger, hinges farther back, and opens below the snout.

HABITAT & ECOLOGY

The most abundant fish in the Chesapeake, with schools resident year-round throughout the Bay and its tributaries. Most common in shallow tidal areas with muddy bottoms and brackish waters, though it can tolerate a wide range of salinities. Feeds by filtering zooplankton, particularly copepods, moving through the water with mouth open like a

tiny whale. To paraphrase Dixon Lanier Merritt: "Behold if you will the Bay anchovy, its mouth is so large that the plankton can't flee." A key food source for larger predators such as bluefish, weakfish, striped bass, and seabirds. Also the target of a bait fishery.

DID YOU KNOW?

On average, adult bay anchovies produce more than 100 trillion eggs per year, with more than 50 billion juveniles surviving to sustain the Bay population. The Bay's other anchovy, the striped anchovy *Anchoa hepsetus*, is less abundant.

Copepods (*Acartia tonsa*)

These small shrimplike crustaceans are the most abundant multicellular animals on Earth. More than seventy species inhabit the Bay; here we describe one of the most common.

DESCRIPTION

Just picture Sheldon J. Plankton from *SpongeBob SquarePants* and you'll have the basic idea. About the size of a rice grain, copepods can be seen darting to and fro if you look very closely at most any bucket of Bay water. Most striking feature is a pair of antennae about as long as the segmented body. Has a single central eye like a miniature cyclops and a 2-pronged tail.

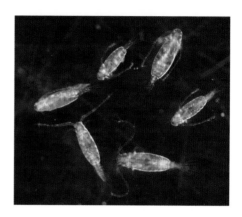

HABITAT & ECOLOGY

A crucial link in the Bay food web, as copepods are in marine food webs worldwide. Uses modified antennae to filter algae from the water, and is itself fed on by many other Bay creatures, including Bay anchovies, Bay nettles, menhaden, and larvae of larger fish such as striped bass. Can reach enormous numbers during spring—more than 1 million per cubic meter, or nearly 4,000 in each gallon—when increasing sunlight, warming waters, and floods of nutrients fuel the year's first bloom of its algal food. By grazing algae, it not only helps transfer energy up the food web but also helps clear the water; scientists estimate that *A. tonsa* can filter up to one-half the volume of a Bay tributary each day.

DID YOU KNOW?

By eating floating algae and detritus and then pooping out heavy, sinking fecal pellets, copepods may help remove excess nutrients from Bay waters, thus enhancing water quality.

Cownose Ray (*Rhinoptera bonasus*)

DESCRIPTION

Averages 3 feet wide but may reach 7 feet. Flattened like a pancake, with 2 triangular "wings" and a long, whiplike tail. Snout shape is distinctive: 2 fleshy lobes when viewed from above or below; together the 4 lobes resemble the nose of a cow. Head is inflated, with eyes on the sides and a harmonica-like mouth below. A small dorsal fin rises near the tail base, just forward of a small, stinging spine. Brown or gray above, whitish below.

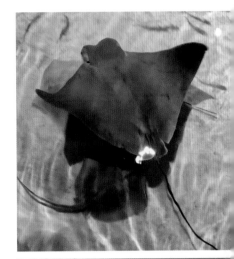

HABITAT & ECOLOGY

A common summertime resident of the mid- to lower Bay, where it regularly swims in squadrons of a dozen or so animals in search of a shellfish meal. Dislodges burrowing clams by flapping its wings to fan away bay-floor sediments, then uses its comblike tooth plates to crush the shells. Prefers softshell clams, but will also eat hard clams and oysters. Predators include cobia, bull sharks, and sandbar sharks.

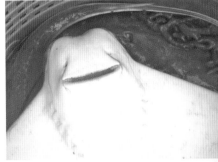

DID YOU KNOW?

Often swim near the surface, where people mistake the curved wing tips for shark fins. Concerns regarding cownose predation on farmed and restored oysters led to efforts to reduce ray numbers through a managed seafood fishery, but with little success to date given market challenges and worries about population impacts on this slow-maturing species. Congregates near Bay mouth prior to fall migration into coastal waters; one such squadron, or "fever," was estimated to contain more than 5 million animals.

Drums and croakers (Sciaenid family)

A large family of bony fishes with 270 species worldwide and 14 species that seasonally inhabit Chesapeake Bay. Many of their common names reference the ability of these fishes to make drumming or croaking noises by rapidly vibrating their swim bladder using specialized muscles. Like birds, each species has a unique sound to help communicate with its closest kin. Croaker and drum choruses can grow loud enough to be heard above water.

Like sciaenids elsewhere, local species play major roles in the Bay food web as both predators and prey; they also support important recreational and commercial fisheries. Here we compare and contrast six common Bay species. Two species, spot and weakfish, are "clean-shaven," with no whiskers beneath the chin. Four have whiskers, or "barbels": Atlantic croaker, black drum, red drum, and Northern kingfish.

Spot

Leiostomus xanthurus. To 14 inches and 2.5 pounds. Dark spot on shoulder, forked tail. Gill cover has smooth seam. Common through summer in shallows of mid to lower Bay, often schooling over oyster reefs. Adults migrate in fall into coastal waters to spawn; currents carry larvae into Bay in early spring; adults follow. Bottom feeders on marine worms, crabs and shrimp, and mollusks. Preyed on by striped bass, weakfish, and sharks. One of the most abundant Bay fishes and a favorite of anglers.

Weakfish

Cynoscion regalis. To 3 feet and 6-18 pounds. Lower jaw longer than upper. Migrate into the Bay in summer to feed and spawn, return offshore in fall. Larvae and juveniles eat copepods, mysid shrimp, and anchovies. Adults are top predators in Bay eelgrass, feeding on marine worms, mollusks, crustaceans, and other fish.

No Barbels

← ─────── **Humpbacked Body** **Drums & Croakers** Elongate Body ──────→
2-part dorsal fin

Barbels

Atlantic Croaker

Micropogonias undulatus. To 27 inches and 9 pounds, but most less than 1 lb. Three-lobed tail. Gill cover has toothed seam. Adults migrate into Bay in spring and occur baywide into fall, when they return to coastal ocean to spawn. Bottom feeder that eats marine worms, crustaceans, and small fishes. Preyed on by striped bass. Bay population fluctuates widely from year to year, likely due to loss of juveniles during cold winters. A favorite of Bay anglers.

Red Drum

Sciaenops ocellatus. To 5 feet and 90 pounds. One or more dark spots near tail. Reddish fins. Spawn during fall in coastal waters; currents carry eggs and larvae into Bay marshes. Eats small shrimp, fishes, and fiddler crabs. Preyed on by dolphins and is a frequent target of recreational and commercial fisheries.

Black Drum

Pogonias cromis. To 4-ft and 110 pounds. Young have 4-5 dark bars that fade with age. Dark fins. Spawn in spring in lower Bay, adults then continue up Bay to feed. Migrate out of Bay in late fall into warmer southern waters. Bottom feeders; use barbels to detect clams, oysters, and crabs and hard dental plates to crush and open the shells.

Northern Kingfish

Menticirrhus saxatilis. To 17 inches and 3 pounds. Dark markings radiate from pectoral fin, tall first dorsal fin with filament on 3rd spine. Only sciaenid that doesn't make sound. Spawn in Bay during summer and migrate offshore in winter. School in shallow waters over firm bottoms to feed on shrimp, crabs, marine worms, and small mollusks and fish.

Summer Flounder (*Paralichthys dentatus*)

DESCRIPTION

Average 15–22 inches and 1–4 pounds; females larger than males. Unmistakable fish that is flattened like a pancake with both eyes on the top of the body. Generally brown and spotted above and white below, but can change color and patterns to match its surroundings. Long dorsal fin stretches all the way from head to slightly pointed tail. A pair of small ventral fins are separated from the long anal fin. Mouth is large compared to other flatfishes. Can be distinguished from winter flounder (*Pseudopleuronectes americanus*) in that it is "left-handed," with its eyes above the mouth on the left side of the body when viewed from above (winter flounder is "right-handed").

HABITAT & ECOLOGY

Can be locally abundant in mid- to lower Bay during summer (hence its common name). Favors inlets and channels, where it shallowly buries into sandbars or eelgrass beds to ambush small fishes; squid; crabs, shrimp, and other crustaceans; small mollusks; and marine worms. Can swim swiftly when hunting or disturbed. May follow schools to the surface, even leaping from the water in pursuit of prey (winter flounder is more sluggish). Migrates into coastal ocean in winter to spawn.

DID YOU KNOW?

The larval stage of this and other flounders initially resembles other fishes, with an eye on each side. As the fish develops, one eye migrates to either the left or right side.

Menhaden (*Brevoortia tyrannus*)

DESCRIPTION

To 15 inches and 1 pound. Large dark spot on shoulder, followed by variable number of smaller dots splattered like paint toward the tail. Deep body is greenish blue on top; silvery sides show brassy tinge above and bluish tinge below along sharp-edged belly. Single, relatively short dorsal fin. Jutting lower jaw and deeply forked tail.

HABITAT & ECOLOGY

Travels in large schools near surface, filtering plankton with its comblike gills, as if a baleen whale had been fragmented into a thousand tiny mouths. Food includes diatoms, copepods, and other small shrimplike crustaceans. These schools in turn serve as key forage for a host of larger predators, including bluefish, striped bass, sharks, weakfish, dolphins, ospreys, and bald eagles. Range from Florida to Nova Scotia; spawning concentrated in coastal waters off the Bay mouth in winter. Eggs hatch at sea; larvae drift into the Chesapeake and other estuaries in spring, where they join adults to feed and grow through the plankton-filled days of summer. Bay and nearby coastal populations support a major commercial fishery in which netted schools are processed into fish oil, bait, fertilizer, and feed for livestock and farmed salmon. The meat is considered too oily and bony for direct human consumption.

DID YOU KNOW?

Called "the most important fish in the sea" for their vital role in feeding larger predators, menhaden are at the center of a heated controversy between commercial harvesters and recreational anglers. Although fishery data shows that the Bay's current commercial catch is sustainable, recreational anglers argue that it deprives striped bass and other menhaden predators of needed forage. The controversy is piqued by the contraction of the commercial fishery into a single company, whose fleet now operates mostly in the Bay and just outside its mouth. The sole remaining processing plant is in Reedville, Virginia.

Oyster Toadfish (*Opsanus tau*)

DESCRIPTION

To 12 inches long. A fish with a face only a mother could love. Mouth is broad with flabby lips; cheeks and jaws bear fleshy "whiskers." Eyes bulge from atop the large head. Flattened body narrows quickly toward rounded tail; taper offset by plump belly and large pectoral fins held like jazz hands to either side. Often rests on throat-mounted ventral fins. Long dorsal fin—which begins with 3 stand-alone spines—runs down the back. Complements its good looks with muddy green skin covered by slimy mucus. Can change color to match surroundings.

HABITAT & ECOLOGY

A year-round Bay resident. Favors oyster reefs, seagrass beds, and other shallow areas. Nestles in reef crannies or hollows a bay-floor den to wait for prey. Has a broad palate, eating crabs, marine worms, shrimp, snails, clams, tunicates, squid, and small fish, including mummichogs, menhaden, puffers, and silversides. Preyed on by sharks.

DID YOU KNOW?

Makes a toad-like grunt to attract a mate. Female deposits the sticky, BB-size eggs—the largest of any Bay fish—on the bottom. Male cleans the nest and protects the eggs even

after they hatch and begin to venture out as tadpole-like larvae. Be wary if you catch a "toad"—they have powerful, snapping jaws and sharp spines on the dorsal fin. Can survive out of water for up to 24 hours.

Lined Seahorse (*Hippocampus erectus*)

DESCRIPTION
This chimerical beast (3–6 inches long) has a horse's head, a monkey's prehensile tail, and a dragon's body. Body flattened sidewise and ringed by bony plates, each armed with 4 blunt spines. Swims vertically by swishing its dorsal fin, which lies about halfway down the back. Color varies widely; often has brown and yellow blotches with lighter concentric lines.

HABITAT & ECOLOGY
Typically found in beds of eelgrass or other underwater vegetation; other haunts include sponges, dock pilings, and crab pots. Uses tail to cling to seagrass stalks or other "structure" for support and camouflage. Retreats to deeper water in winter. Feeds on small crustaceans such as shrimp, amphipods, and copepods, as well as polychaete worms and snails, sucking in prey with its tubular snout. Camouflage and bony plates deter most predators.

DID YOU KNOW?
One of the few animals in which the male nurses the eggs, sustaining up to 150 in his brood pouch after they are deposited there by the female. The young resemble adults at hatching, but are only approximately $1/3$ inch long. Overall population considered vulnerable due to marine pollution, seagrass loss, and harvesting for the aquarium trade elsewhere in its range, including Florida.

Sheepshead (*Archosargus probatocephalus*)

DESCRIPTION

Averages 10–20 inches and 3–4 pounds; record is 29.5 inches and 22 pounds. Almost oval, laterally flattened fish with 6–7 dark bars on silvery green background. Bars fade with age. Blunt snout and small, nearly horizontal mouth with disturbingly humanlike teeth. Single long dorsal fin; front part with 11–12 sharp spines, rear with 11–13 flexible rays. Anal fin has enlarged second spine. Tail is shallowly forked with rounded corners. Resembles black drum, but grows much smaller and lacks chin whiskers, or "barbels."

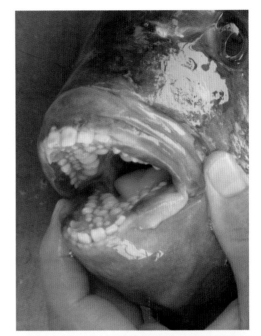

HABITAT & ECOLOGY

Adults prefer tidal creeks and brackish waters with pilings, piers, and other structures. Juveniles favor seagrass beds and muddy bottoms. Adults use impressive chompers to scrape, crush, and eat shelled prey such as barnacles, clams, oysters, and blue crabs. Preyed on by sharks and other large fishes. Migrate offshore in late winter and early spring to spawn. Known to succumb to fish-kill events within low-oxygen "dead zones."

DID YOU KNOW?

Sheepshead are not overly abundant in the Bay, but they are targeted by

anglers for their firm, tasty flesh (though the large scales and sharp dorsal spines make cleaning a chore). Also popular in public aquariums due to their striking markings, which give them the nickname of "convict fish."

Northern Snakehead (*Channa argus*)

DESCRIPTION

To 3 feet and 18 pounds. Snakelike head and body with single long dorsal fin, single long anal fin, and squared-off tail. Body tan with geometric brown blotches along sides. Jutting lower jaw with many sharp teeth. Often mistaken for native bowfin, but the latter has a much shorter anal fin. Also resembles American eel, but eel's dorsal, anal, and tail fins are merged in a single loop.

HABITAT & ECOLOGY

Introduced from Asia, with first report from Bay watershed in a Maryland pond in 2002. Prefers sluggish water with aquatic vegetation and a muddy bottom. Ostensibly a freshwater fish, but tolerant of brackish Bay waters. Now established throughout the Potomac and Rappahannock Rivers, in the upper James, and within a few small drainages on the bayside Eastern Shore. Top predator known to eat at least seventeen species of Bay fishes, including gizzard shad, white perch, and banded killifish. Concerns over continued spread across Bay watershed are abetted by its hardiness—can survive water temperatures of 32°F to 86°F, estivate in mud during drought, hibernate in mud through winter, and live out of water for days if moist. Preferred control measure is a targeted fishery, as the snakehead is a good fighter with tasty meat.

DID YOU KNOW?

Live snakeheads were legally imported to the United States for food and aquariums through the 1990s. Release into local waters and concerns regarding spread and impacts to native wildlife have led to strict state and federal regulations on the import, sale, and possession of these fish or their eggs. For guidance on what to do if you encounter or catch a snakehead, contact or visit the website of Maryland's Department of Natural Resources Fishing and Boating Services or Virginia's Department of Wildlife Resources.

Striped Bass or Rockfish (*Morone saxatilis*)

DESCRIPTION

Males to 3 feet and 20 pounds; females to 5+ feet and 80 pounds. Body marked by 7–8 stripes that may be beaded in younger fish. Has the classic shape of an active predator, with a torpedo-shaped body and a large tail with equal lobes for quick ambush bursts. Two clearly separated dorsal fins, the fore with 9–10 stiff spines, the aft with 7–13 flexible rays. Body green to black above, fading to silver on sides and white on belly.

HABITAT & ECOLOGY

Occupy a wide salinity range from coastal waters to estuaries and rivers. Also stocked in lakes. The Chesapeake holds two populations: those that migrate from ocean waters into Bay tributaries during spring to spawn, and those that inhabit the Bay year-round. Resident fish move into deeper channels in winter and summer. Feed on a wide variety of small fishes and invertebrates. Diet includes anchovy, croakers, eels, herring, menhaden, mummichogs, shad, silversides, crabs, shrimp, marine worms, soft clams, and mussels. Young are eaten by other fishes, including adult stripers. Adults have few predators, but are occasionally taken by sharks, marine mammals, or seabirds. Chesapeake serves as the main spawning grounds for the mid-Atlantic region.

DID YOU KNOW?

A favorite of both recreational and commercial anglers, with an average of more than 4 million pounds harvested commercially in the Bay each year during the early 2000s. This followed a successful effort to restore the population, which had crashed in the 1980s. Recent outbreaks of a bacterial disease and concentration of menhaden harvests into Bay waters have raised concerns regarding the population's continued health and food resources.

Atlantic Sturgeon (*Acipenser oxyrhynchus*)

DESCRIPTION
Regularly 6–10 feet and 100–200 pounds, largest recorded is 14 feet and 811 pounds. The Bay's largest native fish. Readily identified by 5 rows of bony scutes, 4 conspicuous "whiskers," or barbels, beneath snout, and asymmetric tail with a longer upper lobe. Body greenish brown above with a whitish belly. Mouth opens on bottom of head, lacks teeth, and has fleshy lobes that can be extended like a short hose.

HABITAT & ECOLOGY
Spends most of its life in the ocean but enters Bay tributaries to spawn, returning in spring through summer every 3–5 years. Now mostly restricted to James and York Rivers, though historically it likely made spawning runs up all large Bay tributaries. Juveniles remain in their birth river for 4–6 years before moving out to sea. Use their snout to root through the mud for bottom-dwelling creatures such as clams, crustaceans, and worms, which they suck into their mouth like a vacuum. Adults have few natural predators.

DID YOU KNOW?

Sturgeon arose in the Age of Dinosaurs, fed generations of Native Americans and English colonists, and supported a valuable caviar fishery into the twentieth century, when overfishing, pollution, and dams began to threaten this 120-million-year-old lineage. Today, sturgeons are rare worldwide, and are protected in the Bay by state fishing moratoriums and the federal Endangered Species Act. This protection extends to the Bay's other sturgeon species, the shortnose sturgeon *A. brevirostrum.*

> We had more Sturgeon, than could be devoured by Dog and Man, of which the industrious by drying and pounding, mingled with Caviare, Sorell and other wholesome hearbes would make bread and good meate.
>
> —*Capt. John Smith,* Generall Historie of Virginia, *1624*

BAY SHARKS

Scientists have recorded a dozen shark species in the Chesapeake, although some visit only rarely. Sharks enter the Bay during summer both to feed and escape predators, and leave in fall for warmer southern waters. Bay waters also serve as important nursery grounds for sandbars and "duskies." There are no reports of unprovoked shark attacks on people in the Bay waters of either Maryland or Virginia. (Maryland has only one shark attack on record, Virginia only five, all in coastal waters.) Indeed, sharks have much more to fear from people than people do from sharks. Overfishing led to steep drops in shark populations in the mid-Atlantic and elsewhere during the 1970s and 1980s. This included commercial fishing for shark-fin soup and recreational angling, which exploded following release of the movie *Jaws* in 1975. State and federal regulations are now helping these slow-growing animals gradually recover their place as top predators in US coastal waters. Here we describe the five most common sharks in the Chesapeake.

Sandbar Shark (*Carcharhinus plumbeus*)

To 8 feet. Most common large shark in the Bay, which also provides its main nursery grounds. Prefers the lower Bay's saltier waters, where it feeds on small fishes, mollusks, and blue crabs. Pursued by recreational anglers for its tasty meat and harvested commercially for shark-fin soup. Population recovering from overfishing, but slowly, as it doesn't reach sexual maturity until 25 years of age. Distinguishing features include a short, broad snout and a large dorsal fin that originates over the middle of its pectoral fin. Unlike the similar dusky shark, its anal fin lacks a black outline.

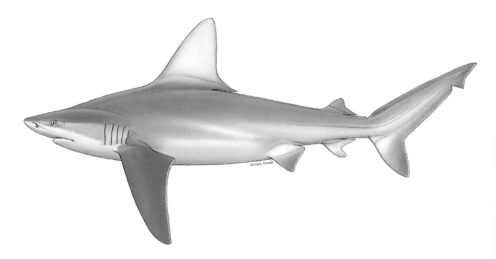

Smooth Dogfish (*Mustelus canis*)

To 5 feet. Common to abundant in the Bay, and may enter the mouths of brackish tributaries. Feeds on the bottom, actively pursuing crabs, shrimp, fish, clams, snails, and marine worms. Name may come from habit of swimming in schools, or "packs." Distinguishing features include a pair of dorsal fins roughly equal in size, and—paradoxically—large, oval, catlike eyes.

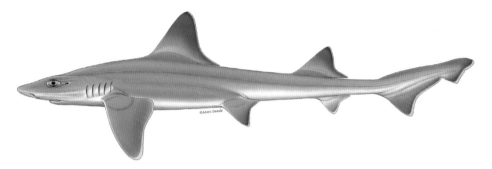

Atlantic sharpnose shark (*Rhizoprionodon terraenovae*)

To 3.5 feet. Rarely seen in the Bay; those encountered are mostly mature males. Eats crabs, squid, shrimp, and small fishes. Distinguishing features include white spots along the sides and a tail that may be outlined in black.

Dusky Shark (*Carcharhinus obscurus*)

To 13 feet. Now rarely seen in mid-Atlantic due to overfishing. Uses shallow waters near Bay mouth as its nursery ground. Eats fishes such as menhaden, bluefish, small sharks, and skates. Once a popular target of recreational anglers, particularly in shark-fishing tournaments due to its large size. Distinguishing features include an anal fin outlined in black.

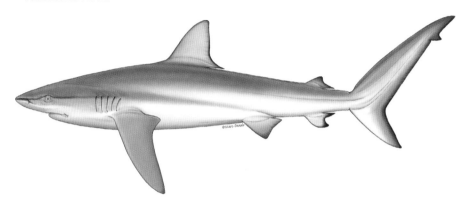

Bull Shark (*Carcharhinus leucas*)

To 7 feet (males) and 11 feet (females). Tolerant of freshwater; occasionally seen in Bay and as far north as the Potomac River. Eats bony fishes, other sharks, rays, sea turtles, and marine mammals. Its aggressive nature and preference for shallow water and large prey make it the most dangerous shark in the Chesapeake for humans, but the risk of an attack is exceedingly low given its rarity. Distinguishing features include small eyes, a tall dorsal fin, and a short, rounded snout.

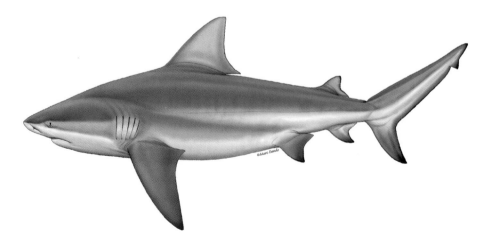

Bottlenose Dolphin (*Tursiops truncatus*)

DESCRIPTION

To 12 feet and 400 pounds. Large marine mammal most often seen "porpoising" along the surface, revealing glimpses of its arched back and hooked dorsal fin. Will also leap clear of the water and ride the bow of fast-moving vessels. Seen in full, it has a stubby snout below an inflated forehead, a single blowhole atop the head, and 2 short flippers.  Body is stout forward of the dorsal fin but tapers quickly toward the horizontal tail. Gray above; sides and belly paler. Males larger than females.

HABITAT & ECOLOGY

Uncommon but regular summertime visitor to the lower and middle Bay, where it preys on fishes such as spot, croakers, and menhaden, as well as shrimp, squid, and crabs. Larger sharks—bulls, tigers, and duskies—are the main predators; also threatened by pollution and fishing gear. Use unique whistles along with clicks, squeaks, and creaks to communicate with other dolphins. Echolocate to navigate, find prey, and detect predators.

DID YOU KNOW?

Bottlenose dolphins usually live about 25 years in the wild, but may double that in captivity. Highly social animals that typically live in pods of a few to more than one hundred individuals. Protected by the Marine Mammal Protection Act. Dolphin-watching tours with trained guides are offered by the Virginia Aquarium; numerous private charters are also available in Virginia and Maryland. To help better understand dolphin behavior in Bay waters, join Chesapeake Dolphin Watch, a community-scientist effort run through the University of Maryland Center for Environmental Science.

Florida Manatee (*Trichechus manatus latirostris*)

DESCRIPTION
To 10 feet and 800–1,200 pounds. Large, slow-moving aquatic mammal with a pair of flipper-like forelimbs. Sausage-like body tapers to a flat, paddle-shaped tail. Face has a whiskered snout and jowls like a bulldog. Nostrils sit atop snout and open upward to facilitate surface breathing. Eyes are small; ears are small holes with no external lobes. Skin is gray, but may appear green due to algal growth. Surfaces to breathe every 3–5 minutes when active.

HABITAT & ECOLOGY
An infrequent summertime visitor to the Chesapeake, one or two manatees are reported from the Bay every few years. Favors shallow, brackish to freshwater areas where it grazes on underwater grasses. Has few natural predators, with isolated evidence of attacks by sharks and alligators in its subtropical home range. Greatest threats are from humans, including boat strikes, propeller strikes, and entanglement in nets. Will "stun" if water temperatures fall below 68°F; individuals that linger in the Bay into fall have therefore been captured and airlifted back to Florida waters, where they normally winter.

DID YOU KNOW?

The manatee's closest relatives include the elephant. The Chesapeake's most famous manatee, "Chessie," made repeated visits to Bay waters between 1994 and 2011. Its identity was confirmed by tagging and the long scar on its left shoulder. Conservation efforts have raised the status of this species from "endangered" to "threatened" in recent years. The US Endangered Species Act makes it illegal to harass, hunt, capture, or kill manatees or any other marine mammal. Report any sightings of a manatee in Bay waters to the appropriate marine mammal response program; call (800) 628-9944 in Maryland or (757) 385-7575 in Virginia.

OTHER MARINE MAMMALS

Bottlenose dolphins are the most common marine mammals in the Chesapeake, but several other species enter the Bay at least occasionally. Humpback whales and harbor seals are fairly common near the Bay mouth during winter; harbor porpoises occur as far north as Maryland.

A good way to observe and learn about the Bay's marine mammals is by booking a trip with the Virginia Aquarium & Marine Science Center in Virginia Beach. They offer 2-hour educational boat tours each year from December through March; these provide opportunities to observe whales, seals, and other winter wildlife in their natural habitat.

If you see any marine mammal swimming freely without injury, enjoy the experience from a distance: at least 50 yards for seals and 100–500 yards for whales. For injured or entangled animals in Virginia waters, call the Virginia Aquarium Stranding Center Hotline at (757) 385-7575. In Maryland, phone the Maryland Natural Resources Police Call Center at (800) 628-9944 (available 24/7 toll-free). Photos, if possible, are always good to help with identification. For your safety, do not approach the animal.

Humpback Whale (*Megaptera novaeangliae*)

To 60 feet and 30–50 tons. Dark above with white on belly, flippers, and tail (light tail patches provide unique "fingerprints" that scientists use to track individuals). Pectoral fins are long and throat is pleated. A favorite of whale watchers, as it often breaches. Uses its sievelike baleen to filter seawater for shrimp, menhaden, and plankton. Groups may gather to concentrate prey by forming a "bubble-net." Historically migrated southward in winter from Arctic to Caribbean breeding grounds, but increasing numbers

are now stopping near and just inside the Bay mouth. Presence in this busy shipping lane is raising concerns about vessel strikes, with one in ten humpbacks in this area having propeller scars or other ship-related injuries.

Harbor Seal (*Phoca vitulina*)

To 6 feet and 300 pounds. Short, dense fur is bluish-gray to tan, with darker mottling. Body is sausage-like, with clawed fore flippers and wide hind flippers. No external ear flap. Mainly seen during winter, but small groups may haul out in spring and summer on riprap near the Chesapeake Bay Bridge-Tunnel. There's one report of a harbor seal near Hopewell, far up the James River. Mainly eats fish, including herring and flounder, but may occasionally consume shellfish. Preyed on by sharks. Now safeguarded from humans by the Marine Mammal Protection Act, but oil spills, boat collisions, and net entanglements still pose a threat.

Harbor Porpoise (*Phocoena phocoena*)

To 5 feet and 135–170 pounds. One of the smallest marine mammals. Dark gray above and white below. Body is stout, with small pectoral fins (some anglers call them "puffer pigs"). Can be distinguished from bottlenose dolphin by much smaller size, blunt beak, triangular dorsal fin, and spade-shaped teeth. (Bottlenose dolphin has noticeable beak, hooked dorsal fin, and conical teeth.) It also rarely leaps from the water. Feeds mostly on small schooling fish, particularly herring. May also eat squid and crustaceans. Typically travels in pods of two to five animals. Visits the Chesapeake Bay from late winter to spring. Primary human threat is accidental capture in gillnets and trawls.

SEA TURTLES

Five of the world's seven sea turtle species are known from the Chesapeake, with up to 10,000 turtles entering the Bay each spring as water temperatures warm. Most are loggerheads; Kemp's ridley, green, leatherback, and hawksbill turtles are far less common. Sea turtles can be distinguished from snappers and diamondback terrapins by their larger size, possession of flippers rather than clawed feet, and inability to withdraw their head or limbs into their shell. All the species are protected under the Endangered Species Act, as populations have been devastated by harvest of eggs and meat, destruction of nesting beaches, bycatch in shrimp and other fisheries, and propeller strikes. If you have the exceptional fortune to encounter a live sea turtle, observe it from a distance of at least 150 feet. If in Virginia, report any hooked or stranded sea turtles (live or dead) to the Virginia Aquarium Stranding Response Program at (757) 385-7575. In Maryland, call the Department of Natural Resources at (800) 628-9944.

Loggerhead (*Caretta caretta*)

Most common sea turtle in the Bay, with a population estimated at nearly 8,000 animals. These are mostly juveniles of 2–3 feet and approximately 100 pounds. Shell is yellow beneath and reddish brown on top, with three scutes across the shoulders immediately behind a single scute at the neck (a trait it shares with Kemp's ridley turtles). Eats blue crabs, horseshoe crabs, whelk, fishes, and sea grasses. Favors channels of major Bay tributaries and largely stays put once it establishes a foraging area. Listed as "threatened" under the Endangered Species Act.

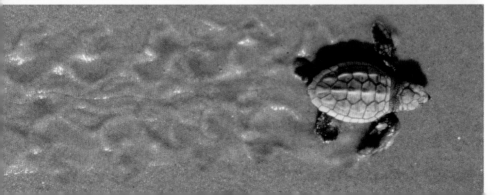

Kemp's Ridley (*Lepidochelys kempii*)

The smallest and rarest of all sea turtles, but second most common in the Bay, with 200–300 juveniles visiting the Chesapeake each summer to feed on blue crabs in eelgrass beds. Shell is grayish, with some white on head and limbs. Distinguished from loggerhead by color, smaller size (Bay animals average about 15 inches long and 20–30 pounds), and possession of 4–5 plates on bridge between upper and lower shell (loggerhead usually has 3). Listed as "endangered" throughout its range.

Leatherback (*Dermochelys coriacea*)

World's largest sea turtle and third most abundant turtle in Bay waters. Adults reach 4–8 feet and weigh up to a ton. Named for their leathery shell, which instead of scutes has firm, rubbery skin with 7 longitudinal ridges. A handful of adults strand in the Bay each year; their average length is about 5 feet. The only black sea turtle in Bay waters, although it often bears white spots on the lower parts of the head, limbs, and body. Mainly eats bay nettles and other jellyfish. Listed as "endangered."

Green (*Chelonia mydas*)

A handful of juveniles are typically seen in Bay waters each year, mostly during late summer and early fall. Their average length is around 1 foot. While adults feed on sea grasses and algae, juveniles feed on both aquatic plants and animals, including jellyfish, mollusks, and crustaceans. Humans harvest both their eggs and meat; they are named from the color of their fat. Listed as "endangered" in United States and "threatened" globally.

Hawksbill (*Eretmochelys imbricata*)

Extremely rare in the Bay. Only two have been reported since 1979, both considered "strays" from the subtropical waters they normally inhabit. Each was less than 1 foot long. These turtles were killed by the millions during the twentieth century to provide "tortoise shell" for combs and brushes, jewelry boxes, and ornaments. This trade was banned in 1977 by the Convention on International Trade of Endangered Species (CITES), but these turtles continue to be listed as "endangered."

Brown Pelican (*Pelecanus occidentalis*)

DESCRIPTION

Giant, pouched bill is unmistakable. Stocky bird with long, curved neck; short, stout legs; and large, webbed feet. Body brownish gray; neck brown in juveniles, white in nonbreeding adults, and dark sable in breeding adults. Adult crown and forehead a yellowed ivory. Aptly described in a limerick by humorist Dixon Lanier Merritt:

> A wonderful bird is the pelican.
> His bill can hold more than his belican.
> He can hold in his beak
> Enough food for a week,
> But I'm damned if I see how the helican.

HABITAT & ECOLOGY

A mostly coastal species that often glides just above the waves in graceful squadrons. Preys on

small, surface-dwelling fish such as menhaden, herring, and silversides using spectacular plunge dives; expels up to 3 gallons of water from expandable pouch before swallowing captured fish whole. Can eat up to 4 pounds of fish per day. Nests mainly on the ground in the Bay area, on coastal islands to deter nest predators such as raccoons and feral cats and dogs. Young also preyed on by laughing gulls, herring gulls, and bald eagles.

DID YOU KNOW?

Populations suffered serious declines in the 1950s and 1960s from thinning eggshells due to pesticides; have recovered markedly since the EPA's 1972 ban on DDT. Number of nests along Atlantic coast increased from about 2,500 in 1970 to almost 15,000 in 2000. Accidental hooking by recreational anglers, entanglement in abandoned fishing gear, and oil spills now pose the biggest threats. Sea-level rise due to global warming threatens to flood nesting sites on low-lying islands in the Chesapeake Bay.

Bufflehead (*Bucephala albeola*)

DESCRIPTION

A small duck of sheltered waters. Head is rounded and large relative to the body, with a short bill. Males are unmistakable with white sidewalls and chest and a large white patch on otherwise dark head and back (these appear black but are actually an iridescent purple-green). Females are grayish brown, with smaller white patch on cheek. Feet are reddish orange. Floats high in the water. Males and females raft in small groups whose near-constant motion is punctuated by quick, sure dives. May spend up to half their time feeding beneath the surface.

HABITAT & ECOLOGY

Buffleheads are winter residents of the Chesapeake Bay watershed, arriving in October from breeding sites in Canada. They prefer nearshore stretches of Bay tributaries and other sheltered waters, both fresh and salt. Their diet in the brackish waters of the Bay typically includes aquatic vegetation, shrimp, crabs, amphipods, isopods, snails, and mussels. Seldom seen on land.

DID YOU KNOW?

Buffleheads are the smallest diving duck in North America. They nest in western and central Canada, almost exclusively in holes dug in trees by northern flickers. Buffleheads became scarce in the early 1900s due to overhunting but recovered following passage of the Migratory Bird Treaty Act between Canada and the United States in 1916.

Canvasback Duck (*Aythya valisineria*)

DESCRIPTION
At 18–22 inches, largest duck in North America. Distinguished by smooth slope from forehead to bill tip and rich fore-aft coloring that bookends the white back. Male has vivid chestnut head, black chest, and dark tail. Female more muted, with a light brown head, gray chest, and gray tail. Tail in both sexes is short and dips toward the water. Takes off by running across the water; one of the speediest ducks in flight, with an airspeed up to 72 miles per hour.

HABITAT & ECOLOGY
Flocks in the Bay's fresher waters during winter, diving to feed on underwater grasses with a preference for wild celery and sago pondweed. Diet has shifted to include clams, snails, and other small invertebrates due to decline in bay-grass acreage. Eggs preyed on by raccoons; young and adults by bald eagles, foxes, snapping turtles, and gulls. A favorite of duck hunters. Nearly half of all canvasbacks once wintered in and around the Chesapeake (the Susquehanna Flats alone are thought to have supported 6 million "cans"), but that's now down to about 20 percent due to decline of bay grasses during the last half of the twentieth century.

DID YOU KNOW?
Species name is based on its taste for wild celery (*Vallisneria americana*). Overall population seems to be slowly recovering from lows seen in the 1970s and 1980s due to habitat loss and poisoning from eating lead shotgun pellets while bottom feeding. The US Fish and Wildlife Service banned the use of lead shot in federal waterfowl hunting areas in 1991. The role of the canvasback as the onetime king of Bay ducks is reflected in its use as the logo of the Decoy Museum in Havre de Grace, Maryland.

Double-crested Cormorant
(*Phalacrocorax auritus*)

DESCRIPTION
Lanky diving bird with dark gray body; neck and breast black in adults, lighter in juveniles. Skin at base of beak orangish yellow; upper beak recurves sharply at tip. Eyes a striking sky blue.

HABITAT & ECOLOGY
Common in fresh- and saltwater habitats throughout the Bay watershed. Swims low in the water; dives for small fish it often swallows while submerged. Occasionally eats crustaceans, insects, and amphibians. May form sizable flocks.

DID YOU KNOW?
Unlike many other waterbirds, cormorants' feathers are not waterproof. This decreases buoyancy—an aid in diving—but requires the bird to perch with wings spread for drying. Waterlogged plumage forces long run atop water surface to gain sufficient speed for flight.

Lesser Scaup (*Aythya affinis*)

DESCRIPTION

Approximately 16–17 inches long, wingspan 29 inches. From afar, male looks like an Oreo cookie, with white flanks sandwiched between a black head, chest, and tail. Closer view reveals more-nuanced coloration: an off-white back delicately marbled with thin, wavy black lines; a blue bill; a yellow eye; and a head with a purplish sheen. Females are mottled brown; many with a white patch next to the bill. Rear of head descends in straight line from tiny peaked "hat," a feature that helps distinguish lesser scaup from the rounded head of the greater scaup (*A. marila*), which it otherwise closely resembles.

HABITAT & ECOLOGY

A common inhabitant of the Bay watershed during winter, forming large flocks on brackish tributaries and lakes, often mixed with canvasbacks and greater scaup. Hunts by diving in shallow water for crabs, shrimp, clams, and fish, but may eat aquatic plants if those animals are scarce. Known to use beak to scythe through bottom for prey while paddling forward. Usually consumes its food underwater. Preyed on by bald eagles and red foxes.

DID YOU KNOW?

Ranges throughout North America, breeding mostly in Canada. Male is usually silent, female more vocal. An early naturalist compared their call to "the sound made by rubbing the finger quickly and lightly over a roll-top desk."

Common Loon (*Gavia immer*)

DESCRIPTION
Ranges from 28–36 inches long with a 6-foot wingspan. Large, long-bodied bird that has been likened to a submarine. Plumage varies through the year. Grayish brown above in fall, with pale cheek, throat, chest, and bill. From late winter through summer breeding season, displays striking black-and-white-checkered back, black head and bill, white breast, and zebra-striped "necklace." Floats low in the water, with short tail often hidden beneath the surface. Stout, daggerlike bill helps distinguish it from double-crested cormorant, whose bill is narrow and hooked.

HABITAT & ECOLOGY
Visits Bay during both fall and spring migration (may be in striking breeding plumage on northward journey). Some birds may overwinter. Favors nearshore waters of Bay's mainstem, where individuals dive for smaller fish such as Atlantic croaker and menhaden as well as invertebrates. Adults have few predators, but may be taken by bald eagles and commercial fishing nets. May gather offshore in large "rafts" at night.

DID YOU KNOW?
This bird is well known for its mournful wail and crazy laughter, but this is most common during summer breeding season on northern lakes and seldom heard on the Bay. Built for swimming and diving, with solid bones and large, webbed feet placed far aft like propellers. Requires long "runway" of up to a quarter mile in order to take flight, and may become stranded if it lands on a small pond.

Red-breasted Merganser (*Mergus serrator*)

DESCRIPTION

The punk rocker of the diving ducks, with a spiky mohawk in both male and female. Long, thin, orangish-red bill also diagnostic. Male is boldly marked with metallic dark green head, black back, and white flanks and neck ring. Female more subdued, with reddish-brown head and grayish-brown back. Swims low in the water. Usually silent.

HABITAT & ECOLOGY

Most likely to be seen in the Chesapeake in winter; prefers saltier waters of mainstem Bay and Atlantic coast. Eats small fish such as sticklebacks and killifishes, as well as crayfish and shrimp. Serrated bill helps grasp its slippery, squirming prey. May "snorkel" along surface with eyes submerged in search of a meal. Can stay submerged for almost a full minute when deep-diving for food.

DID YOU KNOW?

The Chesapeake is also home to two other merganser species, the common merganser (*M. merganser*) and the hooded merganser (*Lophodytes cucullatus*). Common merganser prefers freshwater habitats such as rivers and lakes; hooded favors protected, brackish waters of smaller tributaries and tidal creeks. These species also dive in pursuit of fishes and crustaceans.

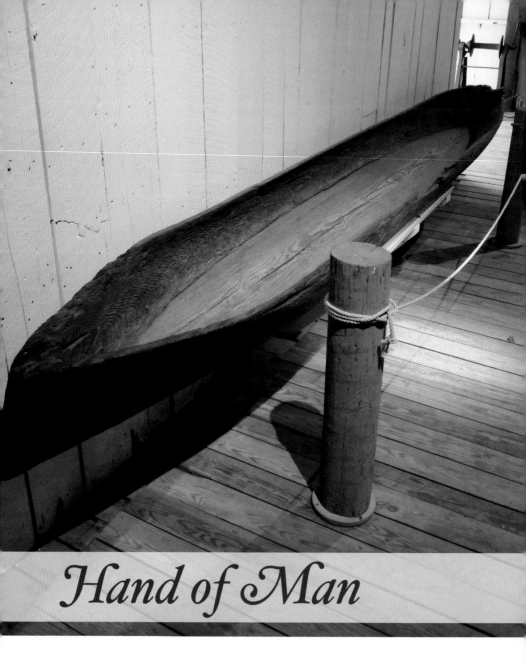

Hand of Man

LOG CANOE

To 30 feet long and 5 feet wide. The Chesapeake's first watercraft was the Native American "dugout" canoe. They shaped these vessels by building a fire atop the felled trunk of a single tuliptree or loblolly pine, scraping away the charred wood with a shell or stone, then repeating this process until they had hollowed a space for buoyancy and up to forty passengers and cargo. They also used "charring," guided by a forked branch, to sharpen the ends of the vessel for easier paddling. One can only imagine the patience and perseverance required for this task, particularly given their lack of metal tools.

Early colonists initially adopted the Indian design, then shifted to multi-log sailing canoes as European deforestation made large trees increasingly scarce. In his delightful book *Harvesting the Chesapeake: Tools & Traditions*, Larry Chowning documents this art in an interview with the last of the log-canoe builders, "Captain Billy" Rollins of Poquoson, Virginia, who crafted a 5-log, 26-foot canoe in 1986. Multi-log canoes used 3, 5, 7, or even 9 logs to form the hull; then added a mast and sails, a retractable keel or centerboard, and "washboards" along the gunnels. The sails allowed a faster trip to and from the fishing grounds, while the centerboard provided stability under sail but could be lifted for working in shallow water. Of course, if there was no wind, the watermen would have to scull or row home. The washboards gave watermen a place to stand while hand-tonging for oysters or pulling crab pots.

Bay watermen sailed multi-log canoes as their primary vessel into the 1920s and, when internal-combustion engines began to replace sails, continued using converted gas-powered canoes as late as the 1970s. Some of these were more than 40 feet long and could carry 200 bushels of oysters. Recreational racing of sailing canoes continues today.

Fine examples of a log canoe are on display at the Chesapeake Bay Maritime Museum in St. Michaels, Maryland, and the Mariner's Museum in Newport News, Virginia.

PUNGY

From 70 to 100 feet long and up to 22 feet wide. These two-masted schooners developed in the early 1700s to carry harbor pilots to ships waiting outside the treacherous shoals at the Bay mouth. The pilots that arrived first got the business, so pungies were built for speed, with large sails and a smooth, hydrodynamic deck. Following the War of 1812, Chesapeake sailors leveraged these attributes and began using pungies to carry perishable goods from port to port within the Bay. Common cargos included watermelons, tomatoes, fish, peaches, grain, people, and mail. Some think the traditional color of pungies—pink and green—echoes the hues of a watermelon as an advertising ploy. The pungies' most unusual cargo was pineapple picked green in Bermuda and allowed to ripen during its delivery to Baltimore.

After New England watermen introduced the oyster dredge to the Bay in the early 1800s, dredging from the larger, more powerful pungies began to replace hand-tonging for oysters from log canoes. Pungies had the larger sails needed to drag a heavy dredge across the bottom, plus the extra heft needed to carry the greater catches that dredging allowed. One drawback was a relatively deep draft, limiting use in the Bay's shallow waters. A final boom in pungy construction followed the Civil War, but rising construction costs, scarcity of local woods, and the advent of gasoline engines slowly led watermen and boatbuilders to switch to smaller bugeyes and skipjacks.

The pungy takes its name from Pungoteague, Virginia, an Eastern Shore community where many of these vessels were built in the mid-1800s.

Historians believe the last pungy was built in 1886, although a replica was built and launched in Baltimore exactly 100 years later. This vessel, the 104-foot *Lady Maryland*, now carries children out on the Bay for the nonprofit Living Classrooms Foundation in Baltimore.

BUGEYE

A bugeye is a two-masted oyster dredger (30–80 feet long, 12–18 feet wide) that combines elements of the log canoe and pungy schooner. Its hull is canoe-like, but made broader by adding more hewn logs (later versions switched to planking). It also inherited the canoe's basic sail plan, already adapted for back-and-forth passes across an oyster bed. From its pungy side, the bugeye got its low profile and rounded log rail, which made it easier to hoist the heavy dredge aboard. The pungy's schooner ancestors bequeathed the bugeye's covered deck, graceful bowsprit, and shallow draft. The shallow draft allowed oystermen to sail to upstream markets during the summer off-season, when they used the vessel for hauling cargo.

The bugeye appeared around 1870 in response to changes in oyster markets and gear. The traditional method of oyster-tonging from log canoes increased during the early to mid-1800s as canals, railroads, and canning expanded markets to burgeoning cities such as Philadelphia and New York. This led to overharvesting of shallow beds by hand tongers and a shift to the deeper-fishing oyster dredge in the years after the Civil War. To protect deeper beds from this heavy, sled-like device, Maryland limited dredging to sail-powered vessels (a restriction that remains today). This legislative compromise set the stage for the bugeye: a vessel large enough to pull a heavy dredge through deep water under sail power only. Its use peaked in the 1880s but continued through the 1960s.

The origin of "bugeye" is uncertain. Some believe it stems from "buckie," a Scottish term for oyster shell. Others think it refers to the two holes for anchor ropes on either side of the vessel's bow, which from the front resemble a pair of eyes.

The restored 53-foot bugeye *Edna E. Lockwood*, a registered National Historic Landmark, is the queen of the historic fleet at the Chesapeake Bay Maritime Museum in St. Michaels, Maryland.

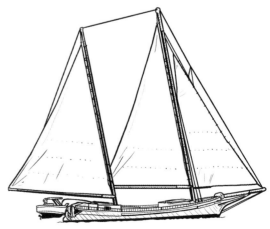

SKIPJACK

Vessel 25–60 feet long and up to 20 feet wide. This distinctive Bay workboat came on the scene in the 1880s. Drawing on elements of the log canoe and sailing skiff, it was cheaper and easier to build than the pungy or bugeye. Features include a single, tilted mast; a triangular mainsail with extremely long boom; a square stern; a small cabin; and a prominent bowsprit. The wooden hull is U-shaped, with a planked bottom and steep sides. Built by hand in small, isolated boatyards, no two vessels were exactly the same.

A fleet of nearly a thousand skipjacks dominated Bay oyster dredging from the 1890s to 1940s, and a few are still in use today due to Maryland's strict limits on the use of powered dredging vessels. (At last count, the web-based Last Skipjacks Project lists thirty-two active vessels.) Several features contribute to the vessel's enduring popularity. Its wide beam provides a stable work platform, its low freeboard eases retrieval of the dredge, and its tilted mast serves double-duty as a crane for unloading oysters at the dock. The sail plan also affords enough power to pull a pair of dredges, while minimizing the number of crew required to handle the boat. But powered dredge boats require even fewer crew, and no wind, leading to the inevitable decline of these elegant sailing ships. Many skipjacks have thus been abandoned, with Maryland's Department of Natural Resources hauling out more than 50 castoff vessels from the waters around Crisfield alone. Of the estimated 2,000 skipjacks built, fewer than 30 remain afloat.

These vessels were originally called "bateau" by watermen, but began to take on their current name in 1900 when a *Baltimore Sun* article compared them to a tuna- or jack-like fish so speedy that it appears to skip over the waves.

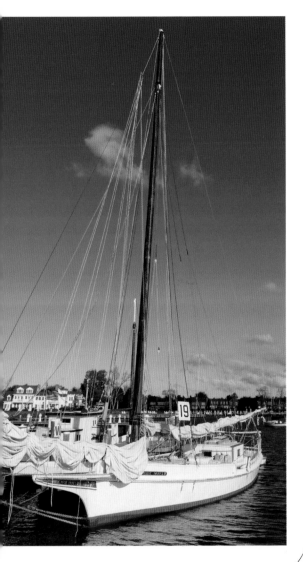

Several Bay museums offer skipjack exhibits and trips aboard refurbished vessels. The Chesapeake Bay Maritime Museum in St. Michaels, Maryland, displays the 52-foot *E. C. Collier* and operates the 46-foot *Rosie Parks*, while the 56-foot *Dee of St. Mary's* operates out of the Calvert Marine Museum in Solomons. The 46-foot *Joy Parks* is on permanent exhibit at the Piney Point Lighthouse Museum. In Virginia, the Reedville Fishermen's Museum operates the 42-foot *Claud W. Somers*, which is listed on both the National Register of Historic Places and the Virginia Register of Historic Places.

SKIFFS

These small vessels (15–18 feet long, 4–5 feet wide) typically have a flat bottom; a pointed, slightly rising bow; and a square stern. Other than a covered bow and a narrow rim around the cockpit, they are generally open to the elements, with enough room for one or two people. A large skeg and centerboard add stability.

Powered by oars or a single sail, they have been the "beginner's" boat for countless generations of children around the Chesapeake. Yet their durability and versatility also make them a popular choice for tending crab pots, working pound nets, tonging oysters, or hunting ducks, particularly within the Bay's shallow tributaries. The blunt-nosed Chincoteague scow played a similar role on the bayside Eastern Shore. Before the advent of the outboard motor, rowing and sailing skiffs were two of the most common boats on the Bay.

The skiff's basic design has today evolved into a wide variety of shapes and sizes. Two fine examples of these adaptable craft are on display at the Mariners' Museum in Newport News, Virginia: the 17-foot *Sinepuxent*, built by Joe Mears in Wachapreague in 1936, and the 22-foot *Yankee*, a late nineteenth-century skiff built in New York and used to tong oysters on the James and York Rivers.

The Patuxent Small Craft Guild at the Chesapeake Bay Maritime Museum in St. Michaels, Maryland, offers classes in skiff building.

DEADRISE

Today's iconic Chesapeake workboat (35–45 feet long, 9–12 feet wide), the deadrise developed during the late 1800s as watermen began traveling farther afield in search of their harvest. Initially just a multi-log canoe with a wide beam for stability and a forward cabin for shelter, it was later built with a planked frame as in a skipjack.

Today's designs retain the forward cabin and spacious aft workspace, while the hull now features a sharp bow that quickly opens into a very shallow "V." This lends the boat its name. As in "dead straight," the "dead" in "deadrise" emphasizes the vessel's almost-flat bottom. The deadrise hull affords a draft of only 2–3 feet, giving these boats wide access to the Bay's generally shallow waters.

Watermen use these boats year-round for harvesting marine life of all kinds, including blue crabs, clams, oysters, eels, and striped bass or rockfish. Over the decades, builders customized the deadrise design for specific uses and areas. A square stern is best for dredging crabs, while a round stern better accommodates oyster-tonging, which involves working both with and against the tide. Planking is generally stouter

for boats working the rougher waters of the lower Bay, while Maryland boats typically have a shallower draft to work the upper Bay's shallow tributaries.

Deadrises are now also widely used for Bay recreation and fishing due to their seaworthiness and historic allure. Most modern boats are fiberglass. The deadrise can use almost any engine, but diesels are preferred because of their reliability.

The state boat of both Virginia and Maryland, deadrises still work all around the Chesapeake. Bay museums also offer educational exhibits and rides aboard refurbished boats. In Virginia these include the 42-foot *Foggy River* at the Reedville Fishermen's Museum and the 35-foot round-stern *Jennie May* at the Deltaville Maritime Museum. Maryland offers the 43-foot draketail *Martha* and the 41-foot dovetail *Dorothy Lee* at the Chesapeake Bay Maritime Museum in St. Michaels.

BUYBOAT

These vessels come in various designs and sizes (40–90 feet long, 12–15 feet wide), but generally share three features: a rear wheelhouse; a long, wide deck to hold lots of cargo; and a deck-mounted crane for loading and unloading.

The origin of the buyboat is easy to grasp. Imagine you're tonging or dredging and have quickly covered your deck with oysters. To make room for more, you can sail for port to offload, but this will take time away from harvesting and cost money for crew and fuel. It would be much better for you and other nearby watermen to simply transfer your catch to another boat while you continue fishing. That roving "middleman" will take a cut, but nowhere near as much as you'd spend on your own trip to and from port.

Buyboats had their heyday in the first half of the twentieth century, circulating among watermen to collect their catches, then delivering their own accumulated cargo to a "scow gang" at the nearest dock for offloading. They were thus designed not for fishing but as "delivery trucks" to load and carry lots of oysters speedily to port.

Today, few if any buyboats operate on the Bay, their demise driven in part by harvest regulations that preclude limitless harvesting. Some were adapted for use in crab dredging, menhaden fishing, or hauling seed oysters to replenish Bay oyster reefs. Others have found new lives as yachts and dive charter boats.

Several Bay museums offer educational exhibits and rides aboard refurbished buyboats. In Virginia these include the 55-foot *Elva C* at the Reedville Fishermen's Museum and the 63-foot, log-bottomed *F. D. Crockett* at the Deltaville Maritime Museum, which in 2012 was added to the Virginia Landmarks Register and the National Register of Historic Places. The Chesapeake Bay Maritime Museum in St. Michaels, Maryland, operates the 65-foot *Winnie Estelle*.

SCHOONERS

These sailing ships (50–130 feet long, 16–26 feet wide) have two or more masts, the one in front typically shorter than the one behind. Their lower sails run parallel to the keel, in what mariners call a fore-aft rig. (In square-rigged ships, the sails run perpendicular to the keel.) Some schooners feature square-rigged topsails; more commonly, they have one or more triangular "jib" sails that extend forward to a long bowsprit. This often bears the vessel's name in ornately carved lettering.

Based on a seventeenth-century Dutch design, schooners reached their peak popularity during the 1800s along the US Atlantic seaboard, where their fore-aft sails proved more adept at harnessing the changeable coastal winds. Earlier square-rigged ships were designed for cross-Atlantic voyages powered by the steady force of the trade winds.

In the Bay, schooners were used to transport freight, carry passengers, and harvest oysters, blue crabs, and fish. Some also operated as privateers against the British. Long, very narrow schooners called "rams" were specifically designed to fit through the

The pungy schooner *Lady Maryland*.

Chesapeake and Delaware Canal. The schooner design later gave birth to bugeyes and pungies, whose shallower draft afforded greater access to Bay shallows. Boatbuilders also married its design to that of the square-rigged, three-masted "merchantmen," leading to the famous Baltimore clippers of the California gold rush and Chinese tea trade.

The golden age of schooners began to wane in the late 1800s as steamships, barges, and railroads came to the fore. But these elegant vessels continue to grace Bay waters, mostly as tourist and educational ships. The 105-foot *Alliance* offers trips out of Yorktown. The 122-foot *Virginia* regularly sails the Bay and can be visited at Nauticus in Norfolk and along with other tall ships during the city's annual Harborfest. In Maryland, the 50-foot *Sultana*, homeported in Chestertown, offers day-long and live-aboard sailing programs. The 100-foot *Pride of Baltimore II* promotes historical maritime education and represents Maryland in ports throughout the world. The 104-foot *Lady Maryland* is operated as an educational vessel by the Baltimore-based Living Classrooms Foundation.

In 1988, the captains of the *Pride of Baltimore II* and the 59-foot *Norfolk Rebel*, the world's only schooner-rigged tugboat, agreed to a race between the two cities. This Great Chesapeake Bay Schooner Race still takes place each October, now with more than 50 schooners and 150 other vessels competing. The schooner *Virginia* set the race record in 2017 with a time of 11 hours, 1 minute, and 41 seconds for the 146-mile competition.

DINGHY TENDER

Vessel 6–11 feet long and 3–5 feet wide. Almost comically petite, these boats are primarily designed to carry people and goods to and from a larger "mother ship" moored offshore, but also see use as recreational sailing craft and rowboats. Design criteria include a sturdy hull to protect against damage caused by impacts with dock pilings and mooring buoys, or when bringing aboard or tethering to the mother ship for transport while under sail. They also have high sides to keep out water and provide buoyancy for passengers and gear, and are lightweight for easy lifting onto a dock or aboard a larger vessel. Their light weight also facilitates transport to and from the "dinghy park" that many marinas provide for short-term storage while owners are onshore. Some of these boats have a deep, rearward expansion of the keel called a skeg, which helps them track straight when towed behind a larger vessel. Many modern dinghies are inflatable.

"Dinghy" is derived from an old Hindi word for a sail or oar-powered passenger vessel.

The typical dinghy is small and simple enough to make building your own boat a reality. Chesapeake Light Craft of Annapolis, Maryland, provides dinghy-building classes and kits and offers a "ShopCam" that allows you to watch boats being built in real time.

HAND TONGS

Envision picking croutons from a salad bar with a pair of tongs as tall as a two-story house. Now imagine that each tong handle is as thick as a baseball bat, crafted from dense hickory, and terminates in a cast-iron rake as broad as the one you use in your yard. Not yet difficult enough? For an added challenge, perform this entire task while standing on the narrow, wet lip of a wave-tossed log canoe, skiff, or deadrise workboat on a chilly February morning. Up to the task? Then you may want to consider trying your hand at hand-tonging for oysters in Chesapeake Bay!

European colonists introduced hand-tonging in the early 1700s as a way to reach oysters growing in deeper offshore waters, after increased harvest pressure had depleted the shoreline and intertidal reefs fished by countless generations of Native Americans. The scissor-like tongs likely began as shorter "nippers" for clawing visible oysters from reefs in the shallow subtidal waters. As harvest pressures continued to mount, the nippers stretched like Pinocchio's nose into longer and longer tongs, some of which eventually reached more than 20 feet in length.

MOORING BUOYS

Parking spaces for boats, these provide a safe and environmentally friendly anchorage for vessels of all sizes, from oceangoing container ships to recreational sailboats. The visible part of the mooring buoy—a white float with a horizontal blue stripe—is like the tip of an iceberg: much smaller than the massive, permanent seafloor anchor that lies beneath. Designed for use where docking facilities are unavailable or made unsafe by heavy seas, the round or tube-shaped buoy offers a loop to which a vessel can moor to the permanent anchor line. A requisite for using a mooring buoy is a tender or dinghy—a small, usually simple craft to carry crew and supplies between the moored vessel and the shore.

Mooring buoys are safer for mariners because their large anchor reduces the chance that a vessel will drag its own smaller anchor and drift during a storm. They're environmentally friendly because they allow multiple boats to sequentially use a single anchor, rather than requiring each boat to drop and retrieve its own. Anchors often destroy or disrupt seafloor communities when deployed and retrieved, so using a single, permanent anchor means less damage to seagrass beds, oyster reefs, and other bottom-dwelling organisms.

Placement of mooring buoys for commercial vessels requires both federal and state permits. Mooring buoys for recreational vessels are under state purview. Federal permits are granted by the US Army Corps of Engineers. State permits are granted by Maryland's Department of the Environment and Virginia's Department of Games and Inland Fisheries, respectively.

POUND NETS

A pound net uses a fence-like "leader"—a net hung between a series of poles placed perpendicular to the shoreline—to direct fish into a series of "hearts" that funnel them into a trap, or "pound," where watermen can remove targeted species with a dip net.

Native Americans long used this fishing method in Bay waters, as shown in Theodor de Bry's 1590 engraving of John White's 1585 watercolor. George Snediker was the first European American to use pound nets in Chesapeake waters, introducing them from Long Island in 1858. Initially spurned and destroyed by Bay fishermen jealous of their effectiveness, they were later adopted and in widespread use by the 1870s. A report by noted American ichthyologist R. Edward Earll noted: "On our visit to the [Mobjack Bay] in 1880, we found that every available site was taken up, and often three, or even four, nets were placed in a line. The leader of one being attached to the outer end of another, for the purpose both of economizing space and of securing the fish that chanced to be passing at a distance from the shore." Indeed, pound nets were so effective that the Bay catch of Spanish mackerel in 1880 reached 1.6 million pounds, 85 percent of the entire East Coast harvest. They were also particularly effective in catching menhaden and anadromous fishes such as shad, migrating up Bay tributaries to spawn.

Pound nets are still used in Bay waters, although they're strictly regulated to prevent overfishing. One of their best features is that non-targeted species or age classes can swim freely in the pound, and are thus likely to go on living and reproducing when freed. They are less friendly to sea turtles and dolphins, which can become entangled in the netting, leading to injury or drowning at high tide. To lessen that chance, modern pound nets use modified leaders whose uppermost netting uses stiff, vertical lines only, greatly reducing the likelihood of entanglement.

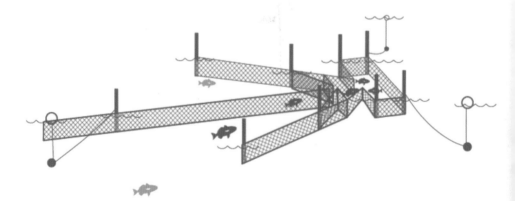

OYSTER CAGES

The Chesapeake is in the midst of a historic shift from the traditional harvest of wild oysters to oyster farming. The most visible signs are the cages and mooring poles sprouting up in nearshore areas around the Bay. The cages are of two main types. Rack-and-bag cages are attached above the seafloor, with an outer rack of vinyl-coated wire and an inner bag of plastic mesh to hold the growing oysters. The Taylor float is a buoyant rectangle of PVC pipe with a mesh floor. Both options protect against oyster predators such as blue crabs, cownose rays, and seabirds; ensure sufficient water flow for the oysters' filter feeding; and are relatively easy to maintain and handle. The poles offer a visible attachment to ease retrieval when rack-and-bag cages are submerged at high tide.

A grower's containment choice depends on their farm setting, boat traffic, and ability to handle the heavy gear, which they must regularly cleanse of barnacles, sea lettuce, and other fouling organisms to maintain water flow. They must also divvy up and disperse the oysters into new bags as the shellfish grow larger and begin to crowd their original homes.

The shift to oyster aquaculture is a response to the century-long decline of the Bay's wild harvest due to overfishing, habitat loss, and disease. While tonging and dredging of natural reefs and planted grounds produced up to 8 million bushels of oysters bay-wide each year during the 1880s, today's annual wild harvests come in at around 20,000

bushels—1/500th of historical totals. At the same time, oyster farming is growing by leaps and bounds throughout the Bay, often using carefully bred, "seedless" oysters that can grow to market size before succumbing to disease. Virginia growers sold approximately 20,000 bushels of farmed oysters in 2005, but more than 320,000 bushels in 2018. Maryland growers sold 22,428 bushels of oysters in 2013 and 74,066 bushels in 2017.

If you like oysters and have a chance, make sure to sample the product! The Virginia Oyster Trail (virginiaoystertrail.com) offers an online travel guide to the growing number of oyster farms and restaurants across the Commonwealth.

CHESAPEAKE BAY LIGHTHOUSES

Brilliant beacons for Bay boaters, dozens of lighthouses grace the shores and shoals of the Chesapeake. Built to warn of navigational hazards, they stretch from Cape Henry Light at the Bay mouth to Concord Point Light at the Bay's head. A visit to one or more of these structures is a must-see for anyone interested in Bay history, commerce, or naval activity. Many are open to the public as part of a park or other public space, and several offshore lights are accessible by charter boat. The Chesapeake Chapter of the US Lighthouse Society runs an annual "Lighthouse Challenge," in which participants visit a changing selection of ten Maryland lights. The society also sponsors a Passport Program, in which anyone collecting stamps at sixty lighthouses earns an official patch. The program helps support lighthouse preservation.

Many of the Bay's lighthouses are historic gems, led by the Cape Henry Light in Virginia Beach. Built in 1792, it was the first lighthouse funded by the fledgling US government and, indeed, the first federally funded public works project of any kind. In 1819 Congress authorized the first Maryland lights, at the entrance to Baltimore Harbor. Those were followed in 1824–25 by lights at Thomas Point Bar near Annapolis, Pooles Island near the mouth of the Gunpowder River, and Concord Point in Havre de Grace, where the Susquehanna River meets the Bay's tides.

In the early 1900s the number of Bay lighthouses peaked at seventy-one. Today, thirty-eight lighthouses still stand in the Bay: twenty-six in Maryland and twelve in Virginia. They are built in six main styles, not all of them "houses." The style and status of existing Bay lights are indicated on the accompanying map.

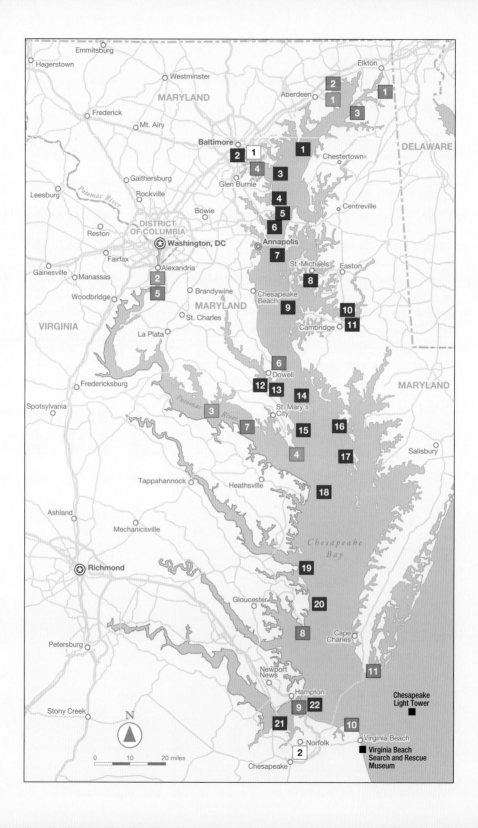

Bay Lights

Dozens of "lights" grace the shores and shoals of the Chesapeake. Here we list them by type, from onshore towers and integral lighthouses to offshore screw-piles, caissons, lightships, and a "Texas Tower." It's always best to call ahead for visiting hours. Also worth a visit is the Beach Surf and Rescue Museum in Virginia Beach. LH = Lighthouse

TOWERS

1. Bethel Bridge LH (replica)
2. Concord Point LH
3. Turkey Point LH
4. Fort Carroll Light
5. Fort Washington LH
6. Cove Point LH
7. Piney Point LH
8. New Point Comfort LH
9. Old Point Comfort LH
10. Cape Henry LH (old)
10. Cape Henry LH (new)
11. Cape Charles LH

SCREWPILE & CAISSON

1. Pooles Island Light
2. Seven Foot Knoll LH
3. Craighill LH
4. Baltimore Harbor Light
5. Sandy Point Shoal LH
6. Thomas Point Shoal Light
7. Bloody Point Bar Light
8. Hooper Strait LH (Display)
9. Sharps Island Light
10. Hambrooks Bar Light

11. Choptank River LH (Replica)
12. Drum Point (original location)
13. Drum Point LH (display)
14. Hooper Island LH
15. Point No Point LH
16. Holland Island Bar LH
17. Solomons Lump LH
18. Smith Point LH
19. Stingray Point LH (replica)
20. Wolf Trap Light
21. Middle Ground LH
22. Thimble Shoal Light

INTEGRAL

1. Fishing Battery Island LH
2. Jones Point LH
3. Blackistone Island LH (replica)
4. Point Lookout LH

LIGHTSHIPS

1. USCG Lightship *Chesapeake*
2. Lightship *Portsmouth*

TEXAS TOWER

1. Chesapeake Light

TOWERS

The earliest Bay lights were simple towers of brick, stone, or wood, often with a spiral staircase leading to an oil-fueled light at the top. Often built on exposed points or spits to better warn ships of these navigational threats, many have succumbed to erosion or been replaced by newer, more landward structures. That explains the "new" Cape Henry Light. Built in 1881, it rises just yards away from its older twin.

INTEGRAL

A popular early design, this is simply a house with a light on top. Only a few remain in the Bay region: Fishing Battery Island Lighthouse at the mouth of the Susquehanna River, Jones Point Lighthouse near Old Town Alexandria in Virginia, the replica Blackistone Lighthouse in St. Clement's Island State Park, and Point Lookout Lighthouse in the Maryland state park of the same name. The Blackistone Lighthouse is only accessible by private watercraft or the St. Clement's Island Museum water taxi.

SCREWPILES

The Chesapeake has accommodated more screwpile lighthouses—forty-two—than anywhere else in the world. The name refers to the construction method, in which seven cast-iron or wooden piles were screwed into the seafloor, carrying the light-bearing structure directly over the water. That structure was traditionally an octagonal, one- to one-and-a-half-story "keeper's house." Screwpiles cost little to build, could be erected quickly, and were particularly well suited for the Bay and other estuaries with soft, muddy, or sandy bottoms. Their Achilles' heel was vulnerability to damage from ice floes, which led most to be replaced by caisson lights. The Thomas Point Shoal Lighthouse, the last remaining screwpile light in the Bay, is available for guided tours.

LIGHTSHIPS

These are anchored vessels equipped with an elevated light to warn other moving vessels of navigational hazards. They were typically used in places too deep or with bottoms too hard for the construction of a screwpile. Originally just a repurposed sailing vessel, lightships later evolved to provide greater stability for the light and enhanced creature comforts for the light-keeping crew, who might spend months at sea. All Bay lightships have now been replaced by navigational buoys. Two historical vessels are available to view: the lightship *Chesapeake* in Baltimore harbor and the lightship *Portsmouth* in the Virginia city of the same name.

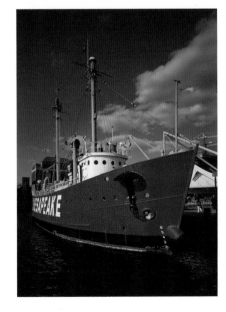

CAISSONS

These lights feature a lighted tower built atop a stone-filled cylinder that has been sunk deeply into the seafloor. The cylinder was typically constructed of cast iron, while the tower might be of either cast iron or brick. Caisson lights were a sturdier, though more costly, replacement for screwpiles. Of the seven caissons built on the Bay, all survive. Three are in Virginia: Wolf Trap (1894), Smith Point (1897), and Thimble Shoal (1914); the other four are in Maryland: Solomons Lump (1895), Hooper Island (1902), Point No Point (1905), and Baltimore (1908).

TEXAS TOWER

Only one of these exists in the Bay region: the Chesapeake Light Tower, 13 miles outside the Bay mouth. Built in 1965, this enormous, 120-foot-high lighted platform resembles an offshore oil rig and was based on the same design.

A DEEPER DIVE

Aschettino, J. M., et al. "Satellite Telemetry Reveals Spatial Overlap between Vessel High-Traffic Areas and Humpback Whales (Megaptera novaeangliae) Near the Mouth of the Chesapeake Bay." *Frontiers in Marine Science*, 7 (2020).

Atlantic States Marine Fisheries Commission. "Atlantic Menhaden" (2020). www.asmfc.org/species/atlantic-menhaden.

Bailey, H. "Dolphinwatch: Understanding Why Dolphins Visit the Chesapeake Bay" (2020). www.umces.edu/dolphinwatch.

Beck, C., R. Pawlitz, and J. Bloomer. "Famous Manatee 'Chessie' Sighted in Chesapeake Bay After Long Absence." *Sound Waves* (St. Petersburg, FL: US Geological Survey, 2011).

Blaylock, R. A. "The Distribution and Abundance of the Bottlenose Dolphin, Tursiops truncatus, in Virginia." Thesis (MA), William & Mary (1984).

———. "Distribution, Abundance, and Behavior of the Cownose Ray, Rhinoptera bonasus (Mitchill, 1815), in Lower Chesapeake." Thesis (PhD), William & Mary.

———. "The Marine Mammals of Virginia: With Notes on Identification and Natural History." VIMS education series, no. 35. (Gloucester Point, VA: Virginia Sea Grant College Program, Marine Advisory Services, Virginia Institute of Marine Science, 1985).

BoatUS Foundation. "Aids to Navigation" (2020). www.boatus.org/study-guide/navigation/aids.

Bradley, S., et al. "Pass It On: Cultural Traditions of the Lower Eastern Shore." Lower Shore Traditions Program (ed.). (Salisbury, MD: Ward Museum of Wildfowl Art, Salisbury University, 2013).

Bugas, P. E., Jr., et al. *Field Guide to Freshwater Fishes of Virginia* (Baltimore: Johns Hopkins University Press, 2019).

Chao, L. N., and J. A. Musick. "Life-History, Feeding-Habits, and Functional-Morphology of Juvenile Sciaenid Fishes in York River Estuary, Virginia." *Fishery Bulletin*, 75(4) (1977). scholarworks.wm.edu/vimsarticles/637.

Chesapeake Chapter: US Lighthouse Society. "Lighthouses" (2017). cheslights.org.

Chesapeake Light Craft. "Rowing Craft: Dinghies" (2018). www.clcboats.com/shop/rowboats/dinghies.

Chowning, L. S. *Harvesting the Chesapeake: Tools & Traditions* (revised and expanded second edition) (Atglen, PA: Schiffer Publishing Company, 2014).

Cox, J. "Humpback Whales, Large Ships on Deadly Course at Bay's Mouth." *Bay Journal* (Seven Valleys, PA: Bay Journal Media, 2020).

Dickon, C. *Images of America: Chesapeake Bay Steamers* (Charleston, SC: Arcadia Publishing, 2006).

Earll, R. E. "The Spanish Mackerel: Its Natural History and Artificial Propagation, with an Account of the Origin and Development of the Fishery" (Washington, 1883).

Florida Museum of Natural History. "International Shark Attack File 2018." www.floridamuseum.ufl.edu/shark-attacks.

Franklin, H. B. *The Most Important Fish in the Sea: Menhaden and America* (Washington, DC: Island Press/Shearwater Books, 2011).

Gill, T. "The Life History of the Sea-Horses (Hippocampids)." *Proceedings of the US National Museum*, 28 (1905).

Goodall, J. L. H. *Pirates of the Chesapeake Bay: From the Colonial Era to the Oyster Wars* (Charleston, SC: The History Press, 2020).

Heinle, D. R. "Free-Living Copepoda of the Chesapeake Bay." *Chesapeake Science*, 13 (1972).

Hicks, B. *Then & Now: Maryland Workboats* (Charleston, SC: Arcadia Publishing, 2009).

Hinman, J. E. "The Intrepid Workboats of the Chesapeake." *The House & Home Magazine* (Tappahannock, VA: JLB Publishing, 2019).

Kirkley, J., and D. Kerstetter. "Saltwater Angling and Its Economic Importance to Virginia" (Virginia Institute of Marine Science, William & Mary, 1997).

Leatherwood, S., D. K. Caldwell, and H. E. Winn. *Whales, Dolphins, and Porpoises of the Western North Atlantic: A Guide to Their Identification* (Seattle: NOAA, 1976).

Leatherwood, S., R. R. Reeves, and L. Foster. *The Sierra Club Handbook of Whales and Dolphins* (San Francisco: Sierra Club Books, 1983).

Luckenbach, M. W., F. X. O'Beirn, and J. H. Taylor. "An Introduction to Culturing Oysters in Virginia" (Gloucester Point, VA: Virginia Institute of Marine Science, William & Mary, 1999).

Lucy, J., T. Ritter, and J. LaRue. "The Chesapeake, a Boating Guide to Weather." Educational series, no. 25. (Gloucester Point, VA: Virginia Institute of Marine Science, William & Mary, 1979).

Maryland Department of Health. "Harmful Algae Blooms" (2020). phpa .health.maryland.gov/OEHFP/EH/Pages/harmful-algae-blooms.aspx.

Maryland Department of Natural Resources. "Bay Grass Identification Key" (2020). dnr.maryland.gov/waters/bay/Pages/sav/key.aspx.

McKay, L., and V. Witmer. "Virginia Oyster Gardening Guide" (Richmond, VA: Virginia Coastal Zone Management Program, 2013).

Miller, C. C. "The Last Skipjacks Project" (2019). lastskipjacks.com/index.html.

NOAA Fisheries. "Marine Life Viewing Guidelines: Whale Watching and Wildlife Viewing in New England and the Mid-Atlantic" (2020). www .fisheries.noaa.gov/new-england-mid-atlantic/marine-life-viewing-guidelines/ whale-watching-and-wildlife-viewing-new.

Odenkirk, J., and S. Owens. "Northern Snakeheads in the Tidal Potomac River System." *Transactions of the American Fisheries Society*, 134(6) (2005).

Pace, L., et al. "Salinity Tolerance of the Sandbar Shark, Carcharhinus plumbeus, and their use of the Chesapeake Bay for Predator Avoidance." *EOS, Transactions, American Geophysical Union*, 87(36) (2006).

Save the Manatee Club. "Save the Manatee" (2020). www.savethemanatee .org.

Schroath, J. A. (ed.). *Guide to Cruising Chesapeake Bay* (Annapolis, MD: Chesapeake Bay Media LLC, 2018).

Sugarman, J. "Pungies, Bugeyes, and Skipjacks: Your Guide to Chesapeake Bay Workboats." *Washingtonian Magazine* (2016).

The Mariners' Museum. "Lighthouses on the Chesapeake Bay" (2002). www.marinersmuseum.org/sites/micro/cbhf/lighthouses/cbl001.html.

The Mariners' Museum and Park. "Chesapeake Bay Workboats" (2002). www.marinersmuseum.org/sites/micro/cbhf/waterman/wat002.html.

Turbyville, L. *Bay Beacons: Lighthouses of the Chesapeake Bay* (Trappe, MD: Eastwind Publishing, 1995).

United States Lighthouse Society. "Alphabetical Lighthouse Listing" (2020). uslhs.org.

Virginia Department of Game and Inland Fisheries. "Northern Snakehead" (2018). dwr.virginia.gov/fishing/snakehead.

Virginia Department of Health. "Virginia HAB Task Force" (May 14, 2020). www.vdh.virginia.gov/waterborne-hazards-control/harmful-algal-blooms/virginia-hab-task-force.

Walker, C. "Crabbing Skiff: A Chesapeake Bay Working Boat from Chapelle." *Small Boats Magazine* (June 2018).

A Day AT THE Beach

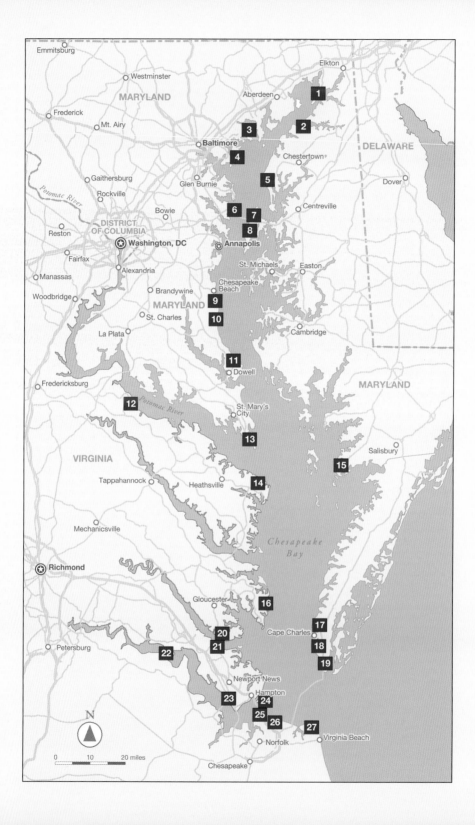

A Day at the Beach

Time on a Chesapeake beach is a true highlight of the Bay experience. Here's a selection of publicly accessible beaches from around the Bay, chosen to showcase the diversity of beach types the region has to offer. NAP = Natural Area Preserve, SP = State Park

1. North East Beach
2. Betterton Beach
3. Gunpowder Falls SP Hammerman Area Beach
4. Rocky Point Park and Beach
5. Rock Hall Beach (Ferry Park)
6. Sandy Point SP
7. Terrapin Nature Park
8. Matapeake SP
9. North Beach
10. Breezy Point Beach
11. Calvert Cliffs SP
12. Colonial Beach Town Pier
13. Point Lookout SP
14. Vir-Mar Beach
15. Crisfield Beach
16. Haven/Festival Beach
17. Savage Neck Dunes State NAP
18. Cape Charles Beachfront
19. Kiptopeke SP
20. Gloucester Point Beach Park
21. Yorktown Beach
22. Jamestown Beach Event Park
23. Huntington Park Beach
24. Buckroe Beach and Park
25. Outlook Beach: Fort Monroe
26. City of Norfolk Beaches
27. First Landing SP

CHESAPEAKE BAY BEACHES have a beauty and feel all their own, enhanced by the constellation of plants and animals highlighted in the following pages. Narrower and shorter than their ocean cousins, Bay beaches usually offer a tranquil demeanor that appeals particularly to families with small children. But when a normally calm beach feels a nor'easter or hurricane, it can be anything but. Plan your visit accordingly.

Three main factors control the size and shape of a beach: sand supply, wave energy, and water level. These change with seasons, winds, currents, and tides, and also interact with the Bay's convoluted shape. These factors make Bay beaches highly dynamic features, and combine to create a hopscotch shoreline that can alternate between sand, marsh, and mud over remarkably short distances. People have also disturbed and harnessed these factors to alter the Chesapeake's beach-scape in ways big and small (see "Hand of Man," p. 124).

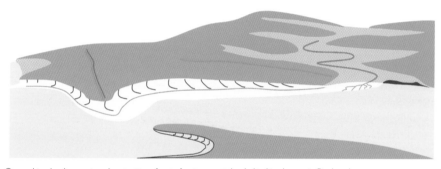

Ownership, development, and protection of waterfront property has led to big changes in Bay beaches.

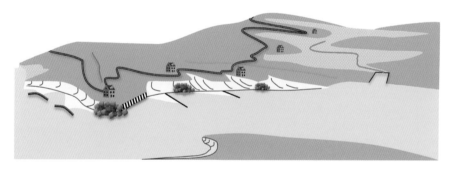

SAND SUPPLY

In the Bay, beach sand is typically supplied through slumping of shoreline bluffs undercut by storm waves. The sand grains, mostly iron-stained quartz and feldspar, are the durable remains of weathered igneous and metamorphic rocks eroded from the Appalachians during the last 300 million years. Carried to the coastal plain by streams and rivers, then reworked by rising and falling seas, the sand beneath your feet could once have been part of a granitic peak soaring as high as today's Himalayas.

YESTERBAY

Heyday on the Bay

Before Bay-spanning bridges eased access to the mid-Atlantic shore and air travel opened new opportunities for seaside vacations in such locales as Hawaii or the Caribbean, Chesapeake beaches were the go-to spot for the region's growing leisure class.

The earliest spot for a bayside vacation was Chesapeake Beach, just 28 miles south of Washington, DC, via a direct railroad or daily steamship traffic from Baltimore. At its height in the early 1900s, the resort town featured hotels, bathhouses, casinos, a race track, a mile-long pier, and a 1,600-foot boardwalk with a band shell, dance pavilion, carousel, and roller coaster. Other early bayfront resorts included Betterton Beach, the "Jewel of the Chesapeake," and Tolchester Beach, both accessible on Maryland's eastern shore by steamship. At Tolchester Beach, vacationers could take tea in the mouth of a preserved whale and rent a woolen, full-length bathing suit for men or a skirted bloomer for women. In 1887 the resort had 500 suits for rent. By 1909 they rented more than 2,000 each day.

Two other notable Bay resorts were established by African Americans in response to segregation at other vacation spots. Highland Beach was founded by Frederick Douglass's son Charles and daughter-in-law Laura in 1893 after they were refused entry to nearby Bay Ridge Beach in Annapolis. Carr's Beach, also near Annapolis, hosted noted Black entertainers such as Billie Holiday, Ray Charles, and James Brown.

Done in by the Great Depression and the advent of the automobile, these sites remain as lovely public beaches, albeit with less of a carnival atmosphere. The grand resort in Chesapeake Beach lives on through displays in the Chesapeake Beach Railway Museum.

Beach sands extend beyond the sandy apron that holds your chair and umbrella—both Bay-ward beneath the water and, in some places, landward into a line of dunes. Sand is carried between these reservoirs by waves, currents, and wind, and any of them can supply sand to another, depending on the conditions.

Erosion of shoreline bluffs provides sand for Bay beaches.

WAVE ENERGY

Waves, tidal currents, and river flow can all winnow lighter and less-resistant particles away from a shoreline, leaving the heavier, more durable sand grains of the typical beach. Wave energy depends on both windspeed and fetch (the area over which the wind blows). In the ocean, a fetch might extend over thousands of square miles and generate huge swells. When these swells near land, they shorten, steepen, and break, dissipating their immense energy by incising and swashing across a wide beach. Fetch in the Chesapeake is limited by the narrowness of its tributaries, as well as its many points, necks, and peninsulas. By blocking the wind, these obstructions keep waves in the Bay relatively small, and its beaches narrow. The exceptions are a few more-exposed beaches near the Bay mouth that occasionally feel an ocean swell.

Bay waves are often gentle, affording safe swimming.

LONGSHORE DRIFT

Driven by the wind, waves can break upon a beach from any seaward direction. But, driven by gravity, their backwash flows in one direction only—downhill perpendicular to the shore face. This dichotomy sets up what is known as longshore drift, where the sand mobilized by breaking waves tends to zigzag along the shoreline in the direction of the prevailing wind.

In the ocean, the consistency of trade winds and daily onshore breezes generates a powerful longshore drift that can carry sand long distances and form large-scale features such as the barrier islands of Virginia and North Carolina's Outer Banks. In the Chesapeake, where winds are more fickle and the shoreline more convoluted, longshore drift acts on a smaller scale but still helps control the size, shape, and location of Bay beaches. Sand entrained in a longshore current will typically move in the direction of the prevailing wind until interrupted by a barrier—whether that's a headland, creek mouth, salt marsh, fallen tree trunk, or groin, as discussed later.

Longshore Drift

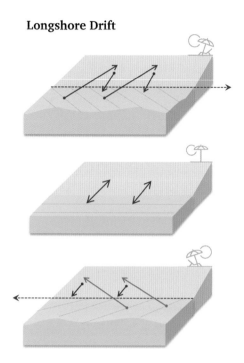

WATER LEVEL

Water level affects Bay beaches on all time scales—from the incessant swash of individual waves to the twice-daily rise and fall of the tide and slow but steady changes in sea level. Sea-level rise—which we discuss in the last chapter—is the factor that most concerns Bay-area governments and landowners. Tidal level and wave height are of greatest concern to beachgoers, as they control the width of the beach and whether you will be relaxing on a float or riding a boogie board. NOAA's Chesapeake Bay Interpretive Buoy System (CBIBS) and Tides & Currents websites are great spots for up-to-date information for planning around these factors.

For thousands of years prior to European colonization, Bay beaches waxed and waned as sand supply, wave energy, and water levels changed in response to climatic and geologic variations. This dynamism posed few problems for beach life or Native Americans, as they simply moved with the shifting sands. Europeans, however, imported a cultural and legal system based on land ownership, which for waterfront properties typically extends to mean low tide (although the intertidal area reverts to public use when the tide returns). Under this system, landowners concerned with property loss due to an eroding sandbank often attempt to slow or stop it with a bulkhead, revetment, or other means. Or they might build a groin to replenish a thinning beach. Indeed, scientists estimate that more than 1,700 miles of tidal shoreline in Maryland and Virginia have been "hardened" using one of these methods.

Top: This CBIBS buoy collects data near the York River mouth.
Bottom: Many Bay beaches use shoreline management techniques to ensure sand for beachgoers.

   European ideas of land ownership have led to widespread efforts to combat natural changes in water level and shoreline erosion. Paradoxically, these attempts at shoreline protection often have the opposite effect, both for the affected landowner and those nearby. By slowing sandbank erosion, revetments remove the source of sand for nearby beaches, which then thin or disappear. By interrupting longshore drift, groins also keep sand from "downstream" beaches, again leading to their thinning or disappearance. Bulkheads bring their own problems, preventing shore life from moving between water and land, often increasing beach scour by reflecting and concentrating wave energy.

   Luckily, scientists and engineers now understand beach dynamics well enough to offer more-effective approaches to shoreline management, including use of living shorelines, breakwaters, sills, and beach nourishment. You will encounter these structures and tactics at many of the Bay's most popular beaches, including many highlighted in this guidebook. In addition to controlling shoreline erosion, these approaches help maintain habitat for beach plants and animals. It is to these we now turn.

Plants

American Beach Grass (*Ammophila breviligulata*)

DESCRIPTION

This clumping, perennial grass has many narrow leaves that arise mostly from base of the plant, around a 3- to 4-foot spike topped by a cylinder of tiny green flowers that ripen in late summer to a light gray seed head. Leaves 2 inches wide and up to 3 feet long, pointed, and alternate with parallel veins. May become rolled with age. Clumps grow from long underground stems, or rhizomes. Often found with sea oats, which have a tawny gold seed head and narrower leaves along entire stem.

HABITAT & ECOLOGY

The most common plant on Bay dunes and vital to their persistence, as it sends up new shoots from its rhizomes whenever buried by blowing sand, eventually producing a stabilizing root network as deep as the dune is high—up to 40 feet! Often forms single-species stands on dune slope nearest water; mixes with bitter panicum, sea oats, seaside goldenrod, and other dune plants farther inland. Provides cover for small animals; seeds attract birds.

DID YOU KNOW?

Often planted to stabilize dunes for shoreline protection, this plant can withstand hot sun, drying winds, and repeated burial, but it is vulnerable to foot and vehicle traffic; hence the familiar signs encouraging beachgoers to stay off the dunes. Leaves once used for baskets and thatch. Genus name *Ammophila* means "sand lover" in Greek.

Beach Panic Grass (*Panicum amarum*)

DESCRIPTION
The lovely, blue-gray hue of this perennial grass distinguishes it from American beach grass and sea oats. Leaves are evergreen and smooth, growing 1–3 feet tall and ¼–½ inch wide in erect to arching clumps that arise from nodes along the underground stems or rhizomes. Flower stalk is up to 6 feet high and topped with a 1-foot-long, compressed mass of small flowers that bloom in fall before ripening to grain-like seeds.

HABITAT & ECOLOGY
One of the most common plants on the landward side of Bay sand dunes. Able to withstand salt spray and burial by windblown sand, although less hardy in these respects than American beach grass and sea oats. Also occurs along the edge of salt marshes. Can survive extended drought and is somewhat winter hardy. Provides cover and habitat for songbirds, waterfowl, and small mammals.

DID YOU KNOW?
Often planted for restoration of coastal dunes, as the clumps and rhizomes help trap and bind blowing sand. Also planted ornamentally for attractive color of foliage. Cherokees used the stems to pad the inside of their moccasins. A favorite food of cattle, sheep, and goats, which has led to overgrazing in some places. "Panic" of common name stems from the Latin *panicum*, a type of millet. Also known as bitter panicum, short dune grass, running beach grass, and sea-beach grass.

Sea Oats (*Uniola paniculata*)

DESCRIPTION

This stately perennial is easily recognized due to its eye-catching seed heads. Up to 6 inches long, they bear clusters of flat seeds that resemble cereal grains like oats and wheat. First green, they ripen to a tawny gold in late summer. Stems are smooth and grow erect to 6 feet; drooping leaves are up to 2 feet long but less than ½ inch wide, tapering to an often brown and curled point. Leaves arise all along stem, unlike the mostly basal leaves of American beach grass, which also sports a dull-gray seed head. Robust roots and rhizomes often visible.

HABITAT & ECOLOGY

A keystone plant of dunes and beaches near the Bay's Atlantic mouth. Stems and rhizomes play a vital role in initiating dunes by catching blowing sand; roots help preserve dunes and beaches by binding sand during hurricanes and nor'easters. Occurs with seaside goldenrod and American beach grass, which dominates north of Bay mouth. Tolerates salt spray, drought, burial by sand, and brief surges of salt water.

DID YOU KNOW?

This plant shouldn't be disturbed due to its important role in stabilizing beaches and dunes. Burial of plant base by blowing sand encourages stems to sprout new rhizomes and stimulates existing rhizomes to spread.

Sea Rocket (*Cakile edentula*)

DESCRIPTION

A low-growing annual with fleshy leaves, pale lavender flowers, and an odd 2-part fruit. Many-branched stems typically ascend to approximately 12 inches, but may also creep in zigzag pattern along the sand. Leaves are simple, alternate, and toothed or weakly lobed. Up to 2 inches long, they are somewhat spoon-shaped and turn yellow in fall. Flowers are ¼ inch wide, with four petals forming a cross. They bloom  May–October. Constricted amidships, the fruit resembles a fleshy green figure eight and holds one to two seeds in its buoyant casing. Stems and leaves taste like horseradish.

HABITAT & ECOLOGY

Grows closer to water than almost any other Bay plant. Inhabits beach-wrack community between high-tide line and dune toe, using nutrients from decaying detritus (often from nearby salt marshes) for growth in otherwise infertile, sandy soil. Fleshy stems and leaves help store water in this sunny, salty environment. In spring, scores of new plants may sprout just above high-tide mark, but few survive into summer.

DID YOU KNOW?

Like several other beach plants, sea rocket responds to burial in sand by growing faster and producing more seeds. Common name has two explanations: the rocket-like shape of its seedpods or its similarity in taste to roquette, or arugula. Native Americans were reported to have harvested the roots for food.

Yucca (*Yucca filamentosa*)

DESCRIPTION

This unmistakable evergreen has a basal pincushion of stiff, sharply pointed, gray-green leaves whose edges are adorned by many fine, curlicued white threads. Leaves 4 inches wide and 2–3 feet tall. Develops a central vertical stalk with multiple branches bearing white, nodding, bell-shaped flowers that bloom June–September. Stalk typically about 6 feet tall but may reach 12–15 feet. Stalk and seedpods persist long after flowering. Grows in isolated clumps.

HABITAT & ECOLOGY

Prefers coastal sand dunes but also grows in inland sites where porous, infertile soils provide dry, desertlike conditions for roots. Tolerant of salt spray. Depends on yucca moth (*Tegeticula yuccasella*) for pollination; moth larvae depend on developing yucca seeds for food.

DID YOU KNOW?

Native Americans used the leaf fibers for baskets, fishing line, and clothing. Immature fruits can be cooked and eaten after seeds are removed; the large petals are used in salads. Name comes through Spanish from Taino, the native language of Haiti; also known as Adam's needle, bear grass, needle palm, and Spanish bayonet. Species name *filamentosa* refers to white threads on leaf edges.

Animals

Coquina Clam (*Donax variabilis*)

DESCRIPTION

These smooth, thin-walled bivalves (½–1 inch) vary greatly in color, with concentric rings (and sometimes rays) of lighter or darker hue against a pastel background of red, blue, and green shades (they've been likened to a "Southern sunrise.") A pair of snorkel-like siphons often poke out between the opened shells, whose interior is commonly purple. Shell lopsided, with one side extending sideways much farther from the umbo.

HABITAT & ECOLOGY

Common in the swash zone of sandy beaches, a habitat it shares with mole crabs. Range in Chesapeake restricted to near the Bay mouth. They filter microorganisms and detritus from the wave-churned swash water, pumping it through their siphons and across the sievelike gills to remove suspended food, with the shell anchored beneath the moving sand by a muscular foot. Preyed on by shorebirds and fishes; humans eat them as a hot or chilled broth after steaming and also harvest the shells for ornamental use.

DID YOU KNOW?

The presence of these wedge, or Pompano, clams indicates a healthy beach. Beach renourishment projects can bury and kill entire coquina colonies, which then require several years to reestablish, and only if unaffected populations remain nearby.

Atlantic Ghost Crab (*Ocypode quadrata*)

DESCRIPTION

Boxlike shell, or carapace, is typically tan to butterscotch on top, creamy white below. Younger crabs may be mottled. Has 10 appendages—8 hairy, stilt-like legs elevate the body above the sand and are used for locomotion; two claws are used to grasp and feed. Both claws are white and fringed with tiny spines, and one is bigger than the other. As if ten limbs weren't enough to keep track of, also has a pair of pincerlike mandibles to place food in its mouth. Eyes are borne on two prominent stalks, à la Mr. Krabs in *SpongeBob SquarePants*.

HABITAT & ECOLOGY

Inhabit sandy tropical and subtropical beaches worldwide. In the Chesapeake region, the ghost crab is restricted to beaches closest to the Bay mouth. An omnivore, it forages above the high-tide line for detritus, vegetation, insects, mole crabs, and sea turtle eggs. Digs tunnel-like burrows up to 4 feet deep, which it uses to shelter from predators, summer's heat, and winter's chill. Preyed on by shorebirds, gulls, and raccoons. Will occasionally dip a leg or two (or eight) in seawater to wet its gills, but otherwise keeps ashore.

DID YOU KNOW?

Ghost crabs have delighted generations of beachgoers with their high-speed, Whac-a-Mole antics. Watch closely as they dig

their burrows and you'll notice they use their legs and claws to fling the excavated sand aside in a characteristic splatter pattern. The fastest crustaceans on land, these "speedsters of the sand" can sprint at almost 10 miles per hour, accelerate rapidly from a standing start, reverse direction without losing much speed, and even spin their body through 180 degrees while continuing to run in the same direction.

Atlantic Horseshoe Crab (*Limulus polyphemus*)

DESCRIPTION

Horseshoe crabs have a 3-part body. Most prominent is the inflated, horseshoe-shaped head, which tapers to a spine on both aft sides. Next is a hinged abdomen edged with movable spines. Last is a stiff, spiked tail, or "telson." You'd be bristly too if your species had been around for 360 million years! Two bean-shaped eyes occupy the highest point of the head; has 7 other inconspicuous eyes plus photoreceptors along the tail. Below are 5 pairs of legs, a single pair of feeding pincers, the book gills, and a central mouth. Grows up to 2 feet long and 1 foot across, with females larger than males. Shell is a lovely tawny brown.

HABITAT & ECOLOGY

As adults, horseshoe crabs crawl along the sandy floor of the coastal ocean in search of small clams, worms, other invertebrates, and detritus. They come ashore to mate—often in large aggregations—from late May through June, with activity in the Chesapeake peaking on sheltered lower Bay beaches during full-moon high tides. Young crabs spend their first 1–2 years in nearshore flats, growing through a series of molts. Tolerate a wide range of temperatures and can survive out of water for lengthy periods as long as their gills remain wet. Eggs are a key food source for migrating shorebirds, and adults are a favorite food of juvenile loggerhead turtles. Eggs and larvae are also important food for many invertebrates and fish, including striped bass and American eels. Individuals can live 20–30 years.

DID YOU KNOW?

"Living fossils" that predate dinosaurs, horseshoe "crabs" are actually most closely related to scorpions and spiders. The remains found on ocean and Bay beaches are typically discarded molts. Medical companies catch and release hundreds of thousands every year to harvest their blood, which contains a compound used to test drugs for bacterial toxins. Also harvested for fishing bait. Harvest pressures have raised concern about the long-term health of the population; other horseshoe crab species around the world have experienced sharp declines.

Isopods (*Ligia exotica*)

Isopods, familiar as pill bugs or roly-polies, are one of largest groups of crustaceans. Most are marine, including *Erichsonella attenuata*, a common but well-camouflaged resident of the Chesapeake's eelgrass beds. Here we focus on a Bay isopod you are more likely to see, the sea roach (*Ligia exotica*).

DESCRIPTION

To 1½ inches. Body is segmented and flattened from top to bottom, with a large pair of antennae and an equal-size pair of forked rear appendages. Has prominent compound eyes. Shell is a mottled gray-brown.

HABITAT & ECOLOGY

A common resident of exposed dock pilings and riprap around the Bay, where large droves will scurry for cover as you approach, darting into the nearest crevice or running full-tilt and upside down onto the underside of a rock. Grazes on algae and diatoms and scavenges bits of detritus and plant debris. Preyed on by some shorebirds. Does not venture into the water; lays its eggs on land.

DID YOU KNOW?

As the name attests, this species is thought to be a non-native "exotic," though it was likely introduced globally hundreds of years ago with the first European sailing vessels and is now naturalized all along the US East Coast, including Chesapeake Bay. Recent genetic studies place its native range in East Asia.

Atlantic Mole or Sand Crab (*Emerita talpoida*)

DESCRIPTION
Built for rapid backward digging, with a streamlined body, 5 short but strong legs, and a tucked-under tail. Egg-shaped body is sandy brown on top and ivory below. Eyes held upright on two nearly transparent stalks, with a nearby pair of feathery antennae. Small enough to cradle in your palm. Females grow to 2 inches and carry their eggs in a bright orange mass beneath the tail. Males are much smaller—rarely exceeding ½ inch long—and often cluster around females.

HABITAT
Restricted to sandy beaches near the Bay mouth. Inhabit the swash zone, one of Earth's most volatile habitats, shifting with the tide to remain within the surge of breaking waves. The upside is proximity to a near-constant broth of wave-stirred plankton and detritus. Feed by scurrying down the beach with each receding wave, then quickly burying their body in the sand while extending their antennae to filter food from the rushing water. Often associated with coquina clams. Preyed on by sanderlings, gulls, and other shorebirds; fishes; and other crabs. Regularly used by anglers for bait.

DID YOU KNOW?
These little diggers delight beachgoers with their Houdini-like ability to disappear in sand, whether on the beach or at the bottom of a pail or sand-castle moat. To catch one, watch for flotillas of V-shaped wakes as waves recede, then quickly dig with a cupped hand at a vertex. They can't bite or pinch, so take a close look before returning them carefully to wet sand during the calm between breakers.

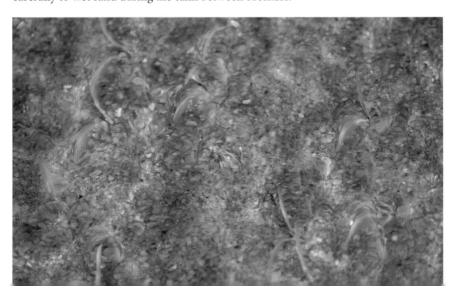

Moon Jelly (*Aurelia aurita*)

DESCRIPTION

Swimming bell is about the size and shape of a Frisbee, with hundreds of fine tentacles that make a short fringe. Both the bell and tentacles are clear to whitish. Central gonads—in the shape of a four-leaf clover—are the most prominent feature. The sting is mild or unnoticed.

HABITAT & ECOLOGY

Found in temperate areas worldwide, and present in lower Chesapeake Bay during summer. Tolerates a wide range of salinity and temperature, but prefers brackish waters between 48°F and 66°F. Favored prey is plankton, including copepods and the free-swimming larvae of mollusks, crustaceans, and fish. Captures prey items on tentacles and the mucus-covered surface of the bell, then uses flagella to pass these to the margins and along eight dorsal canals into the stomach. Can bloom rapidly when prey is abundant, and thus it plays a key role in the Bay food web. Eaten by fish, sea turtles, and birds. Like other jellies, life cycle alternates between the familiar "medusa" form with bell and tentacles and an attached, anemone-like form called a polyp.

DID YOU KNOW?

Both the size and shape of this creature can vary with environmental conditions. Medusae grow larger when food is abundant and shrink when food becomes scarce. Curvature of bell increases with increasing salinity, and vice versa.

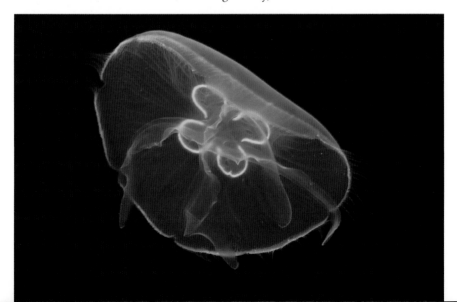

Bay Nettle (*Chrysaora chesapeakei*)

DESCRIPTION

Bell up to 8 inches across, with a convex dome. The 24 tentacles are as thin as spaghetti, several feet long, and closely and evenly spaced around the bell. Four long and ruffled oral arms emerge lasagna-like from beneath the bell's center. Sea nettles in the upper Bay are usually milky white; those in the lower, saltier portions are more likely to have reddish-brown stripes or splotches. The sting is painful but not dangerous unless there is an allergic reaction.

HABITAT & ECOLOGY

Present in the Chesapeake May–October and the most common Bay jelly during summer. Generally confined to brackish waters with salinities between 10 and 16 parts per thousand (seawater is approximately 32–36 ppt) and temperatures of 78°F–86°F. Populations thus peak in years with a warmer spring and higher salinities due to low rainfall. Cap-

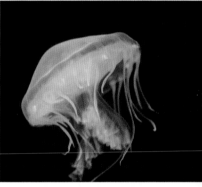

ture prey—mostly comb jellies—in their stinging tentacles, along with copepods and small fishes. Preyed on in Chesapeake Bay by many larger fishes, including Atlantic spadefish and butterfish, as well as leatherback sea turtles. Life cycle alternates between the familiar "medusa" form with bell and tentacles and an attached, anemone-like form called a polyp.

DID YOU KNOW?

NOAA's Chesapeake Bay office offers an online forecast of the likelihood of encountering bay nettles based on water temperature and salinity. This is a good resource to consult before visiting a Bay beach! The bay nettle was known as *Chrysaora quinquecirrha* until 2017, when a genetic study showed it to be a separate species from its sea-nettle cousins of Atlantic waters.

SHOREBIRDS

The Chesapeake is home to more than forty species of shorebirds. Most (thirty-two) are in the sandpiper family, including thirteen species with "sandpiper" in their name (e.g., spotted sandpiper) and many without (e.g., curlews, sanderlings, snipe, whimbrels, and willets). Together, the smaller sandpipers are affectionately known as "peeps." Bay shorebirds also comprise eight plover species, including killdeer. Other Bay shorebirds include the American oystercatcher and black-necked stilt. All have a relatively thin, long bill and long legs, well suited for picking and probing for bivalves, crabs, insects, and other small aquatic prey along open shorelines. Here we offer a few features to help you tell some of the more common shorebirds apart. For full treatment of the Bay's shorebirds, consult the references in "A Deeper Dive."

SPOTTED SANDPIPER

Breast of adult spotted during breeding season (April–August), otherwise white. Juvenile has pale orange legs. Regularly twerks tail in bobbing motion while walking. Frequents brackish and freshwater mudflats. Eats insects, worms, clams, crabs, fish, and spiders.

SANDERLING

Overwintering adult is pale gray above and white below. Breeding adult (less often seen in the Bay) has reddish head and brown back. Common on sandy beaches, where flocks follow waves in and out in search of coquina clams and mole crabs. Also eats insects.

KILLDEER

Boldly marked with two dark bands across breast. Tail is relatively long. Frequents open ground; more likely than other plovers to be found away from water. Eats earthworms, insects and their larvae, crayfish, snails, and seeds.

WILLET

Pale belly; rich brown spots above in summer, drab gray above in winter. Dark wing bisected by white distinctive in flight. Eats fiddler crabs, mole crabs, and other invertebrates from saltwater marshes and along open coastlines.

OYSTERCATCHER

Dark above and white below with unmistakably stout, orange bill. Frequents tidal flats in search of oysters and other bivalves; opens them by using its bill to snip the adductor muscle or smash the shell.

YELLOWLEGS

Long, yellow legs, grayish-brown plumage, and slightly upturned bill. Greater yellow-legs (*Tringa melanoleuca*) similar to lesser (*T. flavipes*) but slightly larger, with bill longer than head. Stabs invertebrates and insects at surface of fresh and brackish wetlands.

Hand of Man

BEACH NOURISHMENT

Beach nourishment is the practice of adding sand to extend a beach seaward. Though more common along ocean shores, beach nourishment does take place within Chesapeake Bay. This includes a few large projects such as a $34.5 million effort in 2017 to nourish a 7.3-mile stretch of Ocean View Beach in Norfolk, Virginia, and numerous smaller projects in conjunction with breakwaters in Virginia and Maryland. The goals are twofold: to reduce erosion of upland banks, and to create more recreational space for beachgoers. The sand is typically derived from dredging of navigation channels, mining of offshore shoals, or quarrying of sand deposits on land. Bay-floor sands are pumped to a project site through pipes in a sand-water slurry; they can also be transferred from a dredge barge to trucks and delivered by land. Though in some ways more natural than seawalls or other "hard" shoreline-protection structures, beach nourishment does

raise environmental concerns, as it can kill seafloor animals and destroy seafloor habitats, both where the sand is extracted and where it is emplaced. Public beach nourishment projects also tend to be controversial because they're expensive and are by nature temporary features that need to be replenished at regular intervals if the forces that originally led to beach erosion aren't addressed.

BREAKWATERS AND TOMBOLOS

As the name implies, breakwaters are elongate piles of rock or other materials placed slightly offshore to combat beach erosion by breaking the energy of incoming waves. Most often seen along the Bay's mainstem, they are frequently constructed in a series along a particular shoreline reach, with short gaps to direct refracted waves and allow

passage by marine life and boats. Every breakwater system is different, carefully designed by scientists and engineers to account for prevailing winds and waves, seafloor and shoreline profiles, and water-level changes due to sea-level rise and storms. Like other kinds of "insurance," their design embodies a trade-off between cost and the degree of protection sought by a waterfront property owner or

community. Designers must also weigh the potential loss of seagrass beds and other seafloor habitat beneath the breakwater footprint.

Unlike groins, breakwaters do not trap sand. A breakwater project thus typically involves beach nourishment as well, with sand added between the breakwater and shore to further curtail wave energy and provide more beach real estate. These sandy spits—called tombolos, from the Italian word for "sand dune"—are usually planted with smooth cordgrass or saltmeadow hay to provide habitat for shore life and further protect against wave energy.

The breakwater system at Yorktown near the mouth of the York River weathered a severe test when Hurricane Isabel blew ashore in 2003 with a 7-foot storm tide. At the storm's peak, 4-foot waves were breaking across the breakwaters and into the adjacent buildings. Although Yorktown's waterfront suffered considerable damage, the breakwaters did their job by preventing even worse destruction.

GROINS

Typically constructed of wood, groins are linear structures placed perpendicular to the shoreline to trap sand on the segment of beach "up-drift" of the longshore current. Groins can widen a beach, but often at the expense of the beaches in their lee—effectively manifesting in coastal real estate the folly of robbing Peter to pay Paul. What sometimes ensues is a series of groins emplaced by adjacent waterfront landowners, each one designed to widen a beach narrowed by the action of their up-drift neighbor. Coastal scientists recommend use of groins only as a last resort, and only on beaches with a copious supply of sand. They also advise use of a "spur" on the down-drift side of the groin to minimize the erosion otherwise likely to take place there due to refracted waves. Due to their drawbacks, resource managers now encourage landowners to switch from groins and other defensive shoreline-protection structures to "nature-based" solutions, such as living shorelines.

By the way, if you're wondering about the origin of the name, the shoreline "groin" is from the Latin *grunium*, for "pig's snout" (itself from *grunnire*, "to grunt"), in reference to how the structure protrudes from the beach into the water. The other, more familiar "groin" is from the Old English *grynde*, a depression or abyss.

LIVING SHORELINES

Traditional, "hard" approaches to managing shorelines—bulkheads, riprap revetments, seawalls—present major drawbacks: They destroy coastal habitat, decrease filtration of polluted runoff, and sever the connection between water and land. For instance, the bulkheads built by waterfront property owners to reduce shoreline erosion often require backfilling and burial of marshland, and block the passage of diamondback terrapins seeking to come ashore to lay their eggs.

Recognizing the drawbacks of shoreline "armoring," coastal scientists and engineers have in the last few decades developed and encouraged an alternative approach called a living shoreline. This involves strategic placement of sand, stone, native plants, and other natural materials to reduce erosion and enhance wetland habitat. They work best on protected, gently sloping shorelines where wave energy is minimal and can be dissipated across a significant distance. That's a common setting along many Bay tributaries and has led to increasing adoption of this more environmentally friendly approach around the Chesapeake. Living shorelines are generally not suitable for the high-energy shorelines of the mainstem Bay or coastal ocean, or where shoreline banks provide little room for dissipation of wave energy.

Properly designed, living shorelines offer numerous ecosystem services. They provide shelter and food for organisms; help keep nutrients, sediments, and other pollutants out of the Bay; and buffer low-lying lands from flooding. They also enhance recreational opportunities and serve as visually pleasing features. In the early 2000s, living shorelines were legally recognized as the preferred method of shoreline protection in both Maryland and Virginia.

REVETMENTS

The laid-back, typically stoned cousin of the bulkhead, revetments are layers of rock "riprap" placed atop a sloped shoreline to dissipate wave energy and reduce erosion. They are often installed along the bank behind a high-energy, wave-swept shoreline after it has been graded to a lesser slope to minimize slumping. Angled, rough surface improves on bulkhead design by absorbing, rather than reflecting, wave energy; revetments are therefore less susceptible to self-inflicted scouring along their underwater edge. Their many nooks and crannies also provide protection for wharf crabs, isopods, and other mobile invertebrates, as well as attached, bottom-dwelling creatures such as oysters, mussels, barnacles, tunicates, and sponges. Length, height, slope, and size of rocks are all engineered for each site's particular "wave climate."

Drawbacks of revetments are that they provide little soil for plant growth and thus filter few nutrients or pollutants from runoff. They can also block or hinder movement of snapping turtles, diamondback terrapins, raccoons, and other creatures whose lifestyle involves traveling between water and land for nesting or feeding. By reducing natural erosion of shoreline banks, revetments also decrease the amount of sediment available to the nearshore sand budget, and can thus force nearby property owners to turn to beach nourishment or groins to maintain their own beachfronts.

A DEEPER DIVE

Bilkovic, D. M., et al. (eds.). *Living Shorelines: The Science and Management of Nature-Based Coastal Protection* (Boca Raton, FL: CRC Press, 2017).

Byrne, R. J. "Shoreline Erosion in Tidewater Virginia." Prepared by Robert J. Byrne and Gary L. Anderson. G. L. Anderson (ed.). (Gloucester Point, VA: Virginia Institute of Marine Science, 1976).

Clark, S. "Dune Science: Flora" (2020). https://dunescience.com/category/flora.

———. "Dune Science: Fauna" (2020). https://dunescience.com/category/fauna.

Fleming, G. P., K. D. Patterson, and K. Taverna. "The Natural Communities of Virginia: A Classification of Ecological Community Groups and Community Types: Maritime Zone Communities." www.dcr.virginia.gov/natural-heritage/natural-communities/ncte.

Greene, K. "Beach Nourishment: A Review of the Biological and Physical Impacts." ASMFC Habitat Management Series (Washington, DC: Atlantic States Marine Fisheries Commission, 2002).

Hardaway, C. S., and R. J. Byrne. "Shoreline Management in Chesapeake Bay." Special report in *Applied Marine Science and Ocean Engineering*, vol. 356 (Gloucester Point, VA: Virginia Institute of Marine Science, William & Mary, 1999).

Hardaway, C. S., et al. "Sands of the Chesapeake" (Gloucester Point, VA: Virginia Institute of Marine Science, William & Mary, 2007).

Hosier, P. E. *Seacoast Plants of the Carolinas* (University of North Carolina Press, 2018).

Lucas, C. "Reproduction and Life History Strategies of the Common Jellyfish, *Aurelia aurita*, in Relation to Its Ambient Environment." *Hydrobiologia*, 451 (2001). 10.1023/A:1011836326717.

Middleton, L. "Nourishing Our Coastal Beaches: Adaptive Strategy or Fiscal Sand Trap?" *Come High Water: Sea Level Rise and Chesapeake Bay* (College Park, MD: Maryland Sea Grant, 2014).

Musick, J. A. "The Sea Turtles of Virginia: With Notes on Identification and Natural History." Virginia Institute of Marine Science (ed.) (Gloucester Point, VA: Virginia Sea Grant College Program, 1988).

National Fisheries Service. "Northeast Marine Mammal & Sea Turtle Protection Guidelines for Recreational Fishermen & Boaters from Maine through Virginia" (US Department of Commerce / NOAA, 2010).

National Research Council. *Beach Nourishment and Protection* (Washington, DC: The National Academies Press, 1995).

Pearse, A. S., H. J. Humm, and G. W. Wharton. "Ecology of Sand Beaches at Beaufort, North Carolina." *Ecological Monographs*, 12 (1942). https://doi-org/10.2307/1943276.

Richardson, H. "Isopods of North America." Bulletin, United States National Museum (Washington, DC: Smithsonian Institution, 1905).

A Marsh Paddle

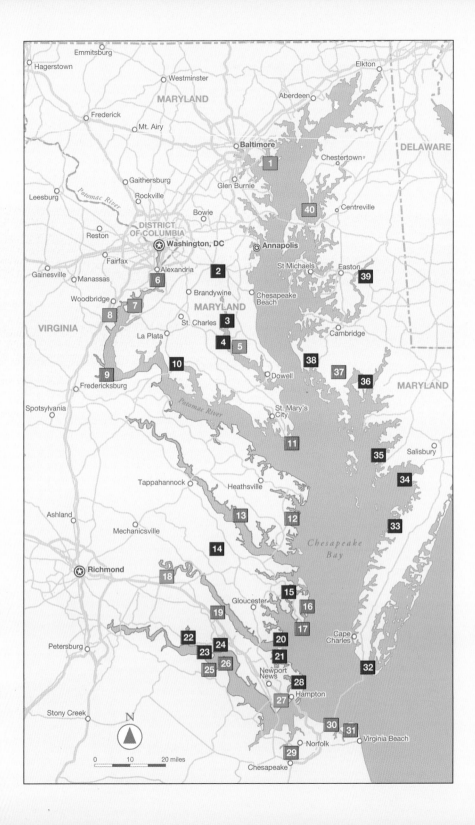

A Marsh Paddle

Marshes are most common and extensive in the lower Chesapeake watershed and along the bayside Eastern Shore. The forty selected here represent an exemplary collection of publicly accessible salt, brackish, and freshwater marshes; those in blue are accessible only by boat, in green by foot (trail or boardwalk), and in orange by either mode. These marshes are conserved by a diversity of federal, state, local, and private organizations; search online for the most current access information, which may vary due to water levels, conservation protections, or hunting restrictions. NA = Natural Area, NAP = Natural Area Preserve, NWR = National Wildlife Refuge, RP = Regional Park, SP = State Park, WMA = Wildlife Management Area

1. Black Marsh NA
2. Patuxent Wetland Park
3. King's Landing Park
4. Hallowing Point—Caney Creek
5. Battle Creek Cypress Swamp
6. Dyke Marsh
7. Mason Neck NWR
8. Metz Wetlands (Neabsco RP)
9. Crow's Nest NAP
10. Allens Fresh NA
11. Point Lookout SP
12. Dameron Marsh NAP
13. Belle Isle SP
14. Dragon's Run
15. Mathews Kayak Trail
16. Bethel Beach NAP
17. New Point Comfort NAP
18. Cumberland Marsh NAP
19. York River SP (Taskinas Creek)
20. Maundy Creek/Big Island

21. Goodwin Islands
22. Chickahominy Riverfront Park
23. Powhatan Creek Blueway
24. College Landing Park
25. Chippokes Plantation SP
26. Hog Island WMA
27. Waterwalk at Central Park
28. Grandview Nature Preserve
29. Paradise Creek Nature Park
30. Pleasure House Point NA
31. First Landing SP
32. Eastern Shore NWR
33. Parkers Marsh NAP
34. Saxis WMA
35. Janes Island SP
36. Fishing Bay WMA
37. Blackwater NWR
38. Taylors Island WMA
39. Choptank River
40. Eastern Neck NWR

THE ICONIC BAY IMAGE for many area residents is likely a great blue heron stalking the edge of a marsh. The Chesapeake is fringed by 9,125 miles of marshland, two-thirds of its 14,415 miles of convoluted tidal shoreline. Thus, unlike the sharp boundary between land and water that typifies ocean beaches or rocky coasts, the Bay's shoreline regularly feathers into open water, offering a beautifully undulant zone of extraordinary biological richness.

Visits to this tidal Serengeti can be challenging (as can living there full-time, as we'll see below). Without proper planning, you may suffer from bug bites or sunburn, lose your way in a meandering channel, or sink to your waist in a muddy tidal flat. But with the right gear, maps, and a tide chart, the upsides—priceless solitude and teeming wildlife—are well worth the risks.

Here we introduce the many factors that combine to animate Bay wetlands, and offer tips for how to leverage them for the most enjoyable visit. We'll proceed by way of a literary paddle, arranging our journey as nature arranges the marsh—by salinity. We'll begin on the tidal creek, the meandering vein whose salty pulse freshens as it carries us inland. Starting at the creek mouth, we'll travel upstream through the tidal salt marsh, both the regularly flooded low marsh and the irregularly flooded high marsh with its salt pannes. We'll then transition through the brackish marsh into the tidal freshwater marsh, where plant diversity blooms as the salt stress is diluted by inland runoff. Next is the tidal swamp, with its water-tolerant shrubs and trees. Our last stop is the marsh edge, the lateral boundary where wetland meets upland bank.

We'll launch our literary voyage from one of the public landings along the Bay shoreline (see map on p. 134). A fine example is on Taskinas Creek within York River State Park between Williamsburg and Richmond, Virginia. This small gem offers in a nutshell the tidal waltz of salt water and freshwater that shapes marshes and their inhabitants all around the Chesapeake. If you don't have your own kayak, canoe, or stand-up paddleboard (SUP), this and many other Bay parks have watercraft to rent.

SALT STRESS

Before we begin our journey, a few words about salt stress. Many independent lines of evidence signify that life arose in the salty embrace of the sea. Signs of our salty origin are everywhere: in the brine of our sweat and tears, and in the key role that sodium and chlorine play in basic biological processes. Without salt, hearts can't beat and sap won't flow.

Maintaining a proper salt balance is a fundamental need of all living things. Land and freshwater organisms typically have elaborate mechanisms for keeping or bringing salt in; marine organisms, for moving salt out or matching the salinity of surrounding seawater. In Bay marshes, these challenges collide—when bathed in salty seawater at high tide, organisms must be able to combat the osmotic pressure driving fluid from their cells and tissues. At low tide and during rainstorms, they must do the opposite—fight the osmotic urge to flood the salty interior of their cells and tissues with diluting freshwater.

Very few plants and animals have surmounted this osmotic challenge—most notably for us, the cordgrasses, anadromous fishes such as herring, and catadromous fishes such as American eels. The benefit of their success is unfettered access to a habitat largely free of competition from other, less osmotically gifted organisms. They have taken full advantage, as demonstrated each time you gaze out on an unbroken expanse of smooth cordgrass stretching to the horizon.

TIDAL CREEK

The tidal creek provides the open-water channel that will carry us through the otherwise often impassable marsh vegetation. The first thing to consider when planning your paddle is the Bay's twice-daily tides. Make sure to go with the flow (literally) by timing your put-in so that you travel upstream with a rising tide and downstream with a falling tide. Doing otherwise requires extra energy, precludes the tide-assisted glides that let you put down your paddle and silently sneak up on wildlife for a quick peek or photo, and will hopefully give you enough water to reach the highest upstream reaches. The only challenge greater than being up a creek without a paddle is being there without any water.

Though you'll be lucky to see them in the often-muddy water, the creek is home to rich fauna, at least seasonally: American eels and shad, blue crabs, diamondback terrapins, herring, jellyfish, mummichogs, oysters, and other marine life. We're more likely to see their aerial predators, including bald eagles, ospreys, and kingfishers.

The water's murkiness is due to a mix of tiny suspended particles of silt and clay, microscopic floating plants known as phytoplankton, decayed detritus from the breakdown of marsh vegetation, and dissolved organic matter. This rich broth hinders visibility, but sustains an incredibly productive food web.

The current in the tidal creek can be surprisingly rapid given the flatness of the landscape. Its twice-daily oscillation—swiftly upstream during flood tides, swiftly downstream during ebbs—helps explain this paradox. In upland creeks, flow speed is controlled by the underlying topography—rapid in steep landscapes, sluggish in flat. In

tidal creeks, flow is powered from the top. At peak tide, the water surface at the head of the Bay's tidal creeks can be 3 feet higher than at the mouth, a gradient that powers a strong downstream ebb current. At low tide, the gradient reverses as the flood tide rushes in. This daily back-and-forth is vital to the marsh, but it can be dangerous for the paddler. Always wear your life vest when on the water!

As you paddle upstream with the flood tide, you'll also quickly notice the sinuosity of the channel. As the crow flies, it's just over a mile from the mouth to the head of Taskinas Creek. As the creek meanders, it's twice as far, with the channel in several places doubling almost all the way back on itself. Many factors help explain these undulations, which curlicue through tidal marshes all around the Bay. Most important are the marsh vegetation, which helps initiate meanders and tends to stabilize them once they form, and the cohesive nature of the fine-grained sediments, another stabilizing force. Make sure you include the meander distance in your float plan so that you don't underestimate how long you'll be on the water.

TIDAL SALT MARSH

The put-in on Taskinas Creek is at its lower, saltier end, and as in salt marshes around the Bay, the vegetation here is dominated by smooth cordgrass. Paddling along its verdant wall, you're likely to encounter droves of scurrying fiddler crabs and herds of periwinkle snails, along with sporadic views of great blue herons and great egrets. If you're lucky, you might even glimpse a more furtive creature, such as a clapper rail, river otter, or muskrat.

Smooth cordgrass (*Spartina alterniflora*) is one of the few organisms with cachet sufficient to put its scientific name on a first-name basis with non-botanists.[1] Outwardly plain, *Spartina* is a wonder, able to withstand regular inundation in full seawater,

---

[1] Botanists, a normally placid and well-behaved group, are deeply troubled by recent calls from taxonomists to reclassify smooth cordgrass from *Spartina alterniflora* to *Sporobulus alterniflorus*. Announcement of the switch at a 2018 meeting of coastal ecologists was met with "expressions of surprise, angst, disagreement, disgust and disbelief." We're sticking with *Spartina* for now.

twice daily scouring by tidal currents, and soil with little or no oxygen. These superhuman feats give it and its cordgrass cousins—big cordgrass and saltmeadow hay—a blade up on other marsh plants not only in the Bay but all along the Atlantic coast.

You can learn more about cordgrasses on pages 148–51, but one adaptation—the rhizome—deserves mention here, as it is shared by many other marsh plants, from lizard's tail to pickerelweed. Often mistaken for a root, this is a modified underground stem that's able not only to send shoots up but to send roots down, allowing rhizomatous plants to build a three-dimensional latticework to stabilize soil even in the face of tidal currents and storm tides (home gardeners will be familiar with this tenacity if they've ever battled crabgrass). Rhizomes also form tubers to stockpile starches for future growth. We tap this reserve each time we eat a potato; marsh plants tap it each spring to initiate their annual resurgence.

Free from competition with less-crafty plants, watered and fed twice each day by the ceaseless tide, and wide open to the sunny sky, mid-Atlantic salt marshes are incredibly fertile, yielding 3–6 tons of detritus per acre per year. This is on par with human agriculture, but without tilling, pesticides, or synthetic fertilizers. This abundance makes the salt marsh a vital habitat and nursery ground for many other organisms. Indeed, nearly 90 percent of commercial and sport fishes depend on salt marsh resources.

Native Americans clearly recognized this bounty as well. Capt. John Smith's map of the Bay's Algonquian chiefdoms shows them closely aligned with nearby marshes. Here they could gather emergent grass stems for house thatch, floor mats, baskets, and other everyday items; and also harvest starchy tubers from arrowhead (aka duck potato), cattails,

The underground stems or rhizomes of *Spartina* help the plant propagate and stabilize the muddy salt marsh soil.

and other rhizomatous plants. English colonists also tapped the marshes, using them to graze cattle and for thatch. Unfortunately, society's view of marshes began to shift during the 1900s as sustainable uses gave way to diking, draining, and filling for water-front development. This continued at a rapid pace until the Clean Water Act of 1972 legislated "no net loss of wetlands" in the Bay and nationwide, bringing the force of law to help preserve marshes and their many ecosystem benefits. We'll talk more about the fate of Bay marshes in the last chapter.

Unfortunately, we can't leave the salt marsh without some mention of the most vexing proof of its productivity—the hordes of mosquitoes, flies, and biting midges (aka "punkies" or no-see-ums) that can quickly ruin an otherwise pleasant paddle. It's best, even on warm days, to wear long sleeves, long pants, closed shoes, and a hat (perhaps even with netting), and to apply a repellent before you depart and again when sweat or splashed water has washed it off. It also helps to paddle during the shoulder seasons of spring and fall and to stay in the more open, windier tidal channel if possible. The one good thing about these noxious critters? They feed a lot of animals we do like, including barn swallows, bats, dragonflies, and amphibians.

HIGH MARSH AND SALT PANNES

The low marsh is bordered on either side by lateral zones of slightly higher elevation, where salt water only reaches during the highest tides—the monthly and seasonal junctures when Earth, Moon, and Sun align to bolster the normal daily tidal range. Bay waters also rise beyond regular tidal heights during hurricanes, nor'easters, and other windstorms.

The high marsh is only inundated during storms or the highest tides.

Evaporation of stranded seawater concentrates salt in salt-panne soils.

Bathed less regularly in salt, these high-marsh areas hold a more diverse flora in which *Spartina* is joined by big cordgrass, black needlerush, salt grass, saltmarsh bulrush, and saltmeadow hay. But the high marsh also contains pockets of concentrated salinity called salt pannes. These form when and where floodwaters collect in any slight dimple in the high-marsh surface. Stranded by the receding tide or storm surge—like a salty wrack line—the ponded salt water is concentrated by evaporation, coating and percolating into the marsh soil at levels up to three times saltier than full seawater. In short, like the proverbial roach hotel, the salt checks in, but it doesn't check out. Only a very few plants can withstand these hypersaline conditions. Chief among them are the glassworts, small succulents that not only tolerate salt but require it to thrive.

TIDAL FRESHWATER MARSH

Paddling farther upstream, we'll eventually reach a zone where upland runoff from streams and brooks provides the lion's share of the water. With little or no salt stress, this freshwater marsh nurtures a rich diversity of aquatic plants. Most common are arrow arum, arrowhead, cattail, and pickerelweed, but there are scores of others as well, with some areas boasting more than fifty species.

Although filled with freshwater, these marshes are still affected by the ocean tide, rising twice each day as high tide dams their downstream flow, and falling twice each day as this hydraulic barrier collapses with the ebb tide. This intermittent flooding and draining imposes stresses not felt in more upland bogs, but these two types of freshwater wetland otherwise support similar communities.

An easy way to distinguish between the salt and freshwater marshes of the Bay's tidal reaches is to visit them in winter. Unlike *Spartina* and most other salt marsh plants, whose leaves persist through the colder months, the plants of the freshwater marsh tend to die back almost completely, leaving an exposed, seemingly unvegetated flat that bears scant resemblance to its summertime lushness. Visit a tidal freshwater marsh a few weeks apart in early spring, and you'll be astounded by the change as the many rhizomatous plants suddenly transform the stored energy of their starchy tubers into a brilliant carpet of emerald-green shoots.

TIDAL SWAMP

At some point in our upstream journey, we'll leave the open, sunlit expanse of the tidal marsh and enter the shaded understory of the tidal swamp, where water-tolerant trees and shrubs such as bald cypress, buttonbush, red maple, river birch, sweet bay, and water tupelo take root. Many of these greet the ground with buttressed roots, or knees, a trait that keeps them upright in the boggy soil. Beneath their canopy—where we may

need to take to foot as the tidal creek narrows to a mere rivulet—we'll be welcomed by masses of spring wildflowers and herbaceous greenery almost junglelike in its verdure, including golden ragwort, jack-in-the pulpit, lizard's tail, marsh marigold, and skunk cabbage. This is also a favorite haunt of crayfish, northern water snakes, snapping turtles, and assorted other creepy-crawlies.

Although the tidal swamp differs in many ways from the marshes downstream, it shares at least two similarities. First is its influence by the ocean tide, which blocks and releases the swamp's downstream flow twice each day. Second is the profusion of insect life—both the vexing sort (mosquitoes, midges, and flies) as well as their stylish and welcome dragonfly predators. Make sure you thank the dragonflies for their service!

MARSH EDGE

The marsh ends where the land surface rises beyond the reach of even the highest tides or storm surge. The marsh terminates gradually in the relatively flat landscapes of the lower Chesapeake and bayside Eastern Shore, more abruptly in the dissected landscapes that prevail as tributaries reach inland toward the fall line. Plants celebrate the higher, drier, less-salty soil with a profusion of shrubby growth dominated by groundsel bush, marsh elder, marsh hibiscus, sea oxeye, and wax myrtle, as well as *Phragmites*, an invasive troublemaker. These often-dense stands provide excellent cover for wildlife and marsh birds such as green herons and yellow-crowned night herons.

YESTERBAY

Bacteria and Bogs

If you've ever slogged through a Chesa-peake tidal swamp, you may have noticed an orange fuzz coating the bottom of slack-water pools or channels. These billowing clumps are formed by iron bac-teria, single-celled, threadlike organisms that gain energy by oxidizing iron dis-solved in groundwater seeps and springs. Their rusty metabolic by-products—iron minerals such as goethite and magnetite—are one of the raw materials used to make bog iron, the metal of the Iron Age. Pro-cessing of bog iron arose in western Asia around 2,000 BCE and blossomed in the peaty boglands of northern Europe and the British Isles during the Middle Ages. When English colonists arrived at what became Jamestown in 1607, they quickly noticed local bog-iron deposits; written records and archaeology provide evidence of small-scale experiments in iron-making

within the first year. They smelted the iron with fires fueled by trees cut from Virginia's rich forestlands—a resource that iron smelting had helped deplete back in England. The earliest large-scale industrial activity in Virginia was a bog-iron smelter built at Falling Creek, near Richmond, in 1619. Destroyed in 1622 in an attack by Powhatan Indians, little remains of this landmark except a small roadside park and historical marker along US 1 just south of today's capital. A modern descendant stands nearby at the Tredegar Iron Works, the largest iron producer in the southern United States before and during the Civil War, and now the main visitor center for Richmond National Battlefield Park.

We've already encountered two marsh paradoxes: the surprising swiftness of the tidal creek, and the hypersaline soil of the salt panne. A third presents itself at the boundary between salt marsh and upland bank, where groundwater often seeps upward to form a narrow ribbon of freshwater plants that is crowded against the shoreline by a broad expanse of their saltwater kin. Peering out through this fringe of cattails and arrow arum, you might falsely assume you're looking at a freshwater marsh when that's actually just a peripheral illusion.

Now that we've introduced the salinity zones where you're most likely to see various marsh fauna and flora, let's take a detailed look at some of their more common and noticeable residents.

Plants

CORDGRASSES

Named for their flowers, which resemble a woven cord, these grasses are the perennial heart of marshes throughout the Bay watershed. They offer refuge and nursery habitat for a wide variety of wildlife, protect shorelines from wave erosion, and provide a rich source of food both as live growth and decayed detritus. Here we introduce three of the Bay's four cordgrass species, whose distribution in the marsh closely follows the upstream salinity gradient.

Smooth Cordgrass (*Spartina alterniflora*)

DESCRIPTION

This perennial grows 1–3 feet tall (short form) but can reach 6 feet near water's edge (tall form). Dies back in winter to a khaki carpet; revives in April and May as maroon shoots send up emerald-green, mostly hollow stems. Narrow, swordlike leaves arise from a triangular stem base. Visible vertical stems connected by underground horizontal stems known as rhizomes. Rhizomes and roots visible on banks of tidal creeks. Blooms August–October with 5–30 flower spikes.

HABITAT

The predominant plant of the Bay's low salt marshes. Occurs in unbroken, single-species stands that may parallel the shoreline for miles. *Spartina* is an "ecosystem engineer" that builds its own habitat by trapping muddy sediments that would otherwise be carried off by tides and currents. Provides food and shelter for many creatures, from periwinkle snails to ribbed mussels, fiddler crabs, great blue herons, marsh rails, muskrats, and white-tailed deer. As *Spartina* dies back each fall, decay of its stems and leaves creates huge volumes of detritus that nurture the marsh food web.

DID YOU KNOW?
Spartina's ability to withstand salty water allows it to colonize huge swaths of tidal land that are off-limits to most other plants. It does so by exuding salt from its leaves and trapping air in root-cell pockets that act as oxygen tanks at high tide. Spreads most commonly by

way of its rhizomes, so large patches can be clones of a single plant. If not blocked by levees or roads, *Spartina* salt marshes are expected to migrate inland with rising seas.

Big or Giant Cordgrass (*Spartina cynosuroides*)

DESCRIPTION

This hearty perennial is by far the tallest of the three Bay cordgrasses, growing higher than a basketball hoop on inch-thick, hollow stems. Strap-like leaves are up to 1 inch wide and 2 feet long; they radiate from stem in overlapping sheaths and are edged by tiny, sawlike teeth. Stems topped by greenish flowers that bloom July–September on 20–40 fingerlike spikes, each with up to 70 ½-inch "spikelets." The only cordgrass whose flowers branch at right angles to stem, lending an antennae-like aspect. Flowers turn tan when in seed.

HABITAT & ECOLOGY

Grows above mean high water in brackish marshes of tidal rivers and creeks, where it often forms dense stands with wild rice in the zone between smooth cordgrass of lower marsh and saltmeadow hay of upper marsh. Vegetation shelters small birds and is used by muskrats to build their lodges. Ducks eat the tender shoots; geese also exhume and eat the underground stems. One of the most productive wetland grasses, adding 3 to 6 tons of organic matter per acre every year to the marsh food web. Propagates both by seed and underground stems; the latter also help stabilize marsh soils. Hosts an extremely uncommon butterfly, the rare skipper.

DID YOU KNOW?

Often used by duck hunters to camouflage their blinds, but carefully so—the leaves are sharp enough to cut exposed skin. Often grows and competes with the invasive *Phragmites.*

Saltmeadow Cordgrass, Salt Hay (*Spartina patens*)

DESCRIPTION

The wiry, dark green stems of this perennial grow 1–3 feet but tend to bend near their base when buffeted by winds or tides, forming low meadows of swirled cowlicks. Leaves are spaghetti thin; roll inward to form an open, drooping tube; and arise from the upper stem in a single plane. Blooms July–September with 2–7 flower spikes; these alternate along the stem, with each bearing 20–50 small, rusty brown "spikelets" aligned in the same direction, like flags in a breeze.

HABITAT & ECOLOGY

Often forms a dark green fringe at the boundary between high salt marsh and upland bank, where it mixes with salt grass and black needlerush, commonly beneath or shaded by marsh elder and groundsel bush. Also forms roughly circular "crop circles" or "pannes" amid the smooth cordgrass of the lower marsh. Dense growth hides songbirds and small mammals, and is a bedding spot for deer. Muskrats use the wiry stems to build their lodges. Detritus from decayed stems and leaves helps nourish the marsh ecosystem. Can spread by seed, but more commonly via its underground stems, or rhizomes. Also found on sandy beaches and low dunes.

DID YOU KNOW?

Salt hay was the main forage for colonial livestock, before widespread clearing of forests for pasture, and some Chesapeake farmers still graze cattle in salt-hay meadows. The rapidly spreading rhizomes are planted to protect shorelines, restore marshes, and stabilize mud flats, dunes, levees, and dredge piles.

Black Needlerush (*Juncus roemerianus*)

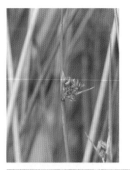

DESCRIPTION

This grasslike perennial occurs in dense, single-species stands of uniform height—typically around 3 feet. Stems are so dark green they appear black from afar, though stands are often speckled with dead, brown stems from previous years. As the name attests, a simple identity test is to walk into a stand: If it's needlerush, you'll be quickly and painfully aware. Stems are short; height comes from the stiff, coarse, sharply pointed leaves. Blooms May–October; yellowish-green flower head leans out from the stem about three-quarters up, resembling a linesman climbing a telephone pole. Horizontal, ground-hugging stems (rhizomes) are coarse, nearly black, and form dense, spreading mats.

HABITAT & ECOLOGY

A common plant of the high marsh, whether salty or brackish. Typically occurs with saltmeadow hay in the zone just landward of saltmarsh cordgrass. Food value is limited, but plant offers superb cover for small mammals such as rice rats and more than sixty bird species, including clapper rails and marsh wrens. It enhances Bay water quality by filtering sediments and pollutants from upland runoff. Its dense system of roots and rhizomes also helps curtail shoreline erosion.

DID YOU KNOW?

Needlerush is seldom eaten by herbivores, but it contributes to the base of the marsh food web through slow release of nutrients during decomposition by microbes. Often used to restore tidal marshes along the Atlantic and Gulf coasts.

Common Reed (*Phragmites australis australis*)

DESCRIPTION

Easily identified by its feathery flower plumes. Up to 1 foot long, these adorn the top of the tall (12–15 feet), round stems. Russet during summer bloom, they fade to khaki in fall and winter. Stems bear long, flat, deciduous leaves of 1–2 inches wide that taper abruptly to a point. Very long (40+ feet), horizontal stems (rhizomes) often grow aboveground. Typically occurs in dense, single-species stands.

HABITAT & ECOLOGY

This introduced species regularly invades marshes and swamps that have been disturbed by diking or fire. Each rhizome can sprout up to twenty sprigs, allowing the plant to outcompete natives such as big cordgrass, cattail, saltmeadow hay, and wax myrtle. Although long considered a weedy invader, *Phragmites* does provide cover for wildlife, filter pollutants from runoff, and protect shorelines from erosion.

DID YOU KNOW?

Long thought to have been introduced by European colonists, recent archaeological and genetic evidence has revealed a native species of common reed (*P. americanus*) that continues to grow in isolated patches around the Bay, with a hot spot along the larger tributaries of Maryland's Eastern Shore. The native form is relatively docile compared to its European cousin, typically occurring in small, sparse colonies along with other native species. Native Americans reportedly used it for mats, musical instruments, and arrow shafts. The two species are difficult to distinguish one on one.

Saltmarsh Bulrush (*Schoenoplectus robustus*)

DESCRIPTION

Hard, triangular stems and conspicuous flower "spikelets" help identify this emergent perennial. Stems are erect and reach 3 feet, with numerous leaves. The 3–5 spikelets bloom April–August and exceed 1 inch in length. Looking a bit like cockleburs, they are reddish brown, cone-shaped, and covered by hook-tipped scales. The fruits are tiny, dark brown nutlets that resemble miniature unpopped corn kernels. Leaves are ½ inch wide, up to 2 feet long, with one side flat and the other rounded. Stems may form a row as they sprout along underground rhizomes.

HABITAT & ECOLOGY

Cover extensive areas of the Bay's low brackish marshes, where they play a key role in the estuarine ecosystem. Seeds are an important food for ducks and geese, while foliage provides cover for nesting birds. Stems and roots provide sustenance for geese and muskrats; the latter also use the foliage to build their lodges. Extensive root system helps stabilize marsh sediments.

DID YOU KNOW?

More accurately known as the leafy three-cornered sedge, this plant was misnamed by European colonists based on a supposed resemblance to the biblical bulrushes that hid the baby Moses in his basket along the Nile. The colonists used the leaves of the sedge to weave floor mats and chair seats; they also ground the starchy tubers to make bread. Today it is regularly planted to improve habitat for waterfowl and wildlife.

Glassworts (*Salicornia* spp.)

DESCRIPTION

Three similar species of these unmistakable succulents occur around the Bay; here we focus on *S. virginica*. It forms dense, jade-green stands of creeping stems with upright branches, both with a woody interior. The branches grow 6–12 inches tall and may form small mounds. Up close, they've been noted to resemble a string of Pop Beads. Leaves are opposite but reduced to miniature scales; the tiny green flowers peek out near the branch ends. Entire plant turns bright red in fall.

HABITAT & ECOLOGY

Glassworts not only tolerate salt but require it to grow. They are most common in high-marsh areas of the lower Bay, where sporadic flooding by "king tides" or storm surge leaves seawater to evaporate in shallow depressions, or "pannes," creating hypersaline salt flats—glassworts are known to germinate in water ten times saltier than seawater. Provides habitat for invertebrates and food for ducks (seeds) and geese (branches). Found with short form of saltmarsh cordgrass.

DID YOU KNOW?

Glassworts are related to cacti and store water in their fleshy stems to help dilute the salty soil water in which they grow. The young stems can be pickled or eaten raw and are considered a delicacy in Europe. The name refers to the ancient practice of burning a European relative of this plant for soda ash to make glass. "Wort" is Old English for "plant."

Groundsel Bush (*Baccharis halimifolia*)

DESCRIPTION

An erect, 6- to 12-foot shrub that can form thickets. Most obvious feature is the cottony fringe of white (female) to cream-colored (male) flowers, which bloom in fall. Brown, woody stems fork into numerous green, hairless twigs. Leaves are alternate and simple. Lower leaves are wedge-shaped and widely toothed (looking a bit like mittens); upper leaves are more lance-shaped and smoother edged. Retains most of its leaves through the winter.

HABITAT & ECOLOGY

Also known as high-tide bush or salt bush, this salt-tolerant plant is one of the most abundant and widespread shrubs in the Chesapeake region. Marks the upper edge of salt marshes, where it often appears between marsh elder at slightly lower elevations and wax myrtle at slightly higher elevations. Also grows in disturbed wet areas along roads and ditches. Provides nectar for bees, moths, and butterflies, including the monarch and common buckeye; as well as food and cover for sparrows and other seed-eating birds.

DID YOU KNOW?

The genus name is from Bacchus, the Greek god of wine, describing a plant with fragrant roots. "Hal" in the species name comes from the Latin word for salt. Male and female plants are necessary for producing seeds. Leaves and

seeds of the female plant are poisonous to sheep and people. Has been introduced to Europe and Australia, where it has become invasive.

Marsh Elder (*Iva frutescens*)

DESCRIPTION
Often confused with ground-sel bush; can be distinguished by leaves, which are opposite, lance shaped, and finely toothed. Small, greenish-white flowers bloom in late fall but, unlike the cottony fluffs of groundsel bush, are almost unnoticeable. Grows 3–8 feet tall.

HABITAT & ECOLOGY
Like groundsel bush, this salt-tolerant shrub is commonly known as high-tide bush. Marks the upper edge of salt marshes, where it grows at slightly lower elevations than groundsel bush and wax myrtle. Also grows in disturbed areas where marshes have been filled. Provides nesting habitat for red-winged blackbirds and marsh wrens and a refuge during high tide for small birds and mammals.

DID YOU KNOW?
The name comes from a purported similarity to the common elderberry, an upland East Coast native. Can be purchased from specialized nurseries for use in stabilizing tidal shorelines and improving wetland habitats.

Salt Grass (*Distichlis spicata*)

DESCRIPTION
This wiry, dark green grass grows 1–2 feet high in thick patches that often resemble a game of pick-up sticks due to back-and-forth bending of stems during storm tides. Stiff, gutter-shaped leaves are 3–6 inches long, narrow as a toothpick, and extend on opposite sides of stem in a single plane. Flowers bloom July–October in flat, tightly packed, light green to pink spikes. Spreads by horizontal, ground-hugging stems that may form dense mats. Salt crystals may coat leaves and stems. Often grows with saltmeadow hay, which has tubular leaves and rusty brown flowers.

HABITAT & ECOLOGY
Mixes with saltmeadow hay to dominate the high marsh. Can tolerate soil salinities greater than seawater and often rims small depressions where storm tides linger and evaporate, leaving their salt behind. Though unpalatable to many forms of wildlife, mallards do eat the seeds, and geese graze the rhizomes after fire or grazing removes the tough stems. A minor food for muskrats and nutria. Foliage offers cover for otters, raccoons, and muskrats, and nesting habitat for rails and other marsh fowl. Helps maintain Bay water quality, as it filters sediments and pollutants from runoff and protects shoreline from erosion.

DID YOU KNOW?
Salt grass was the main source of hay for early colonists. Native Americans obtained salt by licking crystals from the stems. Used by physicians to treat respiratory allergies.

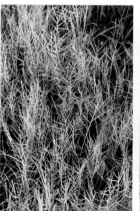

Sea Oxeye (*Borrichia frutescens*)

DESCRIPTION

In dense colonies to 3 feet high, this deciduous shrub is readily identified by its sage-green leaves and yellow, daisylike flowers. Spoon-shaped leaves are opposite, fleshy, and hairy, with a small pointed tip. Blade base typically sports 1–2 small spines. Flowers resemble a brown-eyed Susan, with yellow rays surrounding a brownish-yellow disk. They are borne singly at the ends of the somewhat woody stems and bloom May–August. Reddish-brown seed heads bleach white and persist through winter. Propagates by underground stems (rhizomes).

HABITAT & ECOLOGY

This salt-loving plant is abundant along the upper edge of high salt marshes in dense stands that offer cover for wildlife. Most commonly found with salt grass and sea lavender, occasionally with short form of smooth cordgrass. Attracts many types of butterflies; flowers provide nectar for bees and the salt marsh skipper. Rhizomes help deter erosion. Also found on sandy beaches.

DID YOU KNOW?

This relative of the dandelion is also known as sea daisy, seaside tansy, and sea marigold. Produces masses of seeds with hairlike filaments to catch the wind. Sometimes planted as an ornamental.

Wax Myrtle or Southern Bayberry (*Morella cerifera*)

DESCRIPTION
An evergreen, many-stemmed shrub that typically grows 6–12 feet high. Most noticeable feature is the late-summer berries on female trees. The color of faded denim and the size of BBs, these cluster on short stalks below the leafy stem tips. Lance-shaped, simple leaves are alternate, dark green on top and lighter below, with tiny dots on both sides and a few small teeth near the tip. Both berries and leaves are waxy and emit a spicy odor when crushed. Small, greenish-yellow flowers adorn ends of branches March–April.

HABITAT & ECOLOGY
Commonly found at the upper edge of salt or brackish marshes; also occurs in maritime swamps, coastal dunes, and upland forests. Often associated with groundsel bush in salt marshes, but at slightly higher elevations. Found among dunes with northern and swamp bayberry, highbush blueberry, and yaupon holly. Fruits eaten by migrating tree swallows and wintering myrtle warblers; foliage offers cover for songbirds and wildlife, such as the marsh hare. A host for the caterpillar of the red-banded hairstreak. Roots host bacteria that can extract nitrogen from the air, thus allowing growth in nutrient-poor soils.

DID YOU KNOW?
Colonists boiled the berries to make candles, a practice that continues today. Commonly used in habitat restoration and as a screening hedge in landscaping.

Arrow Arum (*Peltandra virginica*)

DESCRIPTION

An emergent wetland plant with celery-like stalks. Emerald-green, triangular leaves up to 2 feet long and deeply indented at base. Pair of basal leaf lobes have rounded tips (tips in similar arrowhead plant are sharp); all 3 lobes show a light green vein. Leafy reproductive stalk (the "spathe") develops in May or June, then droops and decays to reveal a tubular seedpod. In fall, this "spadix" releases lime-green, corn-like kernels.

HABITAT & ECOLOGY

A dominant plant of shallow freshwater marshes throughout the Bay watershed, often with arrowhead and pickerelweed. Leaves and roots protect the marsh from erosion by absorbing wave energy and binding sediments. Fruit is eaten by wood ducks, rails, and muskrats. Dense vegetation provides cover for birds, insects, and aquatic mammals.

DID YOU KNOW?

The flower stalk produces an odor that attracts flies. Both roots and leaves contain crystals of calcium oxalate, a toxin that deters herbivores (and is the main constituent of human kidney stones). In the same family as jack-in-the-pulpit and skunk cabbage, which share the spathe and spadix flower structure.

Arrowhead or Duck Potato (*Sagittaria latifolia*)

DESCRIPTION

As the name attests, the arrowhead-shaped leaves are this plant's most obvious feature. These are up to 2 feet long, fleshy, and release a milky sap when broken (as does the stem). The sap and several other leaf features help distinguish this plant from arrow arum: The tips of its lower leaf lobes are sharp like an arrowhead (they're rounded like an arrow shaft in arrow arum), and the leaf veins radiate from the leaf base (whereas those in arrow arum branch from a central shaft like the barbs of an arrow's feathers). The white, 3-petaled flowers have a yellow center and arise in whorls from a tall, leafless stalk. Grows alone or in small clumps.

HABITAT & ECOLOGY

Prefers wet soils of fresh to brackish water marshes and swamps, where it often occurs with arrow arum and pickerelweed. Plant dies back in fall, diverting energy to fleshy growths at the end of underground stems. These tubers are an important food source for muskrats and waterfowl, including swans, geese, wood ducks, ruddy ducks, mallards, and canvasbacks. Ducks also eat the seeds.

DID YOU KNOW?

The tubers were an important food source for Native Americans, who roasted or boiled them like potatoes.

Bald Cypress (*Taxodium distichum*)

DESCRIPTION

A deciduous conifer of wetlands and shorelines with roots that form distinctive aboveground "knees" in water-logged soils. Bark is reddish brown with peeling strips; trunk may become fluted at the base with age. Leaves are needlelike, in pairs along branches. Cone resembles a tiny soccer ball. Grows 90–120 feet high and 3–6 feet in diameter.

HABITAT & ECOLOGY

Grows near and in water of swamps and slow-moving streams. Seeds are eaten by wild turkeys, wood ducks, evening grosbeaks, water birds, and squirrels. Bald eagles and ospreys nest in the crown of tall trees; wood ducks, barred owls, and bees nest in cavities. Herons and egrets like to perch on its branches.

DID YOU KNOW?

Bald cypress can reach 1,000 years old and is extremely resistant to toppling in high winds due to a spreading root system. Wood from older trees is rot-resistant and thus prized for use in exterior construction, docks, and boatbuilding. Analysis of tree rings from a bald cypress in the Great Dismal Swamp revealed a severe early 1600s drought, which hindered relations between Native Americans and English colonists.

Buttonbush (*Cephalanthus occidentalis*)

DESCRIPTION
A common, many-stemmed wetland shrub that reaches 12–15 feet. Readily identified by round flowers, swollen stem bases, and fissured bark of older plants. Borne in midsummer, the showy white, fragrant flowers resemble spherical pincushions. Flowers mature in fall to dense, brown seed balls resembling sycamore fruits. Leaves are opposite or in whorls of 3, with smooth edges, a sharp tip, and prominent veins. They attach to stem with dark red petioles. The only wetland shrub with spherical flowers and whorled leaves.

HABITAT & ECOLOGY
Common as dense stands in marshes, swamps, and along the edges of streams and ponds. Offers exceptional wildlife benefits. Foliage provides cover for wood ducks and songbirds and browse for white-tailed deer. Flowers attract butterflies, hummingbirds, and bees; the bees use the nectar to produce a highly valued honey. Seeds eaten by waterfowl, shorebirds, and migrating songbirds. Often found with bald cypress, beech, holly, red maple, oaks, southern bayberry, swamp rose, and switchgrass.

DID YOU KNOW?
Also known as button ball, button willow, honey-bells, and riverbush, this shrub is in the same family as coffee. Showy flowers and fruit make it a popular choice in native gardens; enlarged, stabilizing stem bases encourage its use in controlling shoreline erosion. Native Americans used it medicinally, including chewing the bark to relieve toothache.

Broad-leaved Cattail (*Typha latifolia*)

DESCRIPTION
Narrow, erect stems rise 3–9 feet in dense stands. Long, strap-like leaves typically exceed 1 inch in width and emerge from stem in alternating sheaths. Stem is topped by a distinctive 2-part flower: a lower, hot dog–like cylinder of tightly packed seeds joined to an upper, thinner spike of tiny beige flowers (in the narrow-leaved cattail [*T. angustifolia*], a short gap separates the 2 flower parts, and the leaves are less than 1 inch wide). In fall, the seed cylinder unpacks into tiny, fluffy parachutes for dispersal by wind.

HABITAT & ECOLOGY
Typically grows along the shallow edges of freshwater marshes (the narrow-leaved cattail tolerates a bit more salinity). The underground stems provide food for muskrats and geese; the vegetation offers cover for red-winged blackbirds, swamp sparrows, and other wildlife. Deer will flatten previous year's dried growth for winter bedding.

DID YOU KNOW?
In his 1960s classic *Stalking the Wild Asparagus*, Euell Gibbons called the cattail the "supermarket of the swamp," as almost every part of this plant can and has been used by humans. Bay Indians ate the flower heads, pollen, stalks, stems, and rhizomes; and used the foliage for thatch, floor mats, bedding, clothing, and other household items. Some Bay residents still harvest the tender springtime spike as a delicacy.

Golden Ragwort (*Packera aurea*)

DESCRIPTION

Young plants form a low clump of round, finely toothed leaves that are dark green above and purplish beneath, with each deeply indented where it joins its arching, celery-like stem. Later develops many erect, reddish flower stalks (1–2 feet high) bearing narrow, parsley-like leaves and topped by a cluster of purple buds. Buds open to bright yellow, many-petaled flowers.

HABITAT & ECOLOGY

Prefers rich, moist soils of freshwater swamps and forested wetlands. Basal leaf-clumps persist year-round as splashes of green in otherwise drab winter ground-scape. One of the first marsh plants to bloom in spring, with flowers appearing as early as March and persisting to June. Flowers benefit spring pollinators, particularly skipper butterflies and bees.

DID YOU KNOW?

Also known as golden groundsel and butterweed, this plant is a member of the daisy family. "Ragwort" refers to its raggedly-cut leaves. Can spread by underground stems to form a ground cover in moist, shady landscapes. Touching the leaves may cause mild skin irritation.

Jack-in-the-Pulpit (*Arisaema triphyllum*)

DESCRIPTION

Plant has 2–3 stems. One bears the unusual flower structure, or spathe; the other one or two each supports a 3-part leaf. The spathe consists of a leafy, green to purple sheath (often striped) whose tubular base is topped by a pointed "hood" that starts out erect but later flops over to cover the underlying opening. Within stands a smooth rod (the spadix) with tiny flowers near its base. A cluster of green berries ripens to bright red in late summer.

HABITAT & ECOLOGY

Prefers moist soils of shaded wetlands. Wild turkeys and a few mammals will eat the berries, though these, as well as the leaves and roots, contain calcium oxalate—a chemical toxic to many animals. Emits a fungal smell that draws gnats inside the flower sheath for pollination.

DID YOU KNOW?

The common name refers to the flower's resemblance to a preacher (the "Jack") standing within an old-fashioned pulpit with an overlying "sounding board" (which helped broadcast the sermon before electronic amplification). Native Americans ate the fleshy taproots, but only after drying them for at least 6 months and cooking. In the same family as arrow arum and skunk cabbage, which share the spathe and spadix flower structure.

Lizard's Tail (*Saururus cernuus*)

DESCRIPTION

This wetland perennial is readily identified by its eye-catching flower stalks and heart-shaped leaves. The initially crook-necked stalks slowly unfurl as their tiny white flowers bloom upward from the base. Blooms are fragrant and last May–August. Leaves are alternate, 3–5 inches long, with a pleasant root-beer aroma. The erect, hairy stems grow 1–3 feet tall with many branches, dying back in winter. Typically spreads by underground rhizomes, often forming extensive colonies of genetically identical individuals.

HABITAT & ECOLOGY

Common in brackish and freshwater tidal marshes and along streams and ditches throughout the Bay watershed. Occasionally found with arrow arum, arrowhead, and pickerelweed. Foliage is a favorite food for beavers during late summer; seeds are a minor food source for wood ducks.

DID YOU KNOW?

Both the common and scientific names of this plant (*saurus* is Greek for "lizard"; "*cernuus*" is from the Latin for "tail") are apt given its antediluvian appearance and long history, which stretches back to the Age of Dinosaurs. Part of a small family of aquatic plants now found only in North America and East Asia. These areas were adjacent in the Cretaceous but have since drifted apart.

Marsh Hibiscus (*Hibiscus moscheutos*)

DESCRIPTION
A shrubby plant of marsh edges that grows to 6 feet tall. Its beautifully unmistakable flower has 5 white to pink petals, a crimson center, and a brushy yellow stamen. Diamond-shaped leaves are green, smooth on top and velvety white below, with irregular sawlike teeth. These alternate along the round, reddish, finely haired stem and emit a musky odor when crushed. Seedpod is a small rounded box that persists through winter.

HABITAT & ECOLOGY
Widespread in freshwater marshes and along the upland edge of tidal Bay marshes where groundwater seepage dilutes seawater. Occurs both as isolated clumps and broken hedges. Flowers bloom late July–August and are pollinated by ruby-throated hummingbirds and their very own bee, the rose-mallow bee (*Ptilothrix bombiformis*). Leaves and seeds fed on by caterpillars of both moths and butterflies.

DID YOU KNOW?
Has a number of common names, including rose-mallow, swamp rose-mallow, marsh-mallow, swamp cotton, and wild cotton. These reference its place in the mallow family, which also includes farmed cotton and the European marsh-mallow, whose roots produce a paste that was whipped with sugar to make the original marshmallow candy. The similar seashore mallow (*Kosteletzkya virginica*) brightens the salt marshes of the lower Bay and mid-Atlantic coast.

Marsh Marigold (*Caltha palustris*)

DESCRIPTION

Flowers are bright yellow with 5–9 petal-like sepals and clearly visible veins. They sit on many-branched stems that rise up to 2 feet above a clump of roughly circular leaves with toothed edges. Each of these basal leaves—which by late summer can reach up to 7 inches across—resembles a pizza with one thin slice missing where it attaches to its stalk. Flower stalks bear smaller, alternate leaves. Mature flowers produce a green seedpod.

HABITAT & ECOLOGY

This perennial wildflower blooms April–June in swamps, shaded woods, and creek edges across the Bay watershed. Flowers attract flies and bees; leaves are home to two beetle species. Mammals generally avoid eating the leaves, which contain toxic alkaloids. Although we know little about what might eat its seeds, the seeds of closely related

plants are consumed by wood ducks, sora rails, and some upland gamebirds, as well as voles, chipmunks, and other small rodents.

DID YOU KNOW?

Despite the name, this plant actually belongs to the buttercup family. The species name *palustris* means "marshy" or "boggy," in reference to its preferred habitat.

Pickerelweed (*Pontederia cordata*)

DESCRIPTION

Grows in large, uniform stands directly from the water, with the lower stems submerged. Leaves are waxy and typically heart-shaped, though their shape can vary widely. Veins run in parallel lines from the leaf base. Purplish-blue flowers with yellow spots radiate from a stalk that rises 1–2 feet above the water. These may give the entire marsh a blue hue during the May–October bloom season. Each produces an oblong, corky fruit with a single seed.

HABITAT & ECOLOGY

Forms large colonies along sheltered freshwater shorelines. Vegetation is eaten by geese and muskrats and provides refuge for fish, birds, and small mammals. Seeds are eaten by waterfowl. Flowers are pollinated by bees and butterflies. Stems and leaves die back in winter to leave exposed mudflats; plants regenerate in spring from underground stems. Protects shorelines from erosion by damping waves.

DID YOU KNOW?

As the fruits develop, their weight bows the flower stalk into the water, where it releases its seeds for dispersal by currents. Can be distinguished from arrow arum and arrowhead by the blue flower and parallel venation of the leaves.

Skunk Cabbage (*Symplocarpus foetidus*)

DESCRIPTION

This unusual plant presents two distinct forms. The flower sheath, or spathe—a purplish, leafy structure with an arched hood—emerges in late winter or early spring. Inside develops a club-like flower head (the spadix) resembling a small pineapple. Flower is followed by clumps of large (1–2 feet), bright green, deeply veined leaves on celery-like stalks. Leaves die back by late summer. Both leaves and flower have a skunk-like odor.

HABITAT & ECOLOGY

Prefers moist soils of shaded wetlands. Fetid odor attracts flies and gnats, which themselves fall prey to spiders that use the flower sheath as a hunting blind. Although the leaves contain crystals of calcium oxalate—toxic to many animals—they are eaten by snails, slugs, and moth caterpillars, as well as snapping turtles and bears.

DID YOU KNOW?

One of the few plants capable of generating heat (up to 60°F warmer than its surroundings), which allows the emerging flower sheath to melt through any overlying snow, helps disperse the rotting odor, and provides a warm refuge for pollinators. The roots can contract to offset the upward growth of the underground stems. This keeps the tip of the pre-emergent flower sheath within the relatively warm confines of the soil and out of the freezing air just a few inches above. In the same family as arrow arum and jack-in-the-pulpit, which share the spathe and spadix flower structure.

Sweetbay, Marsh Magnolia (*Magnolia virginiana*)

DESCRIPTION
A shrub or small (30–50 feet) deciduous tree in the Bay watershed, though it can reach 100 feet in the southernly portion of its range along the Gulf Coast. Lance-shaped, simple leaves are alternate, 4–6 inches long, with a dark green top and pale underside. Bark is smooth, gray, and mottled. Flowers and fruits are distinctive. Creamy white, fragrant flowers are 2–3 inches wide with 9–12 petals; they bloom June–July. Fruits look like small, prehistoric pineapples. They bear bright red seeds that dangle from a thread when ripe. Often confused with southern magnolia, a tree of the southeastern United States that has been widely planted as an ornamental.

HABITAT & ECOLOGY
Prefers wet soils near and in swamps and along marsh edges. Foliage and twigs are a favorite browse of white-tailed deer; fatty seeds are eaten and dispersed by songbirds as well as wild turkeys, quail, gray squirrels, and mice. A host plant for tiger and spice-bush swallowtail butterflies and the sweetbay silkmoth.

DID YOU KNOW?
One of the oldest tree families, magnolias shaded dinosaurs. Native Americans used sweetbay leaves as a spice, and made tea from the leaves and bark. During the 1700s, physicians used various parts to treat diarrhea, cough, and fever. Flowers open and close in a 2-day cycle that alternates between a male and female phase to prevent self-pollination. When closed, the flowers generate heat that benefits their beetle pollinators.

Animals

American Eel (*Anguilla rostrata*)

DESCRIPTION

Vary greatly in size and coloration during their intricate life cycle, but consistently distinguished by their snakelike body. Elongated dorsal and anal fins merge around the tail. Can change color to match the bottom, but generally brown on top with white on belly. Youngest life stage visible in the Bay is the translucent "glass eel"; these darken into "elvers," which reach 4–8 inches before transforming into adult "yellow eels." Adult males to 2 feet; females to 5 feet.

HABITAT & ECOLOGY

Anyone encountering glass eels in the shallow, muddy waters of a tidal creek might well assume the creatures had just been born. They are tiny—easily held in your palm—and display all the youthful wriggling of spring. But these juveniles, which migrate up Bay tributaries in March and April, hatched almost a year earlier and a world away—as transparent, ribbonlike leptocephali in the inky-blue waters of the Sargasso Sea south of Bermuda. These larvae ride the Gulf Stream along the East Coast, transforming into glass eels and then elvers as they swim up coastal tributaries. Adult yellow eels spend up to 25 mostly nocturnal years in inland waters before maturing into "silver eels," which return to the ocean to spawn. Diet includes shrimp, crabs, fishes, and carrion. Eels in turn are eaten by many other species, including striped bass.

DID YOU KNOW?

Eel were once common on Bay tables; the commercial harvest is now mostly exported to Europe as a delicacy and to Asia for unagi sushi, or used for bait. Recent population declines in the United States and Canada have led to the species being listed as "endangered" by the International Union for the Conservation of Nature. Dams, fishing pressure, and disease have all been implicated in the drop; East Coast states have responded with stricter harvest regulations. It is illegal to harvest glass eels in Virginia.

Herring and Shad (*Clupeid* family)

Clupeids are a family of mostly marine fishes—herrings, menhaden, sardines, and shad—with 195 species worldwide. Seven species occur in the Bay watershed; here we briefly describe the four anadromous *Alosa* species that leave the ocean for springtime spawning in Bay tributaries. (Catadromous fishes like the American eel do the opposite, spending most of their life in freshwater but spawning in the salty waters of the sea.) The Atlantic menhaden (*Brevoortia tyrannus*), the "most important fish in the sea," earns its very own description on page 38.

DESCRIPTION

Medium-size fishes 1–2 feet long with silvery sides, a greenish-blue back, and a dark spot on the shoulder. Body is laterally compressed (like a pancake standing on edge), with a protruding, bulldog-like lower lip; a single dorsal fin; and a deeply forked tail.

American shad (*Alosa sapidissima*)

Hickory shad (*A. mediocris*)

Alewife (*A. pseudoharengus*)

Blueback herring (*A. aestivalis*)

HABITAT & ECOLOGY

These are schooling fish that eat mostly plankton. They in turn serve as prey or forage for many larger Bay fishes, including striped bass and bluefish, as well as for fish-eating birds such as double-crested cormorants, great blue herons, herring gulls, and ospreys. They thus play a key role in the Chesapeake by enriching the Bay food web each spring with nutrients carried in from the coastal ocean, where these fish spend most of their lives.

DID YOU KNOW?

The spawning migration of shad and herring into Bay waters was a rite of spring for centuries, supporting generations of Native Americans, European immigrants, predatory fishes, and migrating and resident shorebirds and raptors. One shad fisherman was George Washington, who kept careful records of the annual shad harvest from the waters of the Potomac River at Mount Vernon and provided smoked shad from his personal stores to help feed Revolutionary troops during the bitter winter of 1775–76 at Valley Forge. Tragically, this springtime bonanza and cultural touchstone has been undone by overfishing, dam building, and degradation of tributary habitat, with commercial shad fishing banned in Maryland in 1980 and Virginia in 1994. It remains to be seen whether efforts to help restore the fishery—including dam removal, fish ladders, and the Clean Water Act—will one day succeed in bringing the amazing spectacle of the spring shad run back to Bay tributaries.

The Bay's two other clupeid species, the gizzard shad (*Dorosoma cepedianum*) and threadfin shad (*D. petenense*), inhabit freshwaters.

Diamondback Terrapin (*Malaclemys terrapin*)

DESCRIPTION

Named for the jewel-shaped plates of the upper shell or carapace, which may be a uniform greenish black or bear concentric lighter rings. Skin is solid gray to sage green with charcoal spots or splotches. Markings are like fingerprints—no two the same. Carapace widest in rear and may have a central "keel." Webbed feet have stout claws. Horned beak is creamy white to pink; may have dark "mustache." Grow to 12 inches, with females up to two times larger than males. Often only seen as a head periscoped above the waves.

HABITAT & ECOLOGY

The only turtle that lives exclusively in brackish water; found in marshy shallows and tidal rivers throughout the Bay. Hibernates in muddy floor of tidal creeks; lays its eggs on beaches and islands, typically during June, with warmer nests producing more females. Feeds mostly on periwinkle snails, fiddler crabs, and clams, using strong jaws and hard beak to crush shelled prey. Eggs and hatchlings eaten by crabs, crows, gulls, herons, muskrats, foxes, skunks, and raccoons. Raccoons also prey on nesting females.

DID YOU KNOW?

The state reptile of Maryland, this once-abundant creature has long been harvested by people for food, with "terrapin" the Algonquian word for "edible turtle of brackish water." This harvest continues today in Maryland, with additional mortality from drowning in crab pots and propeller strikes raising concerns about the species' long-term survival. Both Virginia and Maryland have responded with legislation requiring or encouraging crabbers to use BRDs (by-catch reduction devices) in their pots.

Snapping Turtle (*Chelydra serpentina*)

DESCRIPTION

This prehistoric Sumo wrestler spills out of its one-size-too-small shell in a profusion of implacable protuberances. Scaly, flipper-like legs end in 5 sharp claws; both jaws terminate in a sharp beak. Rear edge of shell serrated, as is top of tail. Shell of juveniles bears 3 saw-toothed keels; these typically diminish as turtle matures. Can grow very large: Virginia record is 51 pounds with a shell length of 18 inches.

HABITAT & ECOLOGY

Inhabits shallow, vegetated waters, both fresh and brackish, where it often nestles into bottom sediments to wait for prey, with only eyes and nostrils exposed. Eats whatever it can: fish, frogs, toads, crayfish, other turtles, snakes, muskrats, water beetles, ducks, geese, algae, and duckweed. Most often seen in Bay waters April–October; spends winter buried in bottom or in waterside bank. Most often seen on land in late spring, when females emerge to lay eggs. Eggs are eaten by raccoons, skunks, and foxes. Juveniles preyed on by herons, fishes, and snakes. Adults have few predators other than humans.

DID YOU KNOW?

Legally hunted in both Maryland and Virginia for their meat, which some consider a delicacy. Take is increasingly regulated due to concerns of overharvesting. Can be pugnacious on land; to rescue a female crossing a road, keep a scoop shovel in your trunk, or carefully lift by slipping hands under shell on either side of tail, behind the range of long neck and strong jaws. Move to side of road turtle is facing so that it can continue on its way.

Water Snakes (*Nerodia* species)

A quartet of aquatic snakes inhabit the Chesapeake region: the northern cottonmouth (*Agkistrodon piscivorus*) and three species of *Nerodia* water snakes: the brown (*N. taxispilota*), plain-bellied (*N. erythrogaster*), and northern (*N. sipedon*). Here we focus on *N. sipedon*, the only *Nerodia* species found in both Virginia and Maryland. The cottonmouth—the Bay's only venomous aquatic snake—occurs almost exclusively south of Virginia's James River. Unfortunately, people have killed countless *Nerodia* snakes Bay-wide, believing them to be venomous "water moccasins." Below we show how easy it is to tell them apart.

DESCRIPTION

Growing to more than 4 feet long, *N. sipedon* can be identified by its solid dark crossbands, which abruptly switch to blotches about halfway toward the tail. Also note the strongly keeled scales, flattened belly, and round pupils.

HABITAT & ECOLOGY

Nerodia species are typically found near or in freshwater, though they do tolerate some salinity. Brown and plain-bellied water snakes often occupy branches overhanging the water; the latter may hold its mouth open in the underlying current to grab a passing meal.

These snakes prey on a wide variety of fish, as well as frogs, toads, salamanders, and tadpoles. Predators include other snakes, raccoons, largemouth bass, and snapping turtles.

DID YOU KNOW?

Nerodia water snakes can be distinguished from the cottonmouth by their round pupils, narrower head, and markings. Cottonmouth has vertical, catlike pupils; wide, cobra-like "jowls" to accommodate its venom sacs; and dark-lined crossbands that broaden from the backbone toward the belly to form an "hourglass" shape from above. It also, like other venomous snakes, has a heat-sensing pit between each nostril and eye, though this is difficult to see at the distance you should keep from any snake, venomous or not. A final clue that you've encountered *Agkistrodon* is the whitish hue revealed when it opens its "cotton" mouth.

Blue Crab (*Callinectes sapidus*)

DESCRIPTION
Arguably *the* iconic creature of the Chesapeake, this feisty 10-legged crustacean is easily recognized by the bluish cast of its appendages, lateral spines of its olive-green carapace, and paddle-like rear swimming legs. Stalked eyes can fold back into grooves along front of shell. The formidable claws are of equal size, with females' tipped by bright red "lipstick." Shape of "apron" on underside separates males (Washington Monument) from females (dome of US Capitol). Grow by molting; discarded exoskeletons regularly litter Bay beaches.

HABITAT & ECOLOGY
Key players in shallow-water food webs throughout the Bay, from tidal creeks to seagrass beds. Feed on pretty much anything they can catch, including other blue crabs. Favorite main courses are clams, crabs, and polychaete worms, but will add side dishes of fish, snails, insects, shrimp, and detritus as available. Preyed on by eels, drum, spot, croaker, rays, striped bass, oyster toadfish, and sea turtles. Most vulnerable during winter dormancy (to sea stars) and soft-shelled phase just after molting (to wading birds, other crabs, raccoons, and otters).

DID YOU KNOW?
Blue crabs have been the target of a Bay fishery for as long as people have inhabited the Chesapeake region. The Bay harvest long composed about half of all US crab landings, with strict regulations imposed in the early 2000s to halt a troubling drop. As with Inuits' many words for snow, the crabs' importance is reflected in the rich vocabulary developed to describe their molt stages (softies, busters, paper shells, white signs, pink signs, and red signs or peelers); fishing gear (dip nets, pots, longlines, trotlines, scrapes, dredges); and sex and life-stages: Jimmies (adult males); Sallys or she-crabs (immature females); sooks (mature females); and sponge, spawn, blooming, or mother crabs (egg-bearing females).

FIDDLER CRABS (VARIOUS SPECIES)

DESCRIPTION

Males are unmistakable due to one almost comically large claw (females have 2 small claws of equal size). Eight bristly legs extend from shield-shaped shell, which is typically 1–2 inches wide in adults. Eyes borne on 2 short stalks.

HABITAT & ECOLOGY

Large "droves" scamper across muddy marsh edges at low tide. A key link in the marsh food chain, fiddlers scavenge small animals and plant detritus from the mud while themselves falling prey to blue crabs, wading birds, and raccoons. Their burrows help cycle nutrients between the marsh surface and depth, channel oxygen to *Spartina* roots, and can lead to bank erosion and collapse.

DID YOU KNOW?

These "Maestros of the Marsh" are named for the male's habit of rapidly moving its smaller claw toward and away from its mouth while feeding, giving the appearance of drawing a fiddle bow across its larger claw. The male uses its large "fiddle" claw to attract females and guard its burrow. Three species inhabit the Chesapeake Bay region: the red-jointed fiddler crab (*Minuca minax*; shown above), the marsh fiddler (*M. pugnax*), and the sand fiddler (*Leptuca pugilator*).

Devil Crayfish (*Lacunicambarus diogenes*)

DESCRIPTION

The closest the Bay gets to a lobster, albeit in miniature. These reddish-brown crustaceans grow up to 4 inches long, with 10 legs; a pair of large claws and long, whiplike antennae; a narrow, segmented abdomen; and a fanlike tail. Eyes are on movable stalks; gills are tucked beneath the body. Claws often tipped with red. Rarely seen due to their nocturnal, underground habits; presence is most commonly noted by the muddy "chimneys" they build while excavating their burrows.

HABITAT & ECOLOGY

These "mud bugs" inhabit mucky, waterlogged soils of tidal swamps throughout the Bay watershed. They remain within their burrows during daylight to avoid predators and keep their gills moist for effective breathing, emerging at night to scavenge on dead and decaying plants and animals. Prey to more than 200 predatory species, including fishes, raccoons, opossums, red foxes, muskrats, owls and hawks, newts and salamanders, eastern painted turtles, and northern water snakes. Burrows are deep enough (about 2 feet) to reach groundwater during dry spells and avoid freezing temperatures.

DID YOU KNOW?

Like tiny possums, baby "crawdads" stay attached to their mother until their third molt. They then drop off and live independently. People eat crayfish directly and also use them as fishing bait. "Devil" may refer to the red-tipped claws, the burrowing habit, or the painful pinch.

Marsh Periwinkle (*Littoraria irrorata*)

DESCRIPTION

About 1 inch long, this snail has a conical, spiraled shell ringed by narrow grooves specked by reddish-brown flecks. Typically a dusky tan or white, it may appear green due to algal growth. The spire is pointed. Stalked eyes emerge from the top of the muscular foot.

HABITAT & ECOLOGY

Abundant in salt and brackish marshes throughout the Bay, with up to seven individuals per square foot. Almost always occurs with the smooth cordgrass *Spartina* and sometimes with needlerush. Uses its radula (a tongue with teeth) to eat algae and detritus from the exposed marsh surface at low tide; ascends *Spartina* stalks as the tide rises to avoid blue crabs and other predators, which include diamondback terrapins, marsh birds, and small mammals. Chews holes in *Spartina* blades and spreads waste across the cuts to seed the growth of fungi, a preferred food. Releases eggs into the water in spring, where they hatch into free-swimming larvae that develop into small snails by midsummer.

DID YOU KNOW?

Visual experiments show these snails prefer to move toward vertical rather than horizontal bars, suggesting they can see the *Spartina* stems where they shelter. Another study found they can breathe equally well above and below water, dispelling the idea that they climb *Spartina* blades to avoid drowning.

Dragonflies and Damselflies

The raptors *and* sharks of the insect world, these creatures are fierce predators in both of their wildly divergent life stages: the familiar adult fliers and the seldom-seen aquatic larvae. Adult forms share many traits: large compound eyes, six spiny legs, a narrow abdomen with ten segments, and a pair of clearly veined wings. Two obvious differences set them apart: In dragonflies, the eyes are close together and the wings extend outward from the body; in damselflies, the eyes are separated like dumbbell weights and the wings are held vertically above the body when at rest.

Members of both groups spend most of their lives as larval nymphs submerged in freshwater streams, ponds, and swamps. Some species, including common green darners, inhabit brackish marshes. The nymphs live from 3 months to 10 years, depending on species, with ten to twenty molts. They capture prey with a hinged lower lip that can shoot forward with deadly speed, targeting anything equal to or less than their own size. This thankfully includes the larvae of biting insects such as mosquitoes, gnats, and midges. They will also eat tadpoles and fish fry. The nymph emerges from the water when ready to metamorphose into the winged adult form, often climbing up a plant stem to do so.

Typically live a few months as adults, often hanging out on shoreline vegetation. They hunt while in flight, using their legs as a basket to capture flies and other insects from the air, or to pick grounded insects from leaf blades or other landing pads. Will hunt in groups when prey is swarming. Use their sharp eyesight and aerial acrobatics both to hunt and to avoid their own predators, which include birds, fishes, frogs, spiders, water bugs, and other dragonflies. Also mate while in flight; females deposit eggs back in water or nearby.

Consider these insects friends, and make sure to say "Hi" the next time you meet. They're beautiful to look at, don't bite people, and do bite pesky insects such as mosquitoes and gnats. Their presence is sign of a healthy ecosystem.

Here we highlight the features that help tell a few common species apart, including the often starkly different males and females. These creatures are very diverse, with more than sixty dragonfly species in seven families and more than thirty species of damselflies in three families within the Bay watershed. The easiest to identify (and photograph!) are the skimmer dragonflies and broad-winged damselflies, which often perch. Most of the species shown below fall into those two groups. For fuller treatment, consult the references in "A Deeper Dive."

Dragonflies

BAR-WINGED SKIMMER (MALE)
Dusky blue body with black wing bars and dark head.

BLUE DASHER (MALE)
Dusky blue body with black tail tip and green head.

COMMON WHITETAIL (FEMALE, MALE, JUVENILE)
Our most common dragonfly. Name describes male. Adults of both sexes have two dark wing bars; juveniles have three.

EASTERN AMBERWING
The name says it all.

EASTERN PONDHAWK (FEMALE, MALE)
Females have green body and striped tail; males bright blue with green head. Tail spines, or "cerci," are white in both.

FOUR-SPOTTED PENNANT
Brownish blue body with a quartet of brown, sometimes "smudged," wing spots.

GREAT BLUE SKIMMER (FEMALE)
Name describes male (not pictured). Female is brownish with blue eyes. Both have dark spots on wing tips.

HALLOWEEN PENNANT
Jack-o-lantern wing stripes are unmistakable.

NEEDHAM'S SKIMMER (FEMALE, MALE)
Female is yellowish overall; male is reddish. Both have a dark stripe down the tail.

WIDOW SKIMMER (FEMALE, MALE)
Large, dark wing-patches are unique in Bay area; those in male are set off in white.

DAMSELFLIES

EBONY JEWELWING
Iridescent blue body with dark black wings.

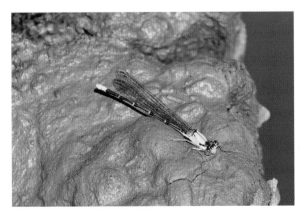

BLUE-FRONTED DANCER (MALE)
Male is bright blue on shoulders and tail. Female (not pictured) is bluish brown.

Bald Eagle (*Haliaeetus leucocephalus*)

DESCRIPTION
Color varies with age. Adults unmistakable with bright white head and tail against dark body and wings; juveniles are a mottled salt-and-pepper everywhere. Feet and sharply recurved beak are a rich yellow. Large bird: 3 feet from head to tail with wingspan of 6–7 feet. Usually silent.

HABITAT & ECOLOGY
Perch or soar in search of fish (carp, catfish, and eels); small mammals (muskrats, rabbits); and reptiles (snakes, turtles). They will also steal fish from ospreys in flight or by harassing them to drop their catch. Will also eat carrion. Lifelong mating pairs build a nest of sticks atop a tall tree near the water, with unobstructed flight lines. Nests can ultimately reach 10–12 feet across and weigh upward of 2 tons! About six in ten Bay-area nests are found in loblolly pines. Eagles concentrate along the low-salinity, fish-rich waters of the Bay's upper tributaries. Have few predators other than humans.

DID YOU KNOW?
Bald eagle populations in the Bay and elsewhere fell precipitously during the 1960s and 1970s, to less than thirty breeding pairs in all of Virginia. Research done at Maryland's Patuxent Research Refuge helped finger the use of DDT, an insecticide that accumulated in predatory birds and weakened their eggshells. With the 1972 ban of DDT in the United States, bald eagle numbers have soared; the Bay now holds around 3,000 nesting pairs. Unfortunately, continued urban development is bringing new challenges to these majestic birds, with loss of suitable nesting trees a growing concern.

Barn Swallow (*Hirundo rustica*)

DESCRIPTION

Lithe, sparrow-size bird distinguished by its long, forked tail; narrow, pointed wings; and striking coloration: iridescent blue and black on top, with a white to pale orange belly and a rufous throat and forehead. Often seen in bat-like flight, dipping and darting above open water or marsh-grass meadows. Flash of belly often visible during high-speed, banking turns.

HABITAT & ECOLOGY

A common warm-season inhabitant of Bay marshes and tidal creeks that subsists almost entirely on flies, mosquitoes, dragonflies, and other flying insects. Builds a muddy bowl for a nest, typically beneath house eaves, bridges, or inside barns (hence the name). Nestlings are vulnerable to a long list of predators including hawks, owls, gulls, and grackles, as well as raccoons, squirrels, rats, and snakes. Raptors will also take adults—if they can match the swallows' aerial acrobatics.

DID YOU KNOW?

These birds both eat and drink while in flight, capturing insects a-wing and using their lower mandible to scoop water from the Bay surface. It's thus fitting that a flock of swallows is called a "gulp." A single adult can eat 60 insects per hour—that's 840 in a 14-hour summer day, or more than 25,000 in a month. If barn swallows didn't exist and someone invented drones that could do that, they would be flying off store shelves.

Clapper Rail (*Rallus crepitans*)

DESCRIPTION
Aka a "marsh hen" or "Seldom Seen Slim," this chicken-size bird has a grayish-brown back and a cinnamon-colored belly with barred flanks. Bill is long, slender, and yellowish orange on bottom. Legs long with noticeably oversized toes. More often heard than seen; series of sharp *kek-kek-kek*s varies in tempo. Seldom flies, even when startled. Body is flattened from side to side to ease passage through dense marsh grasses.

HABITAT & ECOLOGY
Frequents the low salt marsh, where it hunts fiddler crabs from the cover of smooth cordgrass or black needlerush during high tide and along the exposed edges or floor of tidal creeks and muskrat runways at low tide. Will also eat minnows and insects, as well as seeds in winter. Preyed on by great blue herons, gulls, raccoons, dogs, and cats. There is even one recorded from the stomach of a tiger shark! Nests late May–early June on a raised platform of dead vegetation built by the male.

DID YOU KNOW?
King and Virginia rails look very similar but typically inhabit freshwater marshes, not salt. Habitat loss and degradation of marsh habitat have led to local population declines, but overall population is stable. Clapper rails are still hunted legally in Virginia during fall migration.

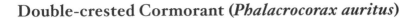

Double-crested Cormorant (*Phalacrocorax auritus*)

DESCRIPTION
Lanky diving bird with dark gray body (2-3 feet tall, 4-foot wingspan); neck and breast lighter in juveniles and black in adults. Skin at base of beak orangish yellow; upper beak recurves sharply at tip. Eyes a striking sky blue.

HABITAT & ECOLOGY
Common in fresh and saltwater habitats throughout the Bay watershed. Swims low in water; dives for small fish it often swallows while submerged. Occasionally eats crustaceans, insects, and amphibians. May form sizable flocks.

DID YOU KNOW?
Unlike many other waterbirds, cormorants' feathers are not waterproof. This decreases buoyancy to aid in diving, but requires the bird to perch with wings spread for drying. Waterlogged plumage also forces a long run atop water surface to gain speed for flight.

Great Blue Heron (*Ardea herodias*)

DESCRIPTION

A large wading bird (4 feet tall; 7-foot wingspan) with stilt-like legs, a long neck, and daggerlike bill. Dusky blue of back continues up nape to patch of blue-jean blue on rear of head and plume. White on chin runs down russet-streaked throat and onto denim-streaked belly. Solid russet on shoulder and thigh. Black wing feathers visible in flight. Call a loud, dinosaurian *kruak*.

HABITAT & ECOLOGY

Arguably *the* iconic bird of the Bay, where solitary individuals stand or stalk along the marsh edge in search of fish, frogs, crayfish, and snakes. Rest and nest in colonial rookeries, mostly in trees. Bald eagles prey on young herons, but adult herons are also known to site rookeries near bald eagle nests, perhaps to gain protection from the eagles' territoriality toward other birds.

DID YOU KNOW?

The "GBH" is one of the few birds familiar enough for its own acronym. More than half the Atlantic coast's great blue heron breeding population nests along Chesapeake Bay.

Great Egret (*Ardea alba*)

DESCRIPTION

Bill of gold and legs of slate, that's what makes an egret great. This resplendent wading bird somehow wears a spotless, all-white dinner jacket while stalking the muddy fringe of Bay marshes. Develops a striking plume of feathers during breeding season that extends from the shoulders past the tail, while space between bill and eye darkens to a lime green. Svelte body and long, S-shaped neck. Emits raucous croak when startled.

HABITAT & ECOLOGY

One of the Bay's iconic wading birds. Year-round residents of the lower Bay, they occupy wetlands throughout the watershed during the mid-April–July breeding season. Mainly eat small fish, including mummichogs and menhaden, but will also take crayfish, shrimp, frogs, snakes, and small mammals. Hunt by patiently wading in shallow waters along the marsh edge with neck extended, then quickly thrusting the bill into the water to nab their prey. Roosts in trees along the water edge.

DID YOU KNOW?

More than 95 percent of great egrets were killed between the late 1800s and early 1900s for their breeding plumes, which were used to adorn ladies' hats. An 1886 issue of *Good Housekeeping* reported that a businesswoman bagged 40,000 seabirds from Cobb Island on Virginia's Eastern Shore to meet the demands of a single hat maker. Populations rebounded quickly following passage of the 1916 Migratory Bird Treaty Act between the United States and Canada.

Belted Kingfisher (*Megaceryle alcyon*)

DESCRIPTION

Stocky, strongly patterned bird with a steel-blue head, back, and "necklace" offset by a white belly and neck ring (the female wears a russet-colored bib across the belly and along the flanks). Head sports a spiky crest and is large in proportion to the body, as is the daggerlike black bill. Kingfishers are wary birds often first noticed by their mechanical "rattle call" as they fly to a more distant perch.

HABITAT & ECOLOGY

A usually solitary, year-round resident of fresh- and saltwater shorelines throughout the Bay. Often perches on shrubs, low tree branches, dock pilings, and other elevated shoreline features to set eyes on aquatic prey (presence is thus a sign of clear water). Will sometimes also hover. Captures prey in beak after quick dive to water surface. In addition to small fish such as mummichogs, eats crayfish, other invertebrates, and even berries.

DID YOU KNOW?

Kingfishers nest in burrows that they excavate within unvegetated sandy banks and cliff faces, usually close to water. Burrows are typically about 3 feet long and 3–5 inches in diameter, with an upward slope to reduce the threat of flooding. Proliferation of unvegetated banks due to road building and gravel mining has increased the number of suitable nesting sites. One of the few bird species in which the female is more brightly colored than the male.

Osprey (*Pandion haliaetus*)

DESCRIPTION

One of the largest of North American raptors: up to 2 feet from head to tail, with a wingspan of 5–6 feet. Generally white below and brown above, with a brown streak from the sharply curved beak, around the eye, and to the neck. Female wears a "necklace" of brown spots across the breast. Wings have a distinctive bend at "wrists" so that wing tips angle backward, forming an "M" in flight. "Finger" feathers at each wing tip are distinctive. The alarm call, a high-pitched *kee, kee, kee*, has been likened to a whistling tea kettle.

HABITAT & ECOLOGY

Ospreys are such a common sight above the Bay during spring and summer that it's easy to forget "our" birds spend almost half the year in South America. Commonly seen soaring above all manner of Bay shoreline, from marshland to sandy beaches. The one constant of their distribution is proximity to water. They build large stick nests near or over water at sites with good visibility and protection from predators. Today, many ospreys nest on man-made platforms. They are plunge feeders that hover to spot fishy prey in the water below before launching a kamikaze-like dive with legs and talons extended. Diet includes perch, shad, and menhaden.

DID YOU KNOW?

Ospreys are the only birds of prey that subsist almost entirely on live fish—hence their common name, "fish hawks." Their populations have increased since the late 1970s, primarily due to the 1972 ban on DDT. The osprey is well adapted to its fishy diet: Toes swivel to hold captured fish during flight, nostrils close to exclude water during dives, and spiny pads on the talons help catch fish. The Bay supports the largest concentration of breeding ospreys in the world. Breeding pairs return to the same nest site, and often remain together for many years. William & Mary's Center for Conservation Biology hosts an Osprey Watch website (www.osprey watch.org) with links to a number of nest cameras around the Bay.

OTHER WADING BIRDS

In addition to great blue herons and great egrets—two common and highly visible species we've already described in detail—the Chesapeake is home to a number of other wading birds. All share a coiled neck, daggerlike beak, stilt-like legs, and splayed toes; a perfect combination for stabbing fish and crabs while stalking Bay shallows and tidal flats. Here we provide a few identifying features to help tell these birds apart. For full treatment of all the Bay's bittern, egret, and heron species (along with ibises, spoonbills, and storks), consult the references in "A Deeper Dive."

NIGHT-HERON

Stocky, large-headed herons that forage for fish at night. Crowns colored as per the names; the yellow-crowned (juvenile pictured) has a stouter bill and longer neck and legs than the black-crowned.

TRICOLORED HERON

Strong contrast between white belly and dark upperparts; unusually long neck and bill. Often runs after prey.

SNOWY EGRET
The great egret's smaller alter ego, with a slate-colored bill and golden-yellow feet.

GREEN HERON
Uncommon, solitary, and secretive, with a rust-colored neck and greenish back.

Beaver (*Castor canadensis*)

DESCRIPTION

A squat, heavy-bodied mammal with thick brown fur; a horizontally flattened, naked tail; webbed feet; an arched back; and a large pair of orange "buckteeth." Rarely seen except as the literal head of a V-shaped wake rippling across a pond. Presence more often noted by gnawed trees, muddy trackways, dams, and lodges. Best viewed at dawn and dusk.

HABITAT & ECOLOGY

Use their large front teeth to fell trees for food (twigs and bark) and dam-building materials (branches and trunks). Their dams enhance the ecology of waterways by slowing runoff, trapping sediments and nutrients, and creating habitat for fish, frogs, turtles, snakes, birds, and other wildlife.

DID YOU KNOW?

These highly aquatic rodents were a keystone species across the Bay watershed and North America until hunted almost to extinction for their pelts—used to make water-resistant hats and coats. Now reclaiming parts of their range, including some Bay tributaries. Rebound is due to restoration efforts by "Beaver Believers," decline in trapping, and scarcity of predators such as wolves and panthers. A particularly impressive beaver dam and pond wows visitors at Calvert Cliffs State Park in Maryland.

Muskrat (*Ondatra zibethicus*)

DESCRIPTION
Shape and motion of tail help distinguish this rabbit-size creature from its fellow Bay rodents: the slightly larger nutria and much larger beaver. Tail—which adds 6–8 inches to the body length—is flattened vertically like a shark's fin and helps propel the animal through the water with its snakelike motion. (Nutria has a round tail it holds still while swimming; beaver tail is flattened like a snowshoe.) Snout is white with black whiskers and yellow teeth (nutria shares white snout but has white whiskers and orange teeth). Fur of muskrat is brown to black.

HABITAT & ECOLOGY
Found in both freshwater and saltwater marshes, where it eats cattails, bulrushes, and many other aquatic plants. Consumes shoots, leaves, and roots; may also eat fish, frogs, and shellfish. Predators include raccoons and bald eagles. Dense populations can almost completely denude a marsh. Uses vegetation and mud to build dome-shaped lodge for protection and food storage; also constructs burrow dens within a creek bank. Turtles will bask atop muskrat lodges.

DID YOU KNOW?
Both the common and species names refer to the musk these animals secrete to communicate with one other and warn intruders. Trapped for fur and meat in both Maryland and Virginia.

River Otter (*Lontra canadensis*)

DESCRIPTION

Tubular, slinky-like body is 3–4 feet long. Short, sturdy legs end in webbed feet. Short, dark brown fur often lighter on chin and chest. Furred, tapered tail is about one-third of the body length. Black, shiny nose sits atop "mustache" of long white whiskers. Head is broad, with eyes and (small) ears set high for surface swimming. Frolicsome behavior—which includes rolling, sliding, and tumbling—helps distinguish from the lunch-pail industriousness of beavers and the straight-line diligence of muskrats. Furred tail is also diagnostic vis á vis those two naked-tailed rodents.

HABITAT & ECOLOGY

Inhabits swamps, salt marshes, rivers, and lakes throughout the Bay watershed. Mostly eats fish, but will also consume crabs, crayfish, frogs, turtles, water beetles, and small mammals such as young muskrats. Hunts singly or in pairs; uses sensitive whiskers to detect underwater prey. Can remain submerged for up to 4 minutes, dive to more than 50 feet, and swim up to a quarter mile underwater. Will travel many miles across land to find new sources of food. Gathers in groups to socialize and play. Often uses dens abandoned by beavers and muskrats.

DID YOU KNOW?

Rivers otters are highly adapted for hunting beneath the waves, with a third, transparent eyelid that allows them to see underwater. Can also close ears and nostrils when submerged. Spend significant time scent-marking territory by urinating, defecating, scratching, and rubbing their scent glands on rocks and trees. Trapped for their fur in Maryland, Virginia, and other Bay states.

Hand of Man

CRAB POT BUOYS

Watermen use these brightly colored floats to mark the location of their submerged crab pots. Indeed, their use is required by law not only for crab pots but also peeler pots, eel pots, and fish pots. Each buoy is marked by a letter—C, P, E, or F—to help game wardens track the different types of fishing activity, and an ID number for monitoring individual crabbers.

Originally crafted from wood and now mostly made of Styrofoam, these buoys have a central hollow through which a top-knotted line passes to secure the underlying crab pot. Unfortunately, recreational vessels regularly sever these lines, marooning the pot on the bottom with no means to locate or retrieve it. The resulting "ghost" pots may continue to trap crabs and other creatures; there are efforts afoot throughout the Bay to find and remove these derelict pots to protect marine life.

Crab pot buoys can also break away from their mooring line during storms; they are frequently seen littering beaches near areas of heavy crabbing activity.

DUCK BLINDS

Often resembling tiki huts or beach cabanas, these structures belong to waterfowl hunters, who camouflage them with everything from marsh grasses and sticks to store-bought netting. When in use, you may also see a "flock" of decoys surrounding the blind to attract waterfowl.

To construct a blind, hunters in both Maryland and Virginia must purchase a state license, with regulations concerning siting, use, and maintenance. Licensing was enacted to minimize conflicts between and among hunters and waterfront property owners. Riparian land owners have first rights in both states to a license in the water Bay-ward of their property; in Virginia, they must also build and actively hunt a blind to maintain those rights.

Hunters may also pursue waterfowl from floating blinds, which requires purchase of a license to a "stake site," typically a tall pole embedded in the bottom to which they can moor their boat. Blinds, whether stationary or floating, may not be sited within 500 yards of each other in Virginia, or 250 yards in Maryland. This is both to reduce competition and to ensure safety.

DECOYS

These imitation waterfowl are used by hunters to entice ducks near their duck blind or skiff (goose decoys are often placed on land to similar purpose). Often hollow for buoyancy, they feature a weighted keel and anchor line for stability in the water. There are two main forms: floaters, with the head held high, and "preeners," with the head twisted back to simulate preening. Hunters carefully place their decoys in flocks or "spreads" whose arrangement depends on season, location, and setting, whether open water, tree-strewn beaver pond, or farm field. Common species include mallards, pintails,

green-winged teal, Canada geese, wood ducks, canvasbacks, redheads, and coots. Duck hunting in the Chesapeake historically centered on the Susquehanna Flats near the Bay's head, where vast meadows of wild celery and other submerged aquatic vegetation sustain large populations of waterfowl.

Today, decoys are available to hunters at low cost in any outdoors store. Typically made of soft plastic, these can be molded and painted to closely mimic the shape, texture, and coloration of any waterfowl species. Yet despite their lifelike details, these modern, mass-produced birds are no match for the wooden decoys traditionally carved by hand in woodshops around the Bay watershed. Originally handmade out of necessity, these decoys are now recognized as a notable form of indigenous and folk art, and celebrated as such in museums and private collections. Today, a new generation of carvers have elevated decoy-making into fine art that is appreciated as "floating sculpture" throughout the region and the world.

Several museums in Maryland offer decoy collections and exhibits describing carving culture. These include the Havre de Grace Decoy Museum in the city of the same name; the Upper Bay Museum in North East; and the Ward Museum of Wildfowl Art in Salisbury. Each of these museums also hosts an annual festival where attendees can admire decoys and purchase them directly from carvers. The Havre de Grace Decoy & Wildlife Art Festival and the Ward World Championship Wildfowl Carving Competition & Art Festival usually take place in spring. The Upper Bay Museum's Decoy and Wildlife Art Festival is held each autumn.

MARSH SILLS

As we have seen, salt marshes are highly resistant to erosion due to the wave-damping action of *Spartina* blades and a network of roots and rhizomes that traps and holds marsh soils despite the ebb and flow of tidal currents. If the marsh has an "Achilles' heel," it's the seaward edge, where waves can wash away the fine-grained sediments and cause slumping of entire blocks of "sod." Erosion here may be aggravated by wakes from passing boats, which bring high-energy waves into a normally calm environment.

The traditional approach to combating marsh erosion is to build a vertical wooden wall, or bulkhead, just seaward of the marsh edge, then to backfill the intervening space with dirt. But bulkheads bring their own problems, preventing shore life from moving between water and land, and often increasing erosive scour by reflecting and concentrating wave energy.

A newer, more effective approach is the marsh sill. What may at first glance appear to be a line of rocks haphazardly dumped a few feet off an eroding marsh edge is actually a carefully engineered structure specifically designed for a site's "wave climate." As such, it accounts for the prevailing wind direction, fetch, maximum wave size, and other factors. The sill dissipates wave energy before it can reach and erode the marsh edge, and provides a living space for oysters, shorebirds, and other wildlife. It also encourages marsh plants to naturally fill in the sheltered water in its lee; this area may also be planted with sprigs of *Spartina* or other species.

Marsh sills are one form of "living shoreline," now legislated as the preferred mode of shoreline protection in both Maryland and Virginia.

A DEEPER DIVE

Beal, E. O., and S. F. Brown. "A Manual of Marsh and Aquatic Vascular Plants of North Carolina with Habitat Data." Technical Bulletin No. 247 (Raleigh, NC: The North Carolina Agricultural Research Service, 1977).

Blossey, B., et al. *Common Reed, in Biological Control of Invasive Plants in the Eastern United States*. R. V. Driesche et al. (eds.) (Morgantown, WV: US Department of Agriculture, 2002).

Correll, D. L., T. E. Jordan, and D. E. Weller. "Beaver Pond Biogeochemical Effects in the Maryland Coastal Plain." *Biogeochemistry*, 49(3) (2000). 10.1023/A:1006330501887.

Daniel, E. K., and W. B. Christopher. "Sediment-Trapping by Beaver Ponds in Streams of the Mid-Atlantic Piedmont and Coastal Plain, USA." *Southeastern Naturalist*, 14(3) (2015). 10.1656/058.014.0309.

Eleuterius, L. N. *Tidal Marsh Plants* (Gretna, LA: Pelican Publishing Company, 1990).

Fleming, G. P., K. D. Patterson, and K. Taverna. *The Natural Communities of Virginia: A Classification of Ecological Community Groups and Community Types: Estuarine System (Tidal Wetlands)*, version 3.2 (March 2020). www.dcr.virginia.gov/natural-heritage/natural-communities/ncestuarine.

Goldfarb, B. *Eager: The Surprising, Secret Life of Beavers and Why They Matter* (White River Junction, VT: Chelsea Green Publishing, 2018).

Hosier, P. E. "What's in a Name? A Lot, It Seems! Can a Coastal Plant Ecologist Quell a Minor Social Media Uprising?" *Coastwatch* (Raleigh, NC: North Carolina Sea Grant, 2019).

Massachusetts Audubon Society (ed.). *A Guide to Northeastern Dragonflies and Damselflies* (Lincoln, MA: Massachusetts Audubon Society, 2007).

Meanley, B. *Birds & Marshes of the Chesapeake Bay Country* (Atglen, PA: Schiffer Publishing Ltd., 1975).

Munroe, K. "Dragonflies of Northern Virginia" (2020). http://dragonfliesnva.com.

Musselman, L. J., and D. A. Knepper. *Plants of the Chesapeake Bay: A Guide to Wildflowers, Grasses, Aquatic Vegetation, Trees, Shrubs and other Flora* (Baltimore: The Johns Hopkins University Press, 2012).

Peterson, P. M., et al. "A Molecular Phylogeny and New Subgeneric Classification of Sporobolus (Poaceae; Chloridoideae; Sporobolinae)." *Taxon*, 63(6) (2014a).

Rothenburg, J., S. Rawlins, and S. LeVan. *Marshnotes: An Introduction to the Salt Marsh*. Calvert Marine Museum (ed.) (Solomons, MD: Calvert Marine Museum Press, 1987).

Silberhorn, G. Wetland Flora Technical Reports (various years) (Gloucester Point, VA: Wetlands Program, Virginia Institute of Marine Science, William & Mary). https://scholarworks.wm.edu/ccrm_wetlandflora.

Silberhorn, G. M., M. Warriner, and K. Forrest. *Common Plants of the Mid-Atlantic Coast: A Field Guide* (Baltimore and London: The Johns Hopkins University Press, 1999).

Tiner, R. W., and A. Rorer. *Field Guide to Coastal Wetland Plants of the Southeastern United States.* (Amherst, MA: The University of Massachusetts Press, 1993).

Virginia Department of Game and Inland Fisheries, Coastal Area. *Discover Our Wild Side: Virginia Birding and Wildlife Trail* (2002).

Virginia Institute of Marine Science and Center for Coastal Resources Management. *Field Guide to Virginia Salt and Brackish Marsh Plants.* CCRM (ed.) (Gloucester Point, VA: Virginia Institute of Marine Science, 2007).

Walter, R. C., and D. J. Merritts. "Natural Streams and the Legacy of Water-Powered Mills." *Science*, 319(5861) (2008). 10.1126/science.1151716.

White, C. P. *Chesapeake Bay Nature of the Estuary: A Field Guide* (Atglen, PA: Schiffer Publishing Ltd., 1989).

A Walk through Woods and Fields

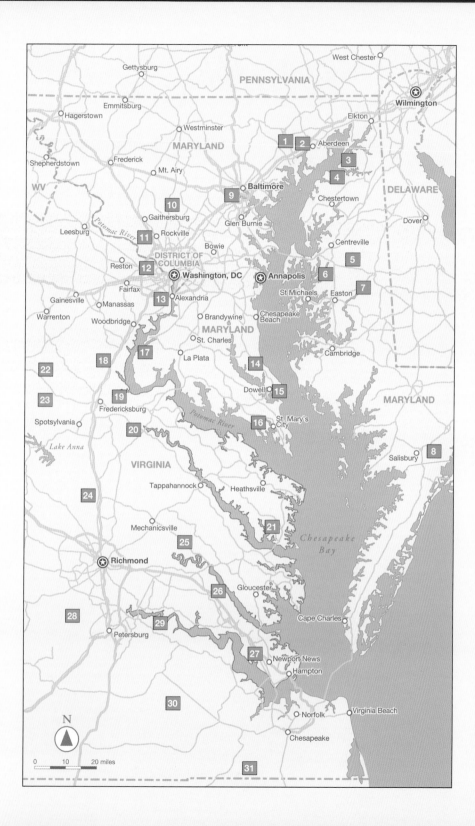

A Walk through Woods and Fields

This guide to the watery wonders of Chesapeake Bay includes a section on woods and fields for good reason: These habitats are key in efforts to maintain and restore the health of Bay waters. Here we highlight public lands with particularly vibrant forest and meadow ecosystems.

NAP = Natural Area Preserve, NRMA = Natural Resources Management Area, NWR = National Wildlife Refuge, SF = State Forest, SP = State Park, WMA = Wildlife Management Area

1. Palmer SP
2. Susquehanna SP
3. Elk Neck SP
4. Sassafras NRMA
5. Tuckahoe SP (Adkins Arboretum)
6. Wye Island NRMA
7. Martinak SP
8. Pocomoke River SP
9. Patapsco Valley SP
10. Patuxent River SP
11. Seneca Creek SP
12. Gold Mine Tract—C&O Canal National Historic Park
13. Glencarlyn Park
14. Parkers Creek WMA
15. Calvert Cliffs SP
16. St. Mary's River SP
17. Chapman SP
18. Prince William Forest Park
19. Crow's Nest NAP
20. Pettigrew WMA
21. Hickory Hollow NAP
22. C. F. Phelps WMA
23. Wilderness & Chancellorsville Battlefields
24. North Anna Battlefield Park
25. Sandy Point SF
26. York River SP
27. Newport News Park
28. Pocahontas SP & SF
29. James River NWR
30. Big Woods SF & WMA
31. Great Dismal Swamp NWR

VIRGINIA doth afford many excellent vegetables, and living Creatures, yet grasse there is little or none, but what groweth in low
Marishes: for all the Countrey is overgrowne with trees, whose
droppings continually turneth their grasse to weeds, by reason of
the ranckness of the ground, which would soone be amended by
good husbandry.

—*Capt. John Smith, 1607*

THIS GUIDE TO THE WATERY WONDERS OF CHESAPEAKE BAY includes a sec-
tion on woods and fields for good reason: Trees, forbs, and grasses help to reduce erosion and filter runoff, and are thus a key part of efforts to maintain and restore the
health of Bay waters. Only by understanding and appreciating the value of our forests
and meadows can we make the changes needed to restore the Bay and its marine life to
their full splendor.

THE ANCIENT FOREST

Like the Bay itself, the forests that surround it are but an eyeblink in the context of geologic time. During the last ice age, mid-Atlantic forests were mostly spruce, pine, and
fir. This boreal forest is now largely confined to Canada, though remnants persist in a
few Bay-area refugia such as the Potomac River headwaters in West Virginia and Bear
Meadows in Pennsylvania. A hardwood forest began to take shape here around 11,000
years ago as the ice age waned, climate warmed, and ocean water began creeping up
the valley of the Susquehanna. The oak, hickory, and pine forest that sustained untold
generations of Native peoples was established by about 5,000 years ago.

WOODLAND INDIANS AND THE FOREST PRIMEVAL

The Native Americans of the Chesapeake Bay region were part of the larger Woodland group, people exquisitely adapted to life in the great Eastern hardwood forest.
Originally hunters and gatherers, they gradually adopted a more sedentary, agrarian
lifestyle as nut-bearing hardwoods replaced the boreal forests of the ice-age Bay, and
corn, beans, and squash were introduced from Mexico. By the time of European contact, they had a yearly routine broken into five seasons. This included a fall harvest
(*Taquitock*), during which they supplemented their crop yields with protein from nuts—
directly from oaks, beech, chestnut, hickory, walnut, and other trees; and indirectly by
hunting deer and turkey, which rely on nuts as a dietary staple. Bay Indians also used
forest products for their weapons (bow and arrows, shields, and swords); canoes (see
the "Boating and Fishing on the Bay" chapter); and houses. A re-created Algonquian
village can be visited at Jamestown Settlement in Virginia and Historic St. Mary's City
in Maryland.

When the English arrived on the Chesapeake's shores in the early 1600s, they marveled at the majesty of the Eastern forest, which to their eyes appeared primeval, with

trees far larger than those in the long-depleted woodlots of Great Britain. Capt. John Smith enthused over cypress with diameters of "3 fathoms" (18 feet) and oaks so tall and straight "they will bear two foot and a half square of good timber for 20 yards long."

But pollen studies and historical accounts suggest that Native Americans had been subtly altering these coastal forests for thousands of years. Early explorers described these as parklike, with Smith writing that "a man may gallop a horse amongst these woods any way, but where the creeks or rivers shall hinder." This openness stemmed mostly from brushfires the Indians set to clear the understory for hunting and gathering of herbs and berries, among other uses. Local tribes also girdled trees to form the small clearings they used to plant

POWHATAN

Held this state & fashion when Capt. Smith was delivered to him prisoner
1607

Captain John Smith described Algonquian houses as "like our Arbors, of small young springs bowed and tied, and so close covered with mats, or the bark of trees very handsomely, that notwithstanding either wind, rain, or weather, they are as warm as stoves."

their crops. These typically measured 100–200 square feet, with the ash providing a rich fertilizer. When, after a few years, farming had depleted the soil, the Indians would move on to create a new clearing, allowing the former opening to return to forest while producing berries and other sustenance. Their impacts were thus few and fleeting. Occasional glades were also formed by disturbances such as windstorms and wildfires.

EUROPEAN DEFORESTATION

European colonists brought clearing and agriculture to an entirely different level, using metal axes and plows to deforest vast swaths of woodland. When Europeans arrived, old-growth forest covered 95 percent of the Bay watershed; by the late 1800s, they had cut two-thirds of this. They felled trees for farms, fuel, fencing, railroad ties, iron production, and timber for buildings and boats (construction of an English warship used up to 2,000 oaks). Deforestation was most pronounced in closely settled areas along the Bay and its tributaries, where 80–90 percent of the landscape was denuded. Indeed, it is difficult to find any remnants of old-growth forest east of the I-95 corridor. The Old-Growth Forest Network maintains a directory of the few that still persist in Maryland, Pennsylvania, Virginia, and other Bay states.

Old-growth chestnut trees like these in the Great Smoky Mountains once covered large parts of Bay headwaters.

This deforestation—comparable to what's occurring today in the Amazon rain forest—profoundly altered Bay hydrology. Raindrops that once would have been hard-pressed to reach the ground without deflection or capture by the foliage of canopy and understory, a carpet of ferns and mosses on the forest floor, or a deep layer of leaf litter now impacted plowed dirt with full force, sluicing tons of soil into Bay waters with each cloudburst. The increase in runoff, turbidity, and siltation lowered Bay salinity, shaded sun-loving bay grasses, smothered oyster reefs, and otherwise altered the marine food web. Because the forest floor was no longer as spongelike, groundwater levels also fell, leading many once-perennial watercourses and springs to become seasonal or dry up completely. Deforestation also led to profound changes in the woodland community, with populations of bear, beaver, elk, and other wildlife drastically curtailed or driven locally extinct due to loss of habitat and overhunting.

A tidal creek before and after upstream clearing shows how deforestation degrades the quality of Bay waters.

TWENTIETH-CENTURY RECOVERY

Following the devastation of the Civil War, abandonment of farms for richer Midwestern cropland, and a switch to coal for heating, new forests began to return to deserted farmland and heavily logged forests across the Bay watershed during the 1900s. This relatively rapid recovery—forests now cover approximately 58 percent of the Bay watershed—proved the natural resilience of Eastern woodlands, and moderated some of the negative consequences of deforestation.

It's important to recognize, however, that these regrown woodlands—the ones familiar to us today—differ fundamentally from the old-growth forests they replaced. The practice of "high-grading"—removing the biggest trees—left only smaller trees to reproduce. One study estimates the current canopy is thus 40 percent shorter than it was at European contact. Changes also resulted underground, where loss of roots disrupted a complex symbiosis with fungi and microorganisms that was key to forest health and renewal. Selective removal of highly valued species such as white oak (for shipbuilding) and white pine (for homes and ships) also promoted the growth of less-beneficial and once-minor species such as red maple. But the most catastrophic shift in forest composition was surely the loss of chestnuts due to blight (see "Yesterbay" sidebar on pp. 218–219).

Today's regrown woodlands are beautiful, but they differ fundamentally from the old-growth forests they replaced.

Protected forest lands, like these in the Blue Ridge Mountains of Virginia, are critical for Bay health.

Forest recovery was aided by the establishment of state and national forests in the early 1900s, with maintenance of water flow and water quality a prime motivation. These forests continue to offer a wealth of ecological benefits and recreational opportunities, from hiking and camping to birding and hunting. The two national forests in the Bay watershed—the George Washington–Jefferson in Virginia and the Monongahela in Pennsylvania—attract more than 5 million visitors annually. State forests—twenty-five in Virginia's portion of the Bay watershed, eleven in Maryland's, eleven in Pennsylvania's, and twelve in New York's—protect millions of acres and are also well worth a visit.

A more recent chapter in forest protection is the riparian buffer. Encouraged in the landmark Chesapeake Bay Watershed Agreement of 2014 and required by state law in both Maryland and Virginia, these are strips of trees maintained or planted along waterways to reduce erosion, filter pollutants, and shade the water. Today the Chesapeake Bay Program estimates that 55 percent of the watershed's 288,000 miles of streambanks and shorelines have these last lines of defense. Financial incentives are helping the program move toward its 70 percent goal, largely by paying farmers to plant and maintain forest buffers along their watercourses.

Densely wooded riparian buffers reduce erosion, filter pollutants, and shade the water.

YESTERBAY

Chestnut Blight

"Chestnuts roasting on an open fire . . ." The opening to Nat King Cole's 1946 classic harkens to a time when the aroma of roasting chestnuts evoked Christmas as much as eggnog or tinsel. Today these holiday treats are mostly a memory, their parent trees devastated by an introduced fungus.

American chestnuts (*Castanea dentata*), forest giants that could reach ten stories tall and 10 feet wide, once dominated Eastern woodlands. More than 4 billion grew from Alabama to Maine, preferring drier, south-facing slopes along the Appalachians and Piedmont, right through the heart of the Chesapeake watershed. For millennia, any rain that fed a Bay tributary had likely splashed a chestnut leaf before reaching the forest floor. It was also a popular urban tree, lining streets in Baltimore, Washington, DC, and other Bay-area cities.

Both native and colonial Americans tapped the chestnut's riches. The strong, rot-resistant wood was widely used in log cabins, barns, flooring, fence posts, and railroad ties. The acorn-size nuts—sweet when raw and nutty when roasted—were a popular ingredient in early American dishes, with trainloads delivered to street vendors in East Coast cities. Homesteaders sold nuts for cash and fattened their hogs and cattle by letting them forage in chestnut forests. The nuts were also a major food source for white-tailed deer, bears, wild turkey, and squirrels. Chestnuts remain a holiday treat

today, but most are from introduced species or imported nuts.

The chestnut blight began around 1900, when a fungus released from imported Japanese chestnuts spread like wildfire across the eastern United States. With no natural immunity, US trees developed cankers and quickly died. By 1940, the once-dominant tree was rare. It persists in some areas as sprouts from stumps of once-mighty trees, but these also quickly succumb to the fungus.

Today a small but dedicated group of scientists, citizens, and students are actively restoring chestnuts to their native range and ecological role. One of their approaches is to breed and plant or graft fungus-resistant hybrids. Another is to inoculate infected trees with a weakened form of a virus that attacks the fungus. Their slow but steady progress offers hope that residents of the Bay watershed will one day be able to enjoy a summer afternoon beneath a spreading chestnut tree.

Those interested in helping restore this magnificent tree should contact The American Chestnut Foundation (acf.org), which is growing more than 30,000 blight-resistant Chinese hybrids at its Meadowview Research Farms in southwest Virginia. The American Chestnut Cooperators' Foundation works with scientists at Virginia Tech to breed blight-resistant chestnuts using only native trees.

The American Chestnut Foundation website offers tips to identify and find wild trees. A 2014 survey by National Park Service staff found small chestnut trees growing in several Bay-area parks, including Catoctin Mountain Park, George Washington Memorial Parkway, Harpers Ferry National Historical Park, Rock Creek Park, and Wolf Trap National Park for the Performing Arts.

NEW THREATS

Protected forestlands are particularly important given the resurgence of deforestation that began in the Bay watershed during the 1970s—this time not for farming, fuel, or timber but mostly to accommodate a burgeoning suburban population. *The State of Chesapeake Forests* notes that more than 750,000 acres of Bay forest—equal to twenty Washington DCs—have been lost since 1982, primarily to sprawling development. That's 100 acres per day.

The latest episode of deforestation is particularly insidious due to its patchy nature. A study in Baltimore County in 2005 showed that roads and developments divide its 133,000 acres of forest into more than 9,000 individual fragments, with less than 0.1 percent in patches larger than 100 acres. Similar disruption has occurred across the Bay watershed, with only 40 percent of forests offering the "interior" refuge of intact woodlands.

Forest fragmentation benefits some "edge" species such as white-tailed deer and wax myrtle, but harms many others, including shade-loving plants; common roadkill creatures such as opossums, raccoons, and box turtles; and large-range predators such as cougars. It also decreases the biodiversity of forests and makes them more susceptible to both wildfire and invasive species such as gypsy moths, hemlock woolly adelgids, Asian stilt grass, and kudzu.

Looking to the future, Bay forests face a number of emerging threats (see the last chapter, "The Once and Future Bay"). Climate change will favor the northward spread of heat-tolerant trees such as oak and loblolly pine, and the loss of northerly species

Suburban sprawl and fragmentation are the biggest threats to today's Bay forests.

Eastern hardwood forests enhance Bay water quality and offer majesty to visitors.

such as maple and beech. It will also indirectly lead to tree loss as rising seas create "ghost forests." Warming is also likely to enhance the abundance of insects such as the emerald ash borer and the prevalence of plant disease.

Although the modern Bay forest differs from its old-growth predecessor, and despite the many challenges it still faces, it remains a global treasure, with some of the largest hardwood stands in temperate latitudes and offerings of beauty and solace to residents and visitors alike. Writers have long compared a walk through a forest with a visit to a grand cathedral—perhaps that's even more true in today's Bay watershed, as incessant threats from human development have hopefully awakened us to the sanctity of these sylvan landscapes and the inherent, ecologic, and economic value of keeping them whole.

FIELDS AND MEADOWS

It's daunting to realize that people create and maintain almost every single clearing in the Bay watershed—from pastures to farm fields, gardens, lawns, parks, golf courses, roads, medians, and parking lots. One cannot help but marvel at the sheer industriousness of this enterprise (especially before the advent of power tools!) and fret over its major impacts on Bay waters. In either case, our opening of the forest canopy has greatly increased the habitat for sun-loving plants. Once confined to a few ephemeral forest glades, they now brighten (unpaved) patches throughout the watershed. Some attribute the human proclivity for tree clearing to a subconscious yearning to re-create our origins on the savanna; if so, this might help explain the serenity that so many feel during a walk through these man-made clearings. Properly managed, fields and meadows can contribute to a healthy Bay; the native grasses and wildflowers described in the following pages are naturally suited for minimizing erosion, reducing nutrient pollution, and providing habitat for pollinators and wildlife.

Meadows are a beautiful yet largely man-made feature of the coastal plain landscape.

Plants

American Beech (*Fagus grandifolia*)

DESCRIPTION

Grows 60–80 feet tall, 2–3 feet in diameter. Bark is distinctive—smooth, thin, and pearly gray, often with patches of sea-green lichen. Leaves are alternate, simple, and diamond-shaped with small symmetrical teeth, a sharp tip, and a distinct central vein. Triangular nuts are brown and prickly. Holds onto bronzed autumn leaves throughout winter, particularly on lower branches. Fingerlike roots knead the forest floor like a baker kneads dough.

HABITAT & ECOLOGY

Common throughout the Bay watershed, preferring moist but well-drained soils. Nuts are an important food source for white-tailed deer, turkeys, songbirds, and wood-peckers, as well as black bears, foxes, and squirrels. Dense canopy often excludes most understory growth other than shade-tolerant beech saplings. Often found in association with a root parasite known as beechdrops, which in summer and fall send up brown shoots (to 10 inches) with small purple and white flowers.

DID YOU KNOW?

Beech bark is a favorite for those who feel a need to carve their initials or other markings into a tree. Although this is unlikely to kill the tree, it can stress it and reduce its growth. More to the point: Would you like someone to give you a lifelong tattoo without your consent? Beechnuts are edible and quite sweet. Enjoy a few on your next autumn hike!

American Holly (*Ilex opaca*)

DESCRIPTION
Readily identified by the spiny and shiny green leaves it holds through winter; red berries (drupes) on female trees; and smooth, light gray bark that becomes warty with age. Leaves are simple, alternate, and waxy. Often-crooked trunk grows 30–50 feet tall and 1–2 feet in diameter.

HABITAT & ECOLOGY
One of the predominant understory trees of the Bay forest. Its berries feed a variety of birds, including blue jays, cardinals, flickers, mockingbirds, mourning doves, red-bellied woodpeckers, robins, towhees, white-throated sparrows, and turkeys. Also eaten by deer, foxes, rabbits, raccoons, squirrels, white-footed mice, and box turtles. Trees provide shelter and nesting sites for bluebirds, thrashers, and other songbirds.

DID YOU KNOW?
Europeans had long considered the English holly a "holy" tree because it remained green throughout the long, dark winter (thence its name). The custom of cutting holly boughs for Christmas decorations (brought to America by the English) led to widespread loss of hollies throughout the Bay watershed and subsequent passage of protective laws in Maryland and Delaware.

Flowering Dogwood (*Cornus florida*)

DESCRIPTION

This small (15–30 feet), otherwise modest deciduous tree takes center stage each spring across the Bay watershed as its creamy white "flowers" open before its leaves unfurl. The real flower—a tight, lime-green cluster—is rather low-key as well; the white, crossed quartet of notched "petals" are actually modified leaves known as bracts. True leaves are opposite, simple, and strongly veined, with a smooth or slightly wavy margin. Fruit is a cluster of 3–5 small red kernels that ripen in fall. Bark is smooth when young but turns blocky with age.

HABITAT & ECOLOGY

The dogwood's beauty isn't just skin-deep, as almost every part of this understory tree provides food for wildlife. The high-fat fruits nurture more than three dozen bird species, including cardinals, grouse, titmice, and turkeys, as well as beavers, black bears, chipmunks, foxes, and squirrels. Foliage and twigs are browsed by deer and rabbits, while the flowers attract bees and butterflies. Prefers moist, rich soils in part shade; leaves will wilt and drop during summer drought. Often found with redbuds and beneath stands of loblolly pine, oak, sweetgum, and tuliptree.

DID YOU KNOW?

A popular ornamental and the state tree of Virginia, but sadly now challenged by the anthracnose fungus. This disease may have been imported along with the Asian kousa dogwood, whose widespread planting as an ornamental also precludes the many wildlife benefits of our native tree. Common name refers to traditional use of stems for making skewers once known as "dogs."

Eastern Red Cedar (*Juniperus virginiana*)

DESCRIPTION
Aromatic evergreen (40–60 feet tall, 1–2 feet in diameter) with small, scaly leaves. Bark is grayish to reddish brown and peels into fibrous strips. Young trees are pyramidal, with upturned branches and a pointed top; older trees are more conical, with horizontal branches. Fruit occurs in clusters of dusty-blue berries (actually highly modified cones). Fluting common on trunks of older trees.

HABITAT & ECOLOGY
Prefers sun and tolerates thin, dry soils; occurs as an early successional species in abandoned fields. Berries are a favorite food of cedar waxwings, and are three times more likely to germinate once they pass through the birds' digestive tract. Also eaten by bluebirds, flickers, goldfinches, mockingbirds, robins, and wild turkeys; as well as bears, coyotes, deer, foxes, rabbits, raccoons, skunks, and possums. Dense foliage provides winter cover for juncos, myrtle warblers, and sparrows and nesting sites in spring and summer for mockingbirds, robins, and sparrows. Deer will also eat twigs and foliage.

DID YOU KNOW?
Aromatic and resistant to decay and insects, red cedar is used in closets and chests to repel moths and other pests. Bay Indians used the wood to construct their dwellings, and burned it in sweat lodges and for purification rites. As the genus name attests, red cedar is actually a juniper.

Loblolly Pine (*Pinus taeda*)

DESCRIPTION

This evergreen conifer reaches 80–100 feet in Bay woodlands. Bark is reddish brown; horizontal gaps bridge vertical furrows to form flat-topped linear blocks built of many thin layers, like a stack of paper plates. Lower limbs self-prune as the tree grows, leaving an open, oval crown. Branches form a shallow "V" at junction with trunk. Needles occur in bundles of three and are about as long as an adult hand (6–9 inches). Cones are 3–4 inches long; with alternating rows of diamond-shaped, sharply pointed seed heads.

HABITAT & ECOLOGY

A common native tree of the coastal plain. Prefers moist to wet soils; occurs from marsh edges to upland sites with shallow water table, including abandoned farm fields. Today often grown in timber plantations. Provides habitat for pine warbler, brown-headed nuthatch, and other songbirds, as well as turkey, white-tailed deer, and gray and fox squirrels. Large trees near marsh edges are a favorite site for osprey and bald eagle nests.

DID YOU KNOW?

"Loblolly" comes from a dark porridge served to sailors, which resembles the mucky soils this tree prefers. Loblollies are the most important timber tree throughout Virginia and the southeastern United States. Their strong, light wood is widely used in home construction.

Longleaf Pine (*Pinus palustris*)

DESCRIPTION

Resembles loblolly pine in form (straight trunk with few branches until open crown) and size (80–100 feet). As the name attests, can be distinguished by its needles, which are longer than an adult hand (10–16 inches). At 6–10 inches, cones are also much larger than those of loblolly. Bark is reddish brown; texture resembles irregular blocks of flaky pastry; not furrowed like loblolly. Tree may "twinkle" on clear days as silvery branch-tip buds reflect sunlight.

HABITAT & ECOLOGY

Found only in the southernmost reaches of the Bay watershed, often in open, park-like settings on sandy to poorly drained coastal soils. Sapling has a fire-resistant "grass phase" in which it remains a foot or so high for several years while channeling its growth into a deep taproot before suddenly shooting skyward. Understory provides choice habitat for quail and excellent browse for white-tailed deer. Turkeys, gray squirrels, and fox squirrels eat the seeds. Open cavities in mature trees are the preferred nesting site for the endangered red-cockaded woodpecker.

DID YOU KNOW?

An important timber tree in the southeastern United States; people also gather and sell its needles for pine mulch and its large cones for decoration and crafts. Listed as "vulnerable" by the International Union for the Conservation of Nature, as range has been much reduced by fire suppression, logging, and development.

Mountain Laurel (*Kalmia latifolia*)

DESCRIPTION

Broadleaf, evergreen shrub or small tree (5–20 feet tall) with twisted, furrowed trunk of reddish hue. Showy late-spring flowers form terminal clusters of pinkish-white cups with radiating purple streaks. Glossy, lance-shaped leaves are alternate to whorled near twig tips. Fruit a round, brown capsule that splits into 5 segments in fall, releasing hundreds of tiny seeds.

HABITAT & ECOLOGY

Slow-growing tree that occupies diverse understory habitats across the Bay watershed. Prefers well-drained soils of south-facing slopes. In the coastal plain it occurs beneath beech, loblolly pine, oaks, red maple, and sweet-gum along with dogwood, hollies, and redbud; in the Appalachians, beneath red spruce and fir along with rhododendrons and mountain holly. Serves as a larval host for the laurel sphinx moth. Browsed by white-tailed deer and rabbits. Seeds require a moist or mossy seed-bed to sprout. Reproduces mainly through suckers.

DID YOU KNOW?

Flowers have a springlike mechanism that spreads pollen when tripped by a nectaring bee. Has grown more common in the Appalachians during the past century, likely from canopy opening due to loss of the American chestnut and defoliation by gypsy moths. Genus named for Peter Kalm, a botanist sent by the Swedish government in 1748 to report on North America's natural resources.

OAKS

Much of the Bay watershed is clothed in what are broadly termed oak-hickory forests. A rich variety of oak species compose this woodland type, depending on local conditions. Tree scientists bring helpful order to this diversity by grouping the many *Quercus* species into red oaks and white oaks. The former, represented here by the northern red oak (*Q. rubra*), includes bear, black, blackjack, cherrybark, laurel, pin, scarlet, shingle, southern red, turkey, water, and willow oak. The white oaks, represented here by the eponymous *Q. alba*, include chestnut, chinquapin, live, overcup, post, swamp chestnut, and swamp white oak. A quick way to tell them apart is to look at the leaf tips: sharp like a flame in red oaks, rounded like a snowball in white oaks.

Northern Red Oak (*Quercus rubra*)

DESCRIPTION

A sizable tree at 70–90 feet tall and 2–3 feet in diameter. Leaves are alternate, simple, 5–8 inches long, with 7–11 sharp, bristle-tipped lobes. Turn crimson in fall. As tree ages, smooth bark develops shallow furrows that resemble figure eight ski tracks. Acorns are about 1 inch long, oval to oblong, and wear a jaunty cap resembling a beret. Require two growing seasons to mature. Tree produces an acorn crop every 2–5 years.

HABITAT & ECOLOGY

This moderate- to fast-growing tree does best on deep, well-drained soils of slopes, ravines, and valley floors. The acorns are an important food for gray squirrels, deer, turkeys, mice and other small rodents, and many other mammals and birds. Animals and insects can eat or damage 8 or more of every 10 acorns; 500 or more acorns may be required to produce a single seedling. Defoliation by the imported gypsy moth may weaken trees enough for disease or other insects to kill them. Often found with dogwood, American holly, redbud, pawpaw, and persimmon.

DID YOU KNOW?

Northern red oak has been widely planted as an ornamental because of its pleasing shape and brilliant fall foliage. Arguably the most popular hardwood in the United States, red oak is widely used in cabinet and furniture making.

White Oak (*Quercus alba*)

DESCRIPTION

A very large tree that can grow 140 feet tall, span 3–4 feet in diameter, and live for 500 years. Leaves are alternate, simple, 4–7 inches long, with 7–10 rounded, fingerlike lobes. Turn dull red or bronze in fall; many persist on tree through winter. Yellow-green male flowers borne on "catkins"; appear with leaves in mid-spring. Acorn is oval to oblong; wears a woolly stocking cap that it doffs at maturity. Matures in one growing season in the early fall. Very light gray bark stands out against the darker bark of almost all other trees; varies in texture with some trees exhibiting long, peelable strips. Smooth patches not uncommon on older trees.

HABITAT & ECOLOGY

This slow-growing tree occupies a wide range of soils and sites. Saplings can persist under the forest canopy for more than 90 years. A boom-or-bust species when it comes to acorns, it can produce huge crops but only does so every 4–10 years. In Virginia, a single tree dropped more than 23,000 acorns in a single "mast" year. Nearly 200 kinds of birds and mammals eat the acorns, including blue jays, crows, red-headed woodpeckers, turkeys, quail, bear, deer, gray squirrels, mice, and raccoons. Deer also browse the twigs and foliage.

DID YOU KNOW?

Woodworkers can tell white oak from red oak because the pores in its growth rings are plugged rather than open. This makes white oak highly waterproof and led to its use for barrels (whiskey and wine) and shipbuilding. It is also widely used for flooring, furniture, and cabinetry. White oak is Maryland's state tree.

Sweetgum (*Liquidambar styraciflua*)

DESCRIPTION
Twigs, fruit, and leaves are all distinctive. Maroon twigs sport tan, corky "wings." Round, spiky fruit looks like a small mace (and can likewise inflict real pain, if stepped on with a bare foot). Spikes occur in pairs that resemble a bird's open beak. Tree holds many of its fruits through winter. Leaves are alternate and simple with 5 pointed lobes and finely toothed edges. Grayish bark is broken into irregular polygons. Twigs and leaves release a pleasant odor when crushed.

HABITAT & ECOLOGY
Prefers bottomlands with rich, moist soil and can tolerate some flooding. Songbirds, mallards, and squirrels eat the seeds; mice and rabbits browse the twigs. Host to the spectacular hickory horned devil, the caterpillar of the regal moth. Beavers use the wood to construct dams.

DID YOU KNOW?
The genus name *Liquidambar* refers to the sap the tree releases to help heal injuries to the bark or limbs. Bay Indians used the sap as chewing gum and mixed a sweetgum tea with pennywort to treat cuts, bruises, and sores.

Sycamore (*Platanus occidentalis*)

DESCRIPTION

Deciduous tree 100–150 feet tall with a diameter up to 12 feet. Bark is distinctive—thin and grading from brown at bottom to peeling "camouflage" patches of cream, green, and gray higher up; often forming a two-tone tree (think graham cracker–brown and marshmallow-white s'more). Crown stands out as a bone-white sentinel among darker trunks in winter forest. Large (6–10 inches) leaves are alternate and simple with 3–5 lobes. Spherical, fibrous, reddish-brown fruits dangle from a long stem through winter like small Christmas ornaments.

HABITAT & ECOLOGY

Seeds are a favorite of juncos, goldfinches, and chickadees; also eaten by squirrels, muskrats, and beavers. Prefers moist soils of bottomlands and marsh edges. Larger trees provide good nesting sites for wood ducks and woodpeckers. A host tree for the eastern tiger swallowtail butterfly.

DID YOU KNOW?

Sycamores occupy stream-edge habitat similar to that of ash trees and thus are an important replacement species as emerald ash borers kill more and more ash trees across the Bay watershed.

Tuliptree, Tulip-Poplar
(*Liriodendron tulipifera*)

DESCRIPTION
The tallest Eastern hardwood, regularly reaches 120 feet in the Bay region, with some trees nearing 200 feet. Broad leaves have 4 lobes. Tulip-shaped, 6-petaled flowers are lime green with an orange ring and a sunburst of banana-colored stamens. Flowers appear in spring, but are often hidden high atop mature trees. Trunk very straight, with few branches before the narrow crown. Bark has cloud-gray furrows. Cone-like fruits release scores of seeds as they ripen; each seed has a sharp, recurved head and a single wing to catch the wind.

HABITAT & ECOLOGY
A fast-growing, pioneer species that thrives in full sun. Prefers rich, well-drained, but moist soils. A favorite nesting tree for songbirds. The nectar-rich flowers attract honeybees and hummingbirds; seeds attract northern cardinals; copious sap attracts yellow-bellied sapsuckers. A larval host for the eastern tiger swallowtail. Will resprout from felled trees; white-tailed deer gladly browse the saplings.

DID YOU KNOW?
Native Americans often used the long, straight trunk to make dugouts; European colonists thus called it "canoewood." Today the soft, light wood is harvested for furniture, pallets, toys, and musical instruments. Despite its popular name, tulip-poplars belong to the magnolia family. ("Tulip" refers to the shape of the flower; "poplar," to the shimmering leaves.)

Eastern Redbud (*Cercis canadensis*)

DESCRIPTION

Often the first tree to bloom around the Bay in spring, this small (20–25 feet), multi-trunked legume bears clusters of bright pink, pealike flowers that unfurl before the leaves do and arise directly from the stems. Fruits are also pealike: flattened, leathery pods with a single row of 4–10 seeds. Initially green, the pods ripen to dark brown in late summer and persist through winter if not dislodged by wind or animals. Leaves are alternate, heart-shaped, 3–5 inches long and wide, with a smooth margin. Smooth brown bark of young trees grows scaly with age, ultimately developing into peeling plates.

HABITAT & ECOLOGY

A widespread but scattered understory tree of open woodlands throughout the Bay watershed. Flowers best along forest edges. Nurtures a wide variety of wildlife. Bees, hummingbirds, and woodland elfin butterflies nectar on the flowers, while cardinals, chickadees, and titmice eat the seeds. White-tailed deer browse the foliage; squirrels eat the bark, buds, and seeds; and woodpeckers search the bark for insects. Trees grow less shade tolerant with age and often suffer from heart rot.

DID YOU KNOW?

Planted as an ornamental throughout the Bay watershed and eastern United States. Genus name refers to the seedpod's resemblance to a weaver's shuttle ("*kerkis*" in Greek). Native Americans used the bark to treat whooping cough and dysentery. The flowers are high in vitamin C and can be eaten raw or cooked.

Red Maple (*Acer rubrum*)

DESCRIPTION
Flowers, fruits, and fall color are all distinctive. The tiny flowers appear before leaves in winter or early spring as a bright gauze of red in the barren forest. The reddish fruit bears 2 winglike samaras on a slender stem; these helicopter down when ripe in spring and early summer or if tossed playfully in the air. Bark of young trees is smooth and light gray; darkens with age and furrows into large, platelike scales. Up to 90 feet tall and 2–3 feet in diameter. In forest, trunk usually branch-free quite far up; develops rounded crown in open areas. Leaves turn a vivid red in fall.

HABITAT & ECOLOGY
One of the most common deciduous trees of eastern North America. A jack of all shades, red maples thrive in wet or dry soils, full sun or shadow, and from coastal wetlands to Appalachian ridgetops. Sprouts profusely from stumps. Twigs are an important source of winter browse for white-tailed deer. Provides habitat for wood ducks, pileated woodpeckers, screech owls, and flickers.

DID YOU KNOW?
Current prevalence in Eastern forests is due in part to loss of American chestnut and elm to disease, and logging of yellow birch and sugar maple. Has also benefitted from fire suppression. Sap may be used to make syrup, though it yields less than sugar maple. Widely used as an ornamental or shade tree.

White Pine (*Pinus strobus*)

DESCRIPTION

Largest conifer in the Bay watershed and eastern United States; mature specimens exceeded 200 feet in virgin forests. Limb arrangement is distinctive: A ring of branches sprouts horizontally near the top of the trunk each year (you can count vertically spaced whorls to estimate tree age). Soft, frosty-green needles are 3–5 inches long and occur in bundles of five. Curved, sappy cones are palm- to hand-size; seed heads are rounded, unlike the sharp seed heads of loblolly and many other pines. Smooth, sage-green bark of young trees develops shallow fissures and grayish, scaly plates as tree matures.

HABITAT & ECOLOGY

Native to the cooler (more northerly or elevated) portions of the Bay watershed, though now planted widely as an ornamental. Deer, beavers, and rabbits browse the foliage; porcupines eat the inner bark. Seeds are eaten by gray squirrels and songbirds. Mature trees are a favorite nesting site for bald eagles and an easily climbable haven for black bears.

DID YOU KNOW?

White pines—aka ship-mast pines—were one of the most important timber trees in early America, and continue to be planted and harvested for lumber and Christmas trees across much of the Bay watershed. Foresters estimate the virgin forests of North America held 600 billion board feet of white pine when European colonists arrived—enough to craft a plank 1 foot wide, 1 inch thick, and 113,636,363 miles long, enough to encircle the Earth 4,500 times. By the late 1800s, almost all of this had been cut, mostly for boats and buildings.

Asian Stiltgrass (*Microstegium vimineum*)

DESCRIPTION

This dark green annual forms extensive, single-species stands with bamboo-like leaves on thin, sprawling stems that rise like stilts 1–2 feet above the ground. Leaves are alternate, 1–3 inches long, and lance-shaped, with a shiny white midvein that helps distinguish this plant from the native whitegrass (*Leersia virginica*). Stiltgrass leaves are also smooth when rubbed, unlike most native grasses, whose leaves are rough in one direction. One or 2 delicate flower spikes crown each stem in late summer.

HABITAT & ECOLOGY

This introduced invasive is a common ground cover in shaded forests, stream bottoms, and moist fields throughout the Bay watershed. Each plant can produce up to 1,000 seeds; these remain in the soil bank for at least 3 years but readily germinate after disturbance by logging, tilling, construction, and heavy animal traffic, including that from hikers and white-tailed deer. Thick foliage shades and outcompetes native plants during growing season but is not eaten by native wildlife; plant dies back completely in fall, leaving the ground open to erosion from winter rains.

DID YOU KNOW?

Also known as Nepalese brown-top and Japanese grass, this Asian native was accidentally introduced to North American around 1920, most likely through its use as a packing material for imported porcelain. Infested areas have decreased biodiversity, lower habitat value for native wildlife, and increased prevalence of other invasive plants, including garlic mustard and Japanese honeysuckle. Contact your local extension agent for control techniques.

Beautyberry
(*Callicarpa americana*)

DESCRIPTION

Fast-growing deciduous shrub (5–8 feet tall) with multiple arching stems that bear clusters of brilliant purple berries in fall. Berries encircle stem where the leaves exit. Leaves are opposite, simple, and ovate with toothed edges, and may be hairy below. They droop during summer drought and emit a strong aroma when crushed. Small, white to pink flowers bloom June–August. Berries persist after leaves have fallen.

HABITAT & ECOLOGY

Prefers woodland edges and disturbed areas with moist soil and partial to full sun. Restricted to southern Bay states; rare in Pennsylvania and absent in New York. Fruit and seeds are eaten and dispersed by more than forty species of songbirds (including American robins, brown thrashers, purple finches, and eastern towhees), as well as deer, foxes, opossums, raccoons, and squirrels. Deer will also browse the foliage. Flowers attract bees and butterflies.

DID YOU KNOW?

Native Americans used branches, leaves, and roots for medicinal purposes. Traditional use of crushed foliage as a mosquito repellant still works! Indeed, recent studies show the active compounds may be as effective as DEET. Genus name *Callicarpa* means "beautiful fruit" in Greek. Shares Greek root *callos* ("beauty") with blue crab (*Callinectes sapidus*; "beautiful swimmer").

Dog Fennel (*Eupatorium capillifolium*)

DESCRIPTION
Weedy perennial, to 6 feet tall, with narrow, feathery leaves arising from woody, reddish, hairy stems that grow in clumps and often persist through winter. Leaves alternate or opposite. Small, greenish-white flowers bloom in large heads, August–October. Stems and leaves release pungent odor when crushed or broken. Member of the aster family.

HABITAT & ECOLOGY
Common across the coastal plain and lower Piedmont. Spreads rapidly through fields, roadsides, clearings, woodland margins, and other open habitats with heavily disturbed soil. Tolerates drought. Seeds eaten by turkeys and swamp sparrows. Attracts bees and wasps. Spreads by both seeds and roots.

DID YOU KNOW?
The Latin name *Capillifolium* refers to the finely threadlike (*Capilli* = "hair") leaves (*folium* = "leaf"). Common name refers to the fennel-like odor, which dogs seem to like; livestock avoid grazing this plant, which is known to be poisonous. Has been used as an insecticide and antifungal; oils have shown promise as a natural insecticide against mosquitoes.

Kudzu (*Pueraria montana*)

DESCRIPTION
"The vine that ate the South." An extremely vigorous non-native that's almost sinister in its exuberance. Best identified by compound, 3-part leaves that are hairy below. These alternate along round, twining stems that become woody with age and can grow hundreds of feet long and up to 10 inches in diameter. Purple, grape-scented flowers bloom June–September in clusters from junction between stem and leaf. Fruit shaped like a peapod but brown and hairy with 3–10 hard seeds. Leaves die back in winter.

HABITAT & ECOLOGY
This non-native invasive prefers disturbed areas such as roadcuts, clearings, and eroding streambanks. Vines can grow up to 1 foot per day and 60–100 feet per year, smothering everything in their path, including shrubs, trees, hillsides, telephone poles, and buildings. Roots are large and fleshy, with as many as thirty vines growing from a single root crown. Tap root can exceed 6 inches in diameter and reach 6 feet below ground; roots of an established vine can weigh as much as a Sumo wrestler. Leaves can extract nitrogen from the air, allowing rapid growth in poor soils. Spreads mostly by runners, but also by seed.

DID YOU KNOW?
Native to Asia, kudzu was first seen in the United States in 1876 during the Philadelphia Centennial Exposition. Enticed by its rapid growth and fragrant flowers, Southerners planted it widely for porch shade; concerns over erosion during and after the Great Depression led the federal Soil Conservation Service to encourage planting throughout the eastern United States. Recognition of its invasive nature led to a course reversal by federal and state agencies during the 1950s, with control measures now estimated to cost hundreds of millions of dollars per year.

Milkweeds (*Asclepias* spp.)

"Milkweeds" are a diverse group that includes nearly one hundred species across the United States. The Bay watershed holds eighteen of these. Here we describe two familiar Bay species: common milkweed (*Asclepias syriaca*) and swamp milkweed (*A. incarnata*).

DESCRIPTION

Erect perennials (3–6 feet) whose stem and leaves release a milky white sap when broken. Leaves are simple and opposite; aromatic flowerheads are pink to light purple and occur in spherical clusters. Seedpods shaped like candelabra light bulbs; open to reveal tightly packed seeds with brown heads and silky white tails. Several traits help distinguish swamp milkweed from its common cousin. Its leaves are smooth and much narrower, its flowerhead has approximately 20 flowers per cluster, its seedpods are smooth, and its central stem may branch. Common milkweed has more-ovate, hairy leaves; a flowerhead with 30–100 flowers; seedpods covered with hair and soft spikes; and an unbranched mainstem.

HABITAT & ECOLOGY

As the name implies, swamp milkweed prefers moist soils along swamps, marshes, rivers, and ditches. It shuns the dry, sunny fields favored by common milkweed. Both plants are a host for the monarch butterfly. Their foliage contains glycosides that monarch larvae absorb while feeding. These compounds render the larvae and adult butterflies toxic to birds and other predators. Also attract many other insects, including the large milkweed bug, common milkweed bug, red milkweed beetle, blue milkweed beetle, and bees.

DID YOU KNOW?

Native Americans used milkweed as a source of fibers and medicine. During World War II, children collected the "floss" from the seedpods, which was used for flotation in life vests. This material is still harvested today for use in pillows and comforters.

Pawpaw (*Asimina triloba*)

DESCRIPTION

A small (20–30 feet), thin tree with long branches. Large (10–12 inches), paddle-shaped leaves cluster near branch tips. Leaves are alternate, simple, and smooth-edged; release a foul odor when crushed. Fruits resemble a plump, dwarf banana; ripen from green to yellow-green and often grow in pairs or multiple clusters. Creamy fruit encases numerous dark brown seeds that are a bit larger than a lima bean. Maroon flowers appear before leaves; look like an upside-down tricorn hat.

HABITAT & ECOLOGY

Prefers rich soils in sunny spots along forest edges or in glades, where it grows in small, crowded, clonal stands. Fruits are a favorite of many woodland mammals, including raccoons, opossums, gray squirrels, and deer. Also eaten by songbirds. Intact seeds are often visible in raccoon scat on fallen logs. Flowers are pollinated by flies and beetles. A host plant for the larva of the zebra swallowtail butterfly.

DID YOU KNOW?

Pawpaws not only look like bananas but taste like them too. Easy to gather from trees for a snack or pawpaw smoothie, although they over-ripen quickly and are a challenge to prepare due to their large number of seeds. Well-liked by Native Americans and English colonists, chilled pawpaw fruit was a favorite of George Washington. Sometimes called the "prairie banana."

Animals

Woodland Box Turtle (*Terrapene carolina carolina*)

DESCRIPTION

An unmistakably beautiful resident of Bay woodlands. High-domed, brightly colored shell with a central keel; some bear flared scutes like a bustle along lower rear margin. Dark brown shell marked with radiating yellow splotches in a wide variety of patterns. Head, neck, and legs often show raised, orangish-yellow spots. Beak on upper jaw presents a fetching "bucktoothed" smile. Lower shell, or plastron, is hinged.

HABITAT & ECOLOGY

A woodland resident that rarely enters water. Eats many different kinds of berries as well as slugs, snails, earthworms, insects, salamanders, and mushrooms. Hinged lower shell provides complete closure for protection against predators, which include rats and hogs. Eggs are eaten by crows, foxes, raccoons, skunks, and dogs. Unfortunately, people in cars pose the greatest threat. Be especially watchful for these shelled pedestrians on summer mornings after a rain.

DID YOU KNOW?

True stay-at-homes, individuals may spend their entire lifetime—up to 100 years—in an area no larger than a football field. Due to mortality from car strikes, fragmentation of woodland habitat, and removal for the pet trade, box turtles are listed as "vulnerable" by the International Union for the Conservation of Nature. Human impacts on these slow-moving, brightly colored creatures began with Native Americans, who harvested them for food and to make rattles. Box turtles can eat mushrooms poisonous to humans; people have died from the toxins after eating turtle meat.

Raccoon (*Procyon lotor*)

DESCRIPTION

"Bandit mask" on face and ringed, "Davy Crock-ett" tail are unmistakable. Fur is coarse and relatively long; color varies from frosted gray to brown. Ears are large and erect; sharp muzzle features long white whiskers. Paws have 5 distinct digits with nonretractable claws. About 2 feet from nose to base of tail; tail itself is about 1 foot long. Back is arched. May hiss, whistle, scream, growl, or snarl if perturbed.

HABITAT & ECOLOGY

Widespread in wild and suburban areas throughout the Bay watershed. Prefers wooded areas near water and spends considerable time in trees. A good swimmer. Will eat almost anything, including frogs, birds and eggs, fish, crayfish, rodents, insects, fruits, nuts, berries, and carrion. Corn may be a large part of diet in rural areas. Solitary (except for mothers with young) and mostly nocturnal; often killed crossing roads at night.

DID YOU KNOW?

"Raccoon" comes from the Algonquian *aroughcun*, which means "he scratches with his hands." The species name *lotor* is Latin for "laundryman." Both refer to the habit of Rubik-cubing its food in water before eating. Once thought to be a washing behavior, experiments have shown this actually helps the raccoon gain a better tactile sense of its food, as wetting the skin increases the responsiveness and sensitivity of the many nerve cells in its highly dexterous hands.

Eastern Gray Squirrel
(*Sciurus carolinensis*)

DESCRIPTION
Short fur is white beneath and grayish brown on head and back; the grizzled tail is bushy and often held curled. Ears are erect and without tufts (unlike the red squirrel of the northern Bay watershed). Dark, round eyes are highlighted by a white eye ring. Often sits on haunches with back arched and forelegs held near the mouth. Leaf nests are clearly visible in bare winter trees.

HABITAT & ECOLOGY
These amazing acrobats inhabit hardwood forests throughout the Bay watershed. Play a key role in the early life history of trees such as oaks and beech by caching nuts below ground, where any unrecovered acorns or beechnuts are primed for germination. One study showed that squirrels fail to retrieve three of every four nuts they bury! Also eat seeds, fruits, bulbs, flowers, frogs, insects, and bird eggs. Predators include raccoons, foxes, snakes, and raptors, as well as cats, dogs, and humans.

DID YOU KNOW?
Uses its bushy tail for balance, warmth, and communicating with other squirrels. Bay populations include a subgroup of dark brown to black individuals, particularly in the more northerly parts of the watershed.

Opossum (*Didelphis virginiana*)

DESCRIPTION

There is no better description of the chimerical "possum" than that penned by Capt. John Smith based on his explorations of the Bay watershed between 1607 and 1609: "An Opassom hath a head like a Swine, and a taile like a Rat, and is of the bignesse of a Cat. Under her belly shee hath a bagge, wherein she lodgeth, carrieth, and suckleth her young."

HABITAT & ECOLOGY

Inhabits all corners of the Bay watershed, from upland woods to fields and swampy forests. Spends much of its time in trees. A nocturnal omnivore that eats insects, carrion, fruits, nuts, eggs, grubs, snakes, and frogs. Predators include owls, hawks, red foxes, cats, dogs, and humans. Despite a sometimes scruffy appearance, they are fastidious groomers who remove and eat up to 5,000 ticks per year, helping to curtail Lyme disease.

DID YOU KNOW?

As North America's only marsupial, opossums carry their babies in a pouch (and later wear their juveniles like a fur coat along their back). Respond to threats by drooling, hissing, and, if that doesn't work, "playing possum" by fainting to the ground in shock.

Foxes (*Vulpes vulpes* and *Urocyon cinereoargenteus*)

DESCRIPTION

Two fox species inhabit the Bay watershed: the red fox (*Vulpes vulpes*) and the gray fox (*Urocyon cinereoargenteus*). Both are the size of small dogs (3–3.5 feet with tail, 7–12 pounds). They share a long, bushy tail; erect, pointed ears; a slender snout; and short legs compared to other canids. Differ primarily in coloration. Red foxes are orangish-red above and white below, with black-backed ears, dark "leg stockings," and a white-tipped tail. Gray foxes are grizzled gray above and ivory below, with reddish sides and a tail striped and tipped in black. Grays also tend to be stouter, with shorter legs and snout. They are also less vocal than red foxes, which will let loose a bloodcurdling scream if disturbed at the den.

HABITAT & ECOLOGY

Occupy a wide range of habitats, from forests, fields, and swamps to city streets. Increasingly abundant in suburban areas with backyard chicken coops. Omnivorous like most members of the dog family, eating mice, moles, rabbits, snakes, squirrels, muskrats, birds, insects, acorns, and carrion. Mostly nocturnal and solitary, except during the breeding and whelping season, which stretches January–May. Red foxes will dig their own burrows or use one abandoned by a groundhog. Grays usually den in hollow trees or brush piles. Preyed on by eagles, coyotes, bears, and mountain lions. Trapped by humans for fur or killed as "pests."

DID YOU KNOW?

Like cats, red foxes have vertical pupils to enhance night vision for hunting. Gray foxes have hooked claws that allow them to climb trees to escape predators or reach food. Both species are sensitive to the low-frequency sounds of rodents moving underground.

White-tailed Deer (*Odocoileus virginianus*)

DESCRIPTION

Short, rather stiff brown hair tints red in summer and gray in winter; offset by white on the belly and throat, inside the ears, around the eyes and nose, and, of course, under the flag-like tail. Fawns are spotted. Males bear antlers during the fall mating season. Adults in the Bay region stand around 3 feet high at the shoulder, with long, slender legs and black hooves.

HABITAT & ECOLOGY

White-tailed deer live on the edge—of the day and forest. Most active at dawn and dusk, deer bed down during the day in thickets or marsh grasses. When active, they frequent the edge between forest and field, browsing on twigs, buds, leaves, and fruits, with acorns and pawpaws two favorites. Predators included wolves and cougars, and now humans. Whitetails spend time in and near marshes and are strong swimmers.

DID YOU KNOW?

Native Americans relied on all parts of the white-tailed deer—meat for food, skins for clothing, sinews for thread, bones and antlers for tools—and created deer habitat by burning forest to encourage shrubby browse. Heavy hunting by English colonists depleted local deer populations, but because they also exterminated predators and increased edge habitat by farming, deer populations rebounded, and today have expanded in step with suburban sprawl. Biologists estimate 900,000 whitetails in Virginia today compared to 400,000 when the English arrived in 1607. This has raised concerns regarding overgrazing, highway safety, and the spread of diseases affecting both humans (Lyme) and deer (chronic wasting disease).

Turkey Vulture (*Cathartes aura*)

DESCRIPTION

Large dark bird with naked red head, ivory beak, and pale legs. Flight feathers and tail are dark on top and lighter beneath. Holds primary feathers apart like spread fingers during flight and when extending its wings to dry and warm in the sun in its "horaltic pose." Often seen soaring, where it presents a "drunken V" as slightly upturned wings rock back and forth. Soars singly or in a "kettle" of several birds. Roosts in trees in smelly congregations.

HABITAT & ECOLOGY

The "Custodian of the Chesapeake," this often-reviled vulture plays a vital role by recycling roadkill and other carrion. Frequents forests, fields, and marsh edges; relies mostly on smell to detect rotting carcasses, as these are often hidden from view by vegetation. In Virginia, three most commonly consumed carcasses are gray squirrels, opossums, and white-tailed deer. Nests in rocky outcrops, low thickets, or hollow stumps away from people. Roosts in loblolly pines, tuliptrees, and other tall trees with relatively open canopies. Eggs and roosting adults preyed on by foxes, opossums, raccoons, and dogs.

DID YOU KNOW?

The naked head is thought to be an adaptation for hygiene, as the skin doesn't trap as much gore from carrion as feathers would. Petroleum engineers were the first to discover the turkey vulture's sharp sense of smell (it had long been thought to detect carrion by sight) when they noticed the birds congregating near pipeline leaks in response to the putrid odor of ethyl mercaptan, a substance added to alert people to the presence of otherwise odorless natural gas.

BUTTERFLIES

The Chesapeake watershed is home to more than 150 butterfly species. Many native plants rely on butterflies for pollination, including big cordgrass, buttonbush, milkweed, pawpaw, redbud, sycamore, and wild bergamot. Adult butterflies in turn rely on native plants to host their caterpillar larvae, several in a narrowly adapted monogamous relationship. Here we describe selected features to help distinguish a few common species from each of the five major butterfly families. For full treatment of the Bay's butterflies, consult the references in "A Deeper Dive."

SWALLOWTAILS
Large butterflies with a "tail" on each of the two hind wings.

Tiger Swallowtail
Wings colored and marked like a tiger. Females have blue along rear margin. Tuliptree is a larval host. State butterfly of Delaware and Virginia.

Zebra Swallowtail
Wings have black and white stripes like a zebra or piano keyboard, and a red triangle near the base of the very long "tail." Nectars on milkweed.

Spicebush Swallowtail
Named for one of the plants that host their humpbacked caterpillar (which also feeds on sassafras).

WHITES AND SULPHURS

Common light-colored butterflies of open fields. Usually keep their wings folded above their backs when at rest.

Cabbage White
Female has two dark spots on white wing, male just one. Tip of forewing dark in both sexes.

Clouded Sulphur
Dark margin on male's wing helps distinguish from similar cloudless sulphur.

Sleepy Orange
Caterpillars of this family tend to be green and hairy, with a lighter stripe or stripes.

BRUSHFOOTS

Most have intricately patterned wings. Appear to have only four legs, as front pair are reduced to brushy stubs.

Monarch

The king of US butterflies. Caterpillar ingests milkweed toxins to deter predators. Migrates south to Mexico for winter. Similar to queen and viceroy.

Common Buckeye

There's nothing common about the bold markings of this meadow dweller. Caterpillar eats plantains.

American Snout

What a schnoz! Use their elongated mouthparts to hang from a twig, camouflaged as a dead leaf.

Painted Lady

Prefers flowered meadows. Caterpillars feed on mallows.

Red Admiral

Prefers forest edges and meadows. Caterpillars feed on nettles.

GOSSAMER-WINGED
Many species have thin hairs along rear wing margins.

Red-banded Hairstreak
Prefers forest edges. Caterpillars feed on oaks and hickories.

SKIPPERS
Small, stout butterflies with hooked antennae tips. Family contains many similar-looking species.

Delaware Skipper
Bright yellow orange above.

Silver-spotted Skipper
The name says it all. Caterpillars feed on plants of pea family.

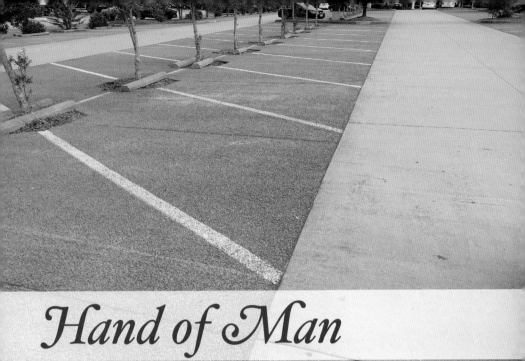

Hand of Man

BAY-FRIENDLY PAVERS

Follow a raindrop. Released by a summer thundercloud, it once had to complete a maze—canopy, branch, furrowed bark, leafed twig, grass blade, moss—to even reach the earth's surface, where its most likely fate was then absorption into leaf litter, loam, and groundwater. Today that same drop may instead plummet to the hard crust of a parking lot or road, joining billions of its kin along with cigarette butts, leaked oil, plastic litter, and other pollutants in a wild stampede corralled by medians and curbs into the nearest storm drain. From there, it's a short trip into an overwhelmed, eroding ravine and straight on to the Bay.

Almost 2 million acres in the Chesapeake Bay watershed are now paved or covered by surfaces that rain can't penetrate—about 3 percent of its total area. The percentage is much higher in urban areas: 51 percent in Baltimore; 46 percent in Washington, DC; and 24 percent in Newport News, Virginia.

Finally awakening to the impacts this stormwater has on Bay health, individuals, businesses, and localities are beginning to replace asphalt and concrete with materials designed to more closely mimic natural, spongy surfaces. Often referred to as the "3 Ps"—permeable, pervious, and porous pavers—all are designed to limit runoff at the source, reduce downstream erosion, and improve water quality by filtering pollutants.

In permeable paving, blocks of concrete or other similar materials are separated by gravel-filled joints that allow water to flow downward into the underlying soil. Per-vious pavers are laced with intercon-nected holes, allowing stormwater to percolate right through. They also let the ground breathe and help sustain life in the underlying soil. Porous pav-ers feature a rigid honeycomb of con-crete or plastic with gravel or grass within the individual cells. They allow parking on apparently grassy surfaces and can help keep gravel in place on sloped paths and driveways.

Paver choice is determined by a site's physical setting and traffic lev-els. All types must be regularly main-tained to preserve full function. If you notice use of any type by a neighbor, business, or locality, take a moment to stop and thank them for helping to improve Bay health!

BAY-FRIENDLY YARDS

Each of the 18 million people in the Chesapeake watershed may care for only a small piece of ground—a grassy lawn, a vegetable patch, a curbside flower garden—but collectively, their individual yard-care decisions have an immense impact on water quality in the Bay. More than 3.8 million acres of the Bay watershed are covered with lawn grasses—nearly 10 percent of its total area. One homeowner's decision whether to apply a lawn fertilizer, weed killer, or pesticide may seem inconsequential, but multiply it by a factor of almost 4 million, and that single drop soon becomes a large bucket.

Recognizing that yard-care decisions have significant impacts on Bay health, scientists and resource managers have established recommendations to promote Bay-friendly care of lawns and gardens. One key goal is to prevent nitrogen-laden runoff from fueling excess algal growth in Bay waters. Algal blooms can release toxins and shade underwater grasses while alive and afloat in the water, and lead to "dead zones" when they die and are eaten by bacteria—a process that consumes dissolved oxygen from surrounding waters.

The first step to a Bay-friendly yard is to consult with a local extension service, master gardener, or certified applicator. These experts can develop a care plan based on your yard's particular conditions. They may suggest ways to minimize lawn area by replacing grass with native ground covers, shrubs, and trees—which also offer food and habitat for wildlife. For remaining lawn areas, they can help decide whether fertilizer is needed, and, if so, the types and amount required to maintain grass cover dense enough to reduce runoff and prevent erosion. They will also recommend that you keep grass clippings and mulched leaves on the yard and out of streets and storm drains, set mower height to 3 inches or more, and regularly aerate the soil to increase its tilth.

WATER BARS

We'll forgive you—particularly on a typi-cally hot and humid summer day in the Bay watershed—if you think a water bar is a new kind of trailside pub for thirsty hikers. The term actually refers to a barrier, usually a peeled log, partly buried at an angle across a sloped trail. Its purpose is to divert runoff from the hard-packed trail surface before it gains sufficient velocity to begin eroding the trailbed. On longer downhill sections, you may encounter several water bars in succession. The logs are usually anchored with stakes or rocks, and by embedding one end in a trailside bank; the downhill end typically terminates in a rock-filled drainage basin to capture its sediment load and help the runoff percolate into the ground.

A big drawback of water bars is that the sediment they divert often ends up clogging the drainage basin and then backing up to fill in along the log riser. Once that happens, the runoff will simply pass over the intended obstruction and likely begin to erode the trail farther downhill as it gains speed.

Alternatives to water bars include "knicks" and "rolling grade dips." A knick is a sub-tle, gently sloped bite-mark dug halfway across a trail to encourage running or standing water to drain. To work, the trail must abut lower ground so the water has a place to go.

Rolling grade dips are most commonly seen on the steepest trail sections. They func-tion somewhat like the smaller mounds that follow the big drop on a roller coaster, using short uphill sections to slow the runoff, which is then shunted aside by a knick. As there is nothing to rot or be dislodged, this technique provides a durable solution that is easy to maintain.

RAIN GARDENS

The hard surfaces that cover many residential lots—roofs, patios, driveways, sidewalks—tend to funnel rainfall directly toward the nearest storm drain, along with any pollutants the water has entrained, including lawn fertilizers, pet wastes, leaked oil, herbicides, and pesticides. Once down the drain, this witch's brew flows directly into the nearest waterway and ultimately into the Bay itself.

A rain garden is an elegant way to stop this problem before it starts. A bowl-shaped depression dug between the places where rainfall concentrates and the low spot where water naturally wants to exit a property, it is filled with spongy soils and planted with native wildflowers and shrubs. The soil allows the otherwise erosive flow to gently percolate down into the water table, while the plants take up nutrients and other pollutants. The vegetation also offers nectar to bees and butterflies, food and habitat for birds and other wildlife, and beauty to neighbors. Use of native plants has the added benefit of greatly reducing or eliminating the need for pesticides and fertilizers to begin with, as they are already well adapted to fend off insects and thrive under local conditions.

A wealth of information is available for anyone interested in creating a rain garden on their residential or commercial property. Contact your local extension agent, or go online for planning tools offered by the Chesapeake Bay Program, Chesapeake Stormwater Network, Pennsylvania Environmental Council, University of Maryland Extension, Virginia Department of Forestry, and many other local, state, and federal agencies.

RETENTION PONDS

Whether tucked behind a shopping mall or visible along a freeway, retention ponds are now one of the more common landscape features around the Chesapeake. Their purpose is to retain and filter the water that surges off roads, parking lots, big-box stores, apartment complexes, houses, and industrial facilities after every rainstorm or snowmelt—water that is often polluted by fertilizers, spilled gas or oil, pesticides, pet wastes, and heavy metals. They are in essence a man-made response to a man-made problem—a not-always successful attempt to replace the absorption and filtration provided naturally by forests, meadows, and wetlands.

The science of "stormwater basins" developed in response to the federal Clean Water Act of 1972 and subsequent state laws to reduce erosion and improve water quality. These basins actually come in two different flavors: With a bottom drain like a bathtub, detention ponds are designed to slow runoff to reduce downstream erosion. Retention ponds are designed to hold water, with the drain raised to a threshold height. Standing water allows retention ponds to develop a functional aquatic habitat, where nutrients and other pollutants can be taken up by marsh plants or broken down by chemical processes in the water and sediments. They thus not only help control the quantity of downstream flow but also may also enhance water quality.

Retention ponds are just one type of "best management practice," a term often heard when discussing methods to maintain or restore water quality in the Bay. Other BMPs include the orange siltation fences and green seed blankets regularly seen around construction sites. We discuss the effectiveness of these methods in "The Once and Future Bay."

RIPARIAN BUFFERS

Many of the BMPs used to help improve water quality in the Chesapeake Bay—detention and retention ponds, pervious pavers, rain gardens, water bars—are designed to control sediment and nutrient pollution near their source.

Riparian buffers, however, are a last line of defense designed to soak up pollutants just before they can enter the "receiving" waters. From the Latin *riparia*, or "shore," "riparian" refers to the land and habitat along a river course. "Buffer" refers to riverside trees and shrubs, whether planted or occurring naturally. Research shows that streamside vegetation is very effective at taking up pollutants with its roots; the above- and belowground biomass also helps reduce bank erosion while shading and cooling the water.

The importance of riparian buffers is reflected by their incorporation into legislation and regulations at both the federal and state level. Virginia's Chesapeake Bay Preservation Act, for instance, requires that a 100-foot riparian buffer "shall be retained if present and established where it does not exist."

In 2014, partners in the Chesapeake Bay Program—all six Bay states and the District of Columbia—renewed their goal to restore 900 miles of riparian buffers in the watershed each year. Although progress has been made, plantings have slowed in recent years due to a lack of resources and other factors. In 2017, only 56 miles of buffers were planted along Bay tributaries, the lowest restoration total in 22 years.

For information on creating or enhancing a riparian buffer for your property or community, contact your local extension agent, or search online for planning tools offered by the New York Department of Environmental Conservation, Pennsylvania Department of Conservation and Natural Resources, University of Maryland Extension, or Virginia Department of Conservation and Recreation.

SHELL MIDDENS

Middens are ancient garbage dumps, with those around the Chesapeake recording the history of Native Americans for at least the past 4,500 years. Bay middens may contain clam shells, crab claws, and fish bones, but are most often dominated by shells of the eastern oyster. They range from small, scattered piles of a few shells—perhaps recording a single seafood picnic—to large sheets and mounds, including one along Virginia's York River that covers ¼ acre to a depth of 6 feet. The larger mounds provide evidence of long-term occupation of a site, at least seasonally.

Middens provide a treasure trove of information about the diet of Algonquian communities as well as their harvest methods and tools, and have been closely studied by scientists for more than a century. Recent research indicates that indigenous populations sustainably harvested Bay oysters for millennia, with oyster size and shape remaining relatively constant despite rapid human population growth and political centralization. Scientists attribute the fishery's long-term sustainability to the Algonquian's relatively low population densities, seasonal mobility, and broad diets. There is also evidence they harvested oysters by hand from nearshore waters, leaving offshore reefs as nursery areas to replenish the shallow harvesting grounds.

Unfortunately, European Americans were not as kind to the oyster resource. They not only developed an unsustainable fishery that ultimately brought the oyster resource to ruin, but also harvested many of the Bay's ancient shell middens for building roads and making mortar.

TRAIL MARKERS

Even experienced hikers know the uneasy feeling of becoming disoriented or lost on a trail. The largely volunteer corps of trail builders around the Bay watershed are here to help, using a simple system of "reassurance markers" to guide hikers on their merry way. These markers are particularly helpful in snow and on little-used trails, where the path may be indistinct.

Right turn ahead!

The type of trail marker you'll see depends on the materials on hand. On a wooded trail, tree trunks provide a natural backdrop for painted or incised "blazes." Usually rectangular or triangular, these may use different colors to mark intersecting trails but are normally of uniform color along a single path—typically a bright hue like yellow to increase their visibility. A single blaze indicates a straight trail segment. A vertical pair of offset blazes indicates a turn: Up and to the right marks a right turn; up and to the left, a left turn.

In areas with few trees and a large supply of loose stone, trails may be marked with cairns: small piles of obviously human-stacked rocks. These are spaced closely enough so that the next cairn is visible in either direction, even during periods of poor visibility such as dense fog.

The most informative marks are trail signs. Often placed at trailheads and junctions, these give trail names, distances, directions, and destinations. They may also identify cultural, ecological, or historical features, as well as regulations, warnings, or closures.

Keep straight!

Left turn ahead!

ORIENTEERING MARKS

Unlike the trail markers used to guide hikers, you're most likely to find these signposts off the beaten path, purposefully tucked away in hidden corners of parks and other public areas around the Bay watershed. A square bisected by orange-and-white triangles is the international symbol of orienteering, a sport in which competitors use map and compass to find a series of checkpoints in the shortest amount of time.

Long popular in Europe (it began as a military training exercise in Sweden in the 1800s), the sport is gaining adherents in the United States and mid-Atlantic, with permanent courses established in Hemlock Regional Overlook Park near Clifton, Virginia; Prince William Forest Park (Triangle, Virginia); Bear Branch Park (Westminster, Maryland); Patapsco Valley State Park-Hilton Area (Catonsville, Maryland); Little Bennett Regional Park (Clarksburg, Maryland); and other areas. Permanent courses have numbered posts, signs, or landscape features that require competitors to answer a feature-based question as proof of visiting. There are also "DIY" events during which flags and/or streamers are hung for a day or a few weeks to mark the checkpoints. The newest wrinkle is electronic contests with no physical markers, in which competitors validate their successful discovery of GPS checkpoints via alerts on their cellphones.

To learn more about orienteering within the Bay watershed, contact or make an online visit to one of the regional clubs. These are headquartered in Richmond (Central Virginia Orienteering Club); Washington, DC (Quantico Orienteering Club); and York, Pennsylvania (Susquehanna Valley Orienteering).

A DEEPER DIVE

Aveni, M., et al. "Recommendations of the Expert Panel to Define Removal Rates for Urban Nutrient Management" (Chesapeake Bay Program, 2013).

Baird, A. R. T., and D. G. Wetmore. *Riparian Buffers Modification & Mitigation Guidance Manual* (Virginia Department of Conservation and Recreation Chesapeake Bay Local Assistance, 2006).

Bergman, R., et al. "Wood Handbook, Wood as an Engineering Material." *General Technical Report FPL-GTR-190* (Madison, WI: US Department of Agriculture, Forest Service, Forest Products Laboratory, 2010).

Britton, K. O., D. Orr, and J. Sun. "Kudzu." *Biological Control of Invasive Plants in the Eastern United States*. R. V. Driesche et al. (eds.) (Morgantown, WV: US Department of Agriculture, 2002).

Brown, L., and T. Elliman. *Grasses, Sedges, Rushes: An Identification Guide* (New Haven, CT: Yale University Press, 2020).

Bureau of Trails. *Best Management Practices for Erosion Control during Trail Maintenance and Construction* (Concord, NH: New Hampshire Department of Resources and Economic Development, Division of Parks and Recreation, 2004).

Burns, R. M., and B. H. Honkala. "Silvics of North America: 1. Conifers; 2. Hardwoods." *Agriculture Handbook 654*, vol. 2 (Washington, DC: US Department of Agriculture, Forest Service, 1990).

Cantrell, C. L., et al. "Isolation and Identification of Mosquito Bite Deterrent Terpenoids from Leaves of American (*Callicarpa americana*) and Japanese (*Callicarpa japonica*) Beautyberry." *Journal of Agricultural and Food Chemistry*, 53 (2005). https://doi.org/10.1021/jf0509308.

Forseth, I. N., and A. F. Innis. "Kudzu (*Pueraria montana*): History, Physiology, and Ecology Combine to Make a Major Ecosystem Threat." *Critical Reviews in Plant Sciences*, 23(5) (2004). 10.1080/07352680490505150.

Frank, A. "Butterflies of the Williamsburg Area." Virginia Master Naturalists and Coastal Virginia Wildlife Observatory (eds.) (Williamsburg, VA: CVWO, 2014).

Golon, S. K., and J. Okay. "Rain Gardens Technical Guide: A Landscape Tool to Improve Water Quality" (Charlottesville, VA: Virginia Department of Forestry, 2014).

Handley, C. O., and C. P. Patton. *Wild Mammals of Virginia* (Richmond, VA: Commonwealth of Virginia Commission of Game and Inland Fisheries, 1947).

Hesselbarth, W., B. Vachowski, and M. A. Davies. *Trail Construction and Maintenance Notebook.* US Department of Agriculture (ed.) (Missoula, MT: USDA Forest Service Missoula Technology and Development Center, 2007).

Jansen, A. "Shell middens and human technologies as a historical baseline for the Chesapeake Bay, USA." *North American Archaeologist*, 39(1) (2018). 10.1177/0197693117753333.

Jenkins, J. A., and M. D. Gallivan. "Shell on Earth: Oyster Harvesting, Consumption, and Deposition Practices in the Powhatan Chesapeake." *The Journal of Island and Coastal Archaeology* (2019). 10.1080/15564894.2019.1643430.

Klapproth, J. C., and J. E. Johnson. "Understanding the Science Behind Riparian Forest Buffers: An Overview" (2009).

Lotts, K., and T. Naberhaus. "Butterflies and Moths of North America" (2020). www.butterfliesandmoths.org.

Maloof, J. "Old-Growth Forest Network" (2020). www.oldgrowthforest.net.

Outen, D. "Baltimore County Forest Sustainability Strategy: Steering Committee Final Draft." Baltimore County Linking Communities to the Montreal Process Criteria & Indicators Project: Baltimore County (Department of Environmental Protection and Resource Management, 2005).

Prince William Conservation Alliance. "Discover Northern Virginia Nature: Butterflies (2020). www.pwconserve.org/wildlife/butterflies/index.htm.

Rockler, A., et al. "Rain Gardens Help Protect Streams and the Chesapeake Bay." University of Maryland Extension (ed.) (Maryland Sea Grant, 2016).

Shepherd, V. "Pursuing an American Dream: Restoring the American Chestnut to Our Forests—and Our Wildlife." *Virginia Wildlife* (Lynchburg, VA: Virginia Department of Game and Inland Fisheries, 2009).

Silberhorn, G. "Red Maple (*Acer rubrum* L.)." *Wetland Flora Technical Reports* (Gloucester Point, VA: Wetlands Program, Virginia Institute of Marine Science, William & Mary, 1991).

———. "Sweet Gum (*Liquidambar styraciflua* L.)." *Wetland Flora Technical Reports* (Gloucester Point, VA: Wetlands Program, Virginia Institute of Marine Science, William & Mary, 1992).

———. "Swamp Milkweed (*Asclepias incarnata* L.)." *Wetland Flora Technical Reports* (Gloucester Point, VA: Wetlands Program, Virginia Institute of Marine Science, William & Mary, 1992).

———. "Loblolly Pine (*Pinus taeda* L.)." *Wetland Flora Technical Reports* (Gloucester Point, VA: Wetlands Program, Virginia Institute of Marine Science, William & Mary, 1993).

———. "Sycamore (*Platanus occidentalis* L.)." *Wetland Flora Technical Reports* (Gloucester Point, VA: Wetlands Program, Virginia Institute of Marine Science, William & Mary, 1994).

———. "American Holly, Christmas Holly (*Ilex opaca* Ait.)." *Wetland Flora Technical Reports* (Gloucester Point, VA: Wetlands Program, Virginia Institute of Marine Science, William & Mary, 1995).

———. "Tulip Poplar, Tulip Tree (*Liriodendron tulopifera* L.)." *Wetland Flora Technical Reports* (Gloucester Point, VA: Wetlands Program, Virginia Institute of Marine Science, William & Mary, 2000).

Sprague, E., et al. (eds.). *The State of Chesapeake Forests* (Arlington, VA: The Conservation Fund, 2006).

Van Dersal, W. R., et al. "Native woody plants of the United States, their erosion-control and wildlife values" (Washington, DC: US Government Printing Office, 1938).

Virginia Department of Forestry. "Common Native Shrubs and Woody Vines of Virginia" (Charlottesville, VA: Virginia Department of Forestry, 2016).

Virginia Department of Game and Inland Fisheries, Piedmont Area. "Discover Our Wild Side: Virginia Birding and Wildlife Trail" (2002).

Walker, M. "Are Pervious, Permeable, and Porous Pavers Really the Same?" *Stormwater Report* (Alexandria, VA: Water Environment Federation, 2013).

Webster, C. R., M. A. Jenkins, and S. Jose. "Woody Invaders and the Challenges They Pose to Forest Ecosystems in the Eastern United States." *Journal of Forestry*, 104(7) (2006). https://doi.org/10.1093/jof/104.7.366.

Williams, M. D. *Identifying Trees of the East: An All-Season Guide to Eastern North America*, 2nd edition (Guilford, CT: Stackpole Books, 2017).

Down TO THE Docks

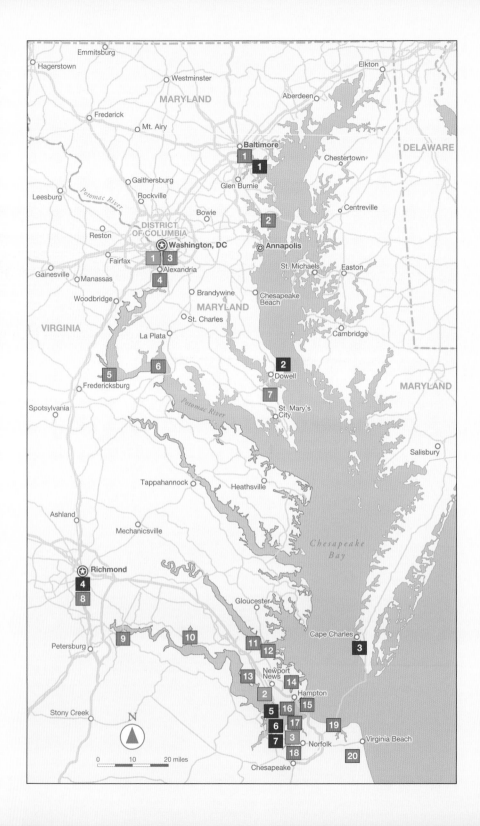

Down to the Docks

The Chesapeake has a rich history and continues to play a major role in maritime commerce and naval activity. Here are some of the Bay's many commercial and military sites, many of which are open to the public, although some require an appointment to visit. The highlighted museums focus on the Bay's role in trade and military affairs.

MILITARY

1. Fort McHenry
2. US Naval Academy
3. Washington Navy Yard
4. Torpedo Factory (Art Center)
5. Battle of Aquia Creek (Civil War)
6. Battle of Mathias Point (Civil War)
7. Patuxent River Naval Air Station
8. Richmond National Battlefield (Drewry's Bluff / Fort Darling / Trent's Reach)
9. Petersburg National Battlefield— City Point Unit
10. Battle of Pig Point (Civil War)
11. Yorktown Naval Weapons Station
12. Yorktown-Gloucester Point (Revolutionary and Civil War battles)
13. Fort Eustis
14. Langley Air Force Base
15. Fort Monroe National Monument
16. Battle of Hampton Roads (Civil War)
17. Norfolk Naval Station, Virginia
18. Norfolk Naval Shipyard
19. Joint Expeditionary Base Little Creek–Fort Story
20. Naval Air Station Oceana

COMMERCIAL

1. Port of Baltimore (Dundalk Terminal, Fairfield Marine Automobile Terminal, Locust Point Marine Terminals, Seagirt Marine Terminal, Sparrows Point)
2. Dominion Energy Cove Point LNG Terminal
3. Port Cape Charles
4. Richmond Marine Terminal
5. Newport News (NN Shipbuilding & Drydock, NN Marine Terminals)
6. Port of Virginia (Norfolk International Terminals, Portsmouth Marine Terminal, Virginia International Gateway)
7. General Dynamics NASSCO Norfolk

MARITIME MUSEUMS

1. US Navy Museum
2. The Mariners' Museum
3. Nauticus (Battleship *Wisconsin*)

WATERBORNE COMMERCE HAS LONG BEEN pursued by the Bay's inhabitants, from Native peoples to European colonists, early American merchantmen, and today's global shipping concerns. The Bay also plays a key role in US military might as home to the world's largest navy base and many other US Navy and Coast Guard properties. Shipbuilding and maintenance likewise have a long history in the area. As detailed below, you can experience the Bay's maritime heritage both by visiting onshore facilities and by observing passing vessels. For information on fishing and recreational vessels, see the "Boating and Fishing on the Bay" chapter.

MARITIME COMMERCE

Commerce in the Bay region began with the arrival of Native peoples more than 11,000 years ago, as revealed by discoveries of notched arrowheads and other artifacts known to have originated outside the mid-Atlantic. During the ensuing millennia, local tribes developed canoe-based trading networks stretching as far as the Great Lakes for materials, such as copper, that were unavailable locally. The history of this Algonquian trade is highlighted at the National Museum of the American Indian in Washington, DC, and the Pamunkey Indian Museum and Cultural Center in Virginia's King William County.

An oxcart descends to the York River in Yorktown, Virginia, an early Bay port that played a key role in early American commerce and military affairs.

Waterside in Norfolk, Virginia, is one of the many vibrant urban waterfronts around the Bay.

Large-scale maritime commerce began in the Bay region with the advent of the "Triangle Trade" in the early 1600s, in which merchant shippers exported tobacco and other cash crops to Europe, then traded European-manufactured goods for human beings from Africa, before returning to the mid-Atlantic with West Indian sugar and enslaved Africans who had endured the infamous "Middle Passage." Virginia's Fort Monroe National Monument commemorates the 1619 arrival of English America's first Africans and their subsequent contributions to the Chesapeake region and nation, as does the National Museum of African American History and Culture in Washington, DC.

Transfer of cargo between ship and shore initially took place at dispersed plantations, but as ships became larger to serve the growing trans-Atlantic trade, Virginia's General Assembly established official deep-draft port towns, beginning with Yorktown in 1633 and adding nineteen others in 1680, including what are now the cities of Hampton, Norfolk, Suffolk, West Point, Urbanna, Alexandria, and Onancock. Major colonial ports in Maryland included Annapolis, Baltimore, Chestertown, Cambridge, and Oxford.

Many of the early port towns retain waterfronts that are well worth a visit. The harbors with narrow approaches or relatively shallow waters now mostly host recreational marinas or commercial fishing operations. Four particularly popular marina districts are those in Annapolis and Cambridge in Maryland and Hampton and Norfolk in Virginia. Fishing fleets are concentrated at Deal, Hoopers, Kent, Smith, and Tilghman Islands in Maryland, and at Cape Charles, Irvington, Newport News, Perrin River, and Tangier Island in Virginia. For a more detailed account, see the "Boating and Fishing on the Bay" chapter.

The localities that combined wide approaches, deep channels and berths, and ready access to roads and railways have developed into today's Chesapeake seaports: Baltimore, Newport News, Norfolk, and Portsmouth. Collectively, these ports processed more than 100 million tons of cargo in 2017, placing fourth in the United States, behind only the Port of South Louisiana, Houston, and New York–New Jersey.

Virginia's major seaport facilities are consolidated in the Port of Virginia, which in 2018 placed sixth among US ports in cargo at 69.8 million tons. Maryland likewise has the Port of Baltimore, which in 2018 placed eleventh in US cargo at 42.9 million tons, and handled a record 850,000 cars. Indeed, Baltimore is the biggest roll-on/roll-off (RO/RO) port in the United States. These ports also offer "intermodal" facilities, in which standardized 40-foot containers are offloaded directly from seagoing vessels onto railway cars or semitrucks, and vice versa, thus saving both time and money. In 2018 the Port of Virginia (POV) processed 1,612,886 container units; the Port of Baltimore (POB), 1,023,161. Laid end to end, these would stretch 19,970 miles, three-quarters around the world.

Though challenged by foreign competition and a global shift toward natural gas, the Bay remains a significant coal port. Norfolk Southern's terminal at Lambert's Point in Norfolk, Virginia, transfers 48 million tons of Appalachian coal per year—one-third of US coal exports—from railcars to ocean colliers along an 1,850-foot pier that can load two ships simultaneously, one on either side. The Dominion Terminal in nearby

Backus Aerial Photography

The Port of Virginia lies near the mouth of Chesapeake Bay.

Newport News has handled 10–15 million tons in recent years, with huge piles awaiting shipment clearly visible to anyone heading over the James River Bridge. The CNX Marine Terminal in Baltimore has an annual "transload" capacity of 16 million tons.

The immense scale of the Bay's port facilities is best appreciated with a visit. Monthly tours of the POV are available by request; tours of the POB are available for school groups.

NAVAL OPERATIONS

The very thing that made Chesapeake Bay a haven for early maritime commerce—seaway access deep into the heart of England's mid-Atlantic colonies—also presented a major vulnerability to the new American nation following the Revolutionary War. The naval battles of that war, and the "second war of independence" in 1812, made clear that to control its future, the infant republic needed a navy to control the Chesapeake. This realization anchored the Bay as an epicenter of US naval operations, a stature it still holds today.

Yet America's interest in developing and sustaining a navy ebbed and flowed with the perceived magnitude of foreign threat. In 1775 the Continental Congress established the first "American Navy," but this initiative waned after the war's end in 1783. It wasn't until 1794, in response to attacks on American merchant vessels by "Barbary pirates," that the US Congress reanimated the effort, with a call to build a fleet of six frigates. Two of these were commissioned for Chesapeake Bay shipyards. The USS *Constellation* was built in Baltimore and launched in 1797. The USS *Chesapeake*, built at Gosport Navy Yard in Portsmouth, Virginia, launched in 1799. Gosport is now the Norfolk Naval Shipyard, the US Navy's largest and oldest maintenance and repair facility. A descendant of the *Constellation*, a tall ship of the same name built in 1854, is berthed in Baltimore's Inner Harbor as a floating museum.

The wisdom of creating an American navy became clear during the War of 1812, when US ships won several early sea victories over the Royal Navy. These triumphs were tempered when a British fleet outgunned American vessels on the Patuxent River and then landed a marine platoon that sacked the newly built US capital (and Capitol) in Washington, DC. Proceeding toward Baltimore, then the Bay's largest city, the British were repulsed not by ships but by the guns of Fort McHenry. You can relive this epic moment in American history with a visit to Fort McHenry National Monument and Historic Shrine.

As foreign trade and US naval reach continued to grow through the 1800s, the need for a naval school became ever more apparent. President John Quincy Adams urged Congress to establish one in 1825, but to no avail. It wasn't until 1845—just after an infamous mutiny by distraught midshipmen aboard the training vessel USS *Somers*— that the US Navy secretary established a land-based naval college, in the bayside hamlet of Annapolis, Maryland. Now the US Naval Academy, this historic institution is open for guided tours year-round. The Bay is also home to the US Coast Guard Training Center in Yorktown.

YESTERBAY

Battle of the Capes

Ironically, one of the first and most consequential naval battles in US history involved no American ships. Known as the Battle of the Capes or the Battle of the Chesapeake, it took place on September 5, 1781, when a French fleet prevented English warships from sailing into the Chesapeake Bay to support General Cornwallis at Yorktown. Just weeks later, under siege near the tip of the Virginia Peninsula, the isolated British general surrendered his troops and ships to the combined forces of Washington and Lafayette, in the last major battle of the Revolutionary War. A celebration of this victory, Yorktown Day, is held on October 19 of each year at Colonial National Historical Park.

The historical importance of this battle is captured in a quote from Michael Lewis in his book *The History of the British Navy*: "The Battle of Chesapeake Bay was one of the decisive battles of the world. Before it, the creation of the United States of America was possible; after it, it was certain."

Historian Emil Reich sounds a similar refrain, writing that the battle "deserves the name of 'British Naval Waterloo of Cape Henry.'"

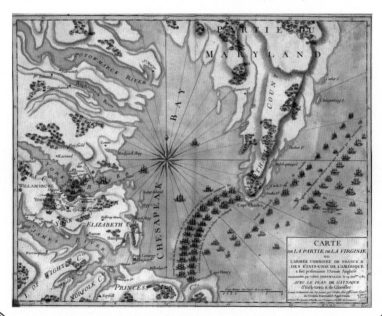

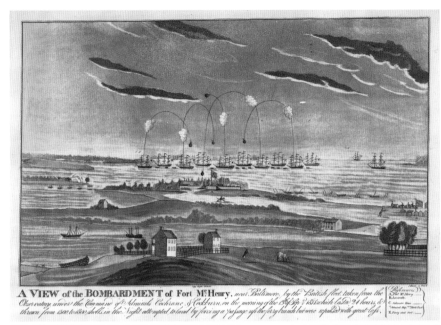

A VIEW of the BOMBARDMENT of Fort McHenry, near Baltimore, by the British fleet taken from the Observatory under the Command of Admirals Cochrane & Cockburn, on the morning of the 13th of Sep. 1814 which lasted 24 hours, & thrown from 1500 to 1800 shells in the Night attempted to land by forcing a passage up the ferry branch but were repulsed with great loss.

BATTLE BETWEEN THE MONITOR AND MERRIMAC.

Top: The bombardment of Fort McHenry during the War of 1812 is immortalized in Francis Scott Key's Star-Spangled Banner. Bottom: The battle between the USS *Monitor* and CSS *Virginia* took place near the mouth of the James River.

Chesapeake Bay continued to play a key role in US naval affairs when, in 1862, the world's first ironclad warships, USS *Monitor* and CSS *Virginia* (formerly the USS *Merrimack*), fought to a standstill in the Battle of Hampton Roads. Restored remains of the

Monitor are on display at the Mariners' Museum in Newport News, Virginia, along with exhibits explaining how these ships transformed the future of naval warfare. Civil War buffs can also visit the sites of naval fortifications at Tyndall's Point Park in Gloucester Point on the York River, and at the City Point Unit of the Petersburg National Battlefield in Hopewell, at the confluence of the James and Appomattox Rivers.

The Chesapeake—particularly Hampton Roads in the lower Bay—remains a center of US naval activities. Naval Station Norfolk is the world's largest naval base, with fifteen piers and almost one hundred homeported ships, including aircraft carriers, cruisers, destroyers, amphibious vessels, and submarines. The naval presence includes ownership of 36,000 acres and 6,750 buildings; more than 100,000 military personnel; and more than 40,000 civilian employees. All told, the Hampton Roads Navy community totals some 318,000 people. Washington Naval Yard, on the Potomac, is the US Navy's ceremonial and administrative center and home to the National Museum of the US Navy.

The US Navy is also seen and heard in the skies above the Chesapeake, with naval air stations in both Virginia (Oceana) and Maryland (Patuxent River). These facilities support the pilots and aircraft that protect Navy ships and project their reach inland. The Bay region now also projects its reach to the stars, with major NASA facilities, including the Langley Research Center in Hampton, Virginia, and the Goddard Space Flight Center in Greenbelt, Maryland.

Naval Station Norfolk is the world's largest navy base.

YESTERBAY

Piracy

No account of maritime history in the Chesapeake would be complete without mention of piracy. Pirates and their legally mandated brethren, the privateers, roamed Bay waters for more than 200 years. Most notorious was Edward Teach, aka Blackbeard, whose legendary career came to an inglorious end in 1718, when, at the behest of Virginia Lt. Governor Alexander Spotswood, Capt. Robert Maynard outdueled the pirate in a bloody fight and carried Blackbeard's head back to Hampton, Virginia, on the bowsprit of his ship. The event is commemorated each year in June with the Blackbeard Pirate Festival on the Hampton waterfront.

A pirate treasure also bankrolled the founding of William & Mary in Williamsburg when the Reverend James Blair struck a deal with buccaneers Lionel Wafer, John Hinson, and Edward Davis. Arrested in Hampton Roads in 1688 after returning from the South Pacific with a wealth of pirated goods, the trio agreed to endow a college charter if Blair would help them hold on to the rest of their disputed loot. In 1691, Blair delivered, writing to the British Crown, "I do humbly certify that the Petitioners have devoted and secured towards the carrying on the pious design of a free School and College in Virginia, the Summe of three hundred pounds, providing that the order be given for restoring to them their money." William & Mary, now America's second-oldest university, was chartered by royal decree in 1693.

The story behind the founding of Naval Station Norfolk brings the maritime history of the Chesapeake full circle. The base developed from an assemblage of naval vessels during the 1907 Jamestown Exposition at Sewell's Point. Thus, an event to commemorate the 300th anniversary of a fateful meeting between Native canoes and English barques launched the modern chapter in the ongoing chronicle of the Bay's role in nautical affairs, with vessels whose speed and bulk early Bay peoples could barely fathom.

Plants

Sea Lettuce (*Ulva lactuca*)

DESCRIPTION

Tissue-thin, translucent green fronds (6–12 inches) with ruffled edges that resemble leaves of lettuce forgotten in your fridge. Found attached to solid surfaces such as riprap, pilings, and driftwood; floating freely in the water; and washed up on shore. Occurs year-round, with large blooms in summer. Dries to black or white sheets with the texture of gift-bag tissue paper.

HABITAT & ECOLOGY

Grows in shallow waters throughout the Bay except for the very uppermost reaches. An important food source for amphipods, snails, and sea urchins. Eaten by Atlantic brant and mute swans. Thrives in nutrient-rich areas and can be a nuisance species near wastewater outfalls, fouling lines and fishing nets. Live growth can shade and kill seagrasses; bacterial decay of dead fronds that have sunk to the bay floor may contribute to low-oxygen "dead zones."

DID YOU KNOW?

A good source of vitamins A and C, sea lettuce is eaten in salads and soups, and used to make ice cream and medicine. Due to its tolerance for high nutrient levels, it's also been used as a "canary in the coal mine" to monitor pollution trends. A "macroalgae," *Ulva* has no distinct tissues. All the cells are more or less alike, with a single chloroplast for photosynthesis. Each leaf is only two cells thick.

Animals

Mummichog (*Fundulus heteroclitus*)

DESCRIPTION

A member of the "top minnow," or killifish family, these "mud minnows" (3–4 inches) are often seen just beneath the surface. Upturned mouth and rounded tail fin. Body about four times longer than wide; snout about as long as eye. Males are steel blue above and creamy yellow below, with obvious vertical stripes. Colors intensify during breeding season. Females are brownish above, pale below; stripes faint or lacking. Males have a larger dorsal fin; their anal fins are also larger and more muscular, as they use them to clasp the female during spawning.

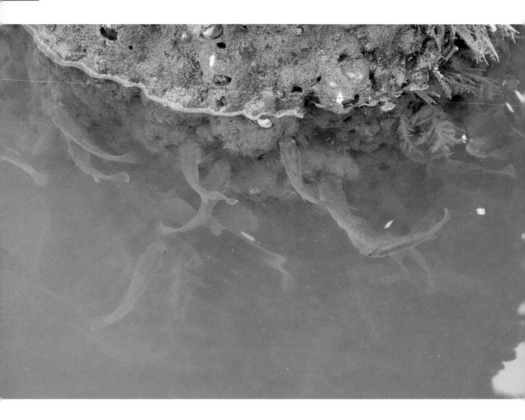

HABITAT & ECOLOGY
Abundant in tidal creeks, salt marshes, seagrass flats, ebb-tide pools, and other near-shore waters Bay wide. True homebodies, individuals may spend an entire summer within a 200-foot stretch of shoreline. Migrate to creek mouths or slightly offshore during winter; may bury in mud to escape the cold. Tolerate low oxygen and a wide range of salinities (0–120 ppt [parts per thousand]) and water temperatures (40°F–90°F). Use upturned mouth to feed at surface on algae, mollusks, crustaceans, insect larvae, other small fishes, and plants such as eelgrass. Major food source for wading birds, seabirds, and many commercially valuable fish.

DID YOU KNOW?
"Mummichog" is a Native American term meaning "going in crowds," referring to this species' schooling habits. People harvest these fish for medical and environmental research, sportfish bait, and control of mosquito larvae.

Bay Barnacle (*Balanus improvisus*)

DESCRIPTION

These small animals outwardly resemble miniature, inch-high volcanoes. Shell is a chalky white cone of 6 fused plates that stop short of their peak to leave an open crater. Crater is stoppered by 2 hinged beaks, like the maw of a nestling bird. Chalky color often obscured by coating of mud.

HABITAT & ECOLOGY

Nestled groups of barnacles cover solid surfaces— dock pilings, seawalls, riprap revetments, boat hulls, turtle shells—all along the salty shores of the lower Bay. They filter plant and animal plankton from the water by opening their "beak" and unfurling six feathery pairs of feeding appendages. Though well protected, barnacles are preyed on by marine worms, marine snails, and shorebirds. Barnacle larvae are an important food source for small fish.

DID YOU KNOW?

The Chesapeake is home to four species of barnacle. Often mistaken as mollusks due to their hard shell, barnacles are actually crustaceans. Indeed, their free-swimming larvae are almost indistinguishable from those of shrimp. As they mature, the larvae settle, cement their head to a hard surface, and secrete their enclosing fortification. The noted nineteenth-century biologist Louis Agassiz described a barnacle as "nothing more than a little shrimp-like animal, standing on its head in a limestone house and kicking food into its mouth."

Bryozoans

DESCRIPTION
Appear to the naked eye as twiggy or encrusting growths on submerged solid surfaces. Easily confused with hydroids, but magnification reveals an animal with a very different body plan: a colony of tiny soft-bodied zooids, each with ciliated tentacles that arise from a horseshoe-shaped structure atop the mouth. The zooids reside within a variety of structures ranging from flat sheets of rectangular boxes to erect branching tubes. When they extend their tentacles to feed, the colony takes on a fuzzy appearance, hence the common name, "moss animal."

HABITAT & ECOLOGY
Found on pilings, shells, seagrasses, buoy lines, driftwood, boat hulls, etc., throughout the Bay's saltier waters. Extend their ciliated tentacles into the surrounding water to capture plankton, marine larvae, and other microscopic organisms. Eaten by blue crabs and other crustaceans, small fish such as mummichogs, and other Bay organisms. Some bryozoans use chemical defenses to deter predators.

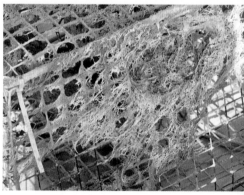

DID YOU KNOW?
The Bay holds at least nineteen species of bryozoan. One mossy species—*Anguinella palmata*, or what watermen call "hair"—fouls crab pots. Another species—the aptly though grotesquely named dead man's fingers—resembles the yellowish phase of the red beard sponge. Growth of bryozoans on ship hulls, crab pots, power-plant intakes, and other preferably unencumbered surfaces is a costly problem in the Bay and other coastal areas worldwide. One bryozoan—*Pectinatella magnifica*—is unusual in that it occurs not in salty waters but in freshwater lakes and ponds.

Ribbed Mussel (*Geukensia demissa*)

DESCRIPTION

Ribbed bivalve (2–4 inches long) with a dark, thin shell typically shaped like a curved teardrop. Interior is pearly white with a smooth, untoothed hinge. Often grows upright, with its "beak" anchored by thin, byssal threads. Shell's thin, organic outer "skin," or periostracum, regularly wears away near the beak. Larger than hooked mussel (*Ischadium recurvum*) and lacks the hooked mussel's strongly recurved beak.

HABITAT & ECOLOGY

Common intertidal resident of the saltier middle and lower Bay. Filters plankton from the water at high tide. Typically grows in the low marsh, in a win-win partnership with smooth cordgrass. Mussels help fertilize plant growth by excreting nutrient-rich wastes, and grow in dense colonies (up to 130 per square foot) that help protect against marsh erosion. Grass stems in turn shade and cool the mussels when exposed at high tide and help protect against blue crabs, marsh crabs, shorebirds, and other predators. Resilient to storms and other disturbances, as it can reattach if dislodged.

DID YOU KNOW?

Ability to filter much smaller plankton cells than other bivalves lends this species a key role in enhancing the clarity and quality of Bay waters. Age can be determined by counting the annual growth ribs on its shell. Although edible, they are tough and less tasty than the popular blue mussel (*Mytilus edulis*). That species is limited to the cooler, saltier waters near the Bay mouth.

Eastern Oyster (*Crassostrea virginica*)

DESCRIPTION
If it grows in isolation, the cupped shell of this iconic Chesapeake Bay bivalve is typically shaped like a tear-drop, with a pattern of concentric rings and radiating ribs that lend a somewhat waffled appearance. The other shell is a thin, flat disc. Shape is highly variable when individuals grow crowded together in reefs. Shells are creamy white with tan markings, and often covered by barnacles and other invertebrate growth.

HABITAT & ECOLOGY
This "ecosystem engineer" is one of the Chesapeake's keystone species. In the pre-colonial Bay, masses of intertidal oysters armored many shorelines, and offshore reefs were so widespread they impeded navigation. These aggregations offered food, living space, and refuge for countless other creatures, including blue crabs and oyster toadfish. Because oysters feed by filtering plankton and detritus from the water, their vast early populations also helped keep the Bay clear enough for growth of seagrasses.

DID YOU KNOW?
Oysters nourished countless generations of Native Americans; became a staple for colonists; and, with the advent of dredges, railroads, and canning, began supplying homes and oyster bars throughout early America. Tragically, overharvesting, disease, and declines in water quality have devastated the Bay's oyster population, with harvests dropping from around 8 million bushels in 1880 to fewer than 10,000 bushels per year in the 1990s. The recent advent of oyster farming and sanctuary reefs provides hope for a return of these tasty shellfish to our tables—and to their ecological role.

Red Beard Sponge (*Microciona prolifera*)

DESCRIPTION

Resembles a plant but is actually an animal (8–12 inches). Unmistakable thicket of orangish-red "branches" radiate in an irregular pattern. Branches are rubbery and perforated by small, scattered pores. Grows attached to submerged solid surfaces, but often seen lolling in shallow water or rolled along by shoreline waves after being dislodged by a storm.

HABITAT & ECOLOGY

The most common sponge in the Chesapeake. Lives on oyster reefs, barnacles, pilings, rocks, and other hard surfaces in the shallow, saltier waters of the middle and lower Bay. Filters phytoplankton and other small particles from water drawn through a network of tiny canals by the beating of hairlike cilia. Bushy form provides refuge in its numerous nooks and crannies for copepods, marine worms, crabs, and other small invertebrates. Preyed on by sea slugs, sea stars, and sea turtles.

DID YOU KNOW?

Like many other sponges, the red beard contains microscopic rods composed of silica. Known as spicules, these glassy, needlelike structures help support the sponge but can irritate human skin when handled or brushed against while swimming. The red beard can regrow into a new organism after being squeezed through a fine sieve.

Tunicates or Sea Squirts (*Molgula manhattensis*)

DESCRIPTION

The size, shape, and consistency of grapes, these translucent to latte-colored sea creatures attach to hard, submerged surfaces and bear 2 chimneylike siphons on their free-standing end. Often sport a fuzzy coat of bryozoans or hydrozoans on their rubbery skin, or "tunic." Each "grape" is a separate organism, but these often grow in dense clusters. Can squirt a forceful stream of water if disturbed while exposed at low tide. Resemble small anemones when siphons are retracted.

HABITAT & ECOLOGY

Found attached to pilings, riprap, shells, driftwood, and flotsam around the Bay, these organisms feed by filtering plankton from water that is drawn through their incurrent and exhalant siphons by the beating of cilia. Preyed on by crabs, eels, and fishes.

DID YOU KNOW?

Close study of larval tunicates shows they have a notochord, nerve cord, and gill slits, traits they share with other chordates such as humans. That's right, these small sea creatures are more closely related to you and me than the sponges and corals they resemble as adults! They resorb these structures once the tadpole-like larva attaches its head to the seafloor and metamorphoses into the adult form.

Wharf Crab (*Armases cinereum*)

DESCRIPTION

Like the Bay's other common intertidal crustaceans, the marsh crab and fiddler crab, these wee fellows have 10 jointed legs (the first pair modified into claws) and a much-reduced "tail" that's tucked under the body. The claws are small and of equal size (unlike male fiddlers); their shell is almost square and rather flat, with the eyes on short stalks in the front corners (fiddler eyes are near the midline and on longer stalks). Typically some shade of brown, with a single "tooth" behind each eye (marsh crabs have a purple, inflated shell with two of these "eye teeth").

HABITAT & ECOLOGY

Skilled climbers often found on pilings, docks, smooth cordgrass blades, bald cypress knees, and other Bay protuberances. Favor the high marsh and may travel hundreds of feet inland. Eat living and decayed plant material (with a particular taste for marsh elder), small fiddler crabs, marsh periwinkles, amphipods, isopods, aphids, and spiders. Preyed on by blue crabs, clapper rails, fishes, and racoons. Hide beneath debris or in shallow, self-dug burrows at high tide.

DID YOU KNOW?

Experiments on tiny treadmills show these crabs have a unique metabolism among running animals. Unlike ghost crabs, they require very little oxygen to sprint; and unlike fiddler crabs, they don't appear to compensate by going into anaerobic oxygen debt like a marathoner. More elastic leg joints or more efficient muscle fibers may explain their locomotory superpowers.

GULLS, TERNS, AND SKIMMERS

What do you call a seagull in the Chesapeake? A bagel! Gulls, terns, and skimmers—all kin in the family Laridae—are some of the most frequently encountered birds along Bay shorelines. Gulls, with their raucous calls, brazen temperament, and taste for human food, are particularly hard to miss. You've likely seen them congregate like tattooed stevedores along a working waterfront, hang out like noisy teens in a mall parking lot, or dive-bomb beach picnics like uninvited in-laws. Terns are more refined, practicing graceful aerial dives for fish a polite distance offshore. Skimmers are perhaps the most sophisticated of the lot, joining in small groups to glide inches above calm waters, occasionally dipping their beaks to sip in small fishes. Populations declined sharply in the early 1900s due to harvesting of eggs and hunting for feathers to adorn women's hats. The Migratory Bird Treaty Act of 1918 initiated their resurgence; gulls in particular have benefitted from increases in human population and garbage.

A set of common features unite these otherwise disparate birds. The body is typically dark above and white below, wings long and pointed, beak relatively short, feet webbed, and tail either square or forked. They also tend to breed in colonies on islands, shoals, and other sites isolated from terrestrial predators. Clear differences in adult plumage aid identification, but juveniles molt through a bewildering progression of plumages that can and do confuse even skilled birders. These plumage stages include juvenile (first basic), formative, first alternate, second basic, second alternate, definitive basic, and definitive alternate. Here we highlight a few features to help distinguish among eight of the Chesapeake's more common adult larids, referencing the breeding plumage most wear in the Bay. For full treatment, consult the references in "A Deeper Dive."

Laughing Gull (*Leucophaeus atricilla*)

To 16 inches long and 0.6 pound, wingspan of 3 feet. *Ha, ha, ha* . . . call is unmistakable, as are adults in breeding plumage: Head has black cap; bill and legs are red; eyes are outlined top and bottom with white. Sexes similar. Rarely strays far from salt water, favoring beaches, marshes, and sandbars. Eats crabs, fishes, snails, insects, scraps from fishing boats, and other human refuse. Will also follow farm plows to snatch unearthed grubs and worms. Migrates into the Bay in early spring to begin breeding. Nests in small colonies on sandy or rocky shores and salt-marsh islands. Leaves in fall for southern wintering grounds. Once almost extinct from hunting for hat feathers, now the most abundant breeding seabird on the US East Coast.

Herring Gull (*Larus argentatus*)

To 2 feet long and 3.3 pounds; wingspan of 4–5 feet. Abundant, widespread, and adaptable. Bay holds resident and migratory populations. In summer, breeding birds are white except for light gray back and wings. In winter's nonbreeding plumage, head and neck are streaked with grayish brown. Wing tips black with white spots year-round. Bill light yellow with a drab red spot; eye rimmed with orange. Preys on and scavenges fishes, invertebrates, insects, earthworms, mammals, eggs, other seabirds, carrion, and human refuse. Nests in many different habitats, including Bay salt marshes and barrier beaches.

Ring-billed Gull (*Larus delawarensis*)

To 21 inches long and 1.2 pounds; wingspan to 4 feet. Black band around yellow bill gives this gull its name and serves as an easy identifier. Adults white in front and below; their pearl-gray wings are tipped in black with white spots. Younger birds mostly mottled brown. Sexes similar. The most inland of Bay gulls, often seen near farm fields, golf courses, landfills, lakes and reservoirs, and parking lots. Coastal birds frequent beaches, mudflats, and boat ramps. Will eat whatever, including small fish, earthworms, insects, grain, small rodents, and garbage. Most return to breed at the colony where they hatched. Nest inland, near freshwater, and are likely to return to the same breeding spot each year.

Great Black-backed Gull
(*Larus marinus*)

One of the world's largest gulls (to 2.5 feet long and 4.5 pounds; wingspan of 5.5 feet). Adults recognized by size; dark wings and back; large, snow-white head; red eye ring; and big yellow bill with bright red spot. A year-round resident of the upper Bay and expanding its range southward into Virginia; often at the expense of herring gulls. Favors big-water shorelines and fishing piers. Eats almost anything: fishes, insects, invertebrates, mammals, other gulls, seabirds, and waterfowl. Will eat carrion and garbage, but prefers live, natural prey. May steal food from other birds. Generally nests in loose colonies or as single pairs.

Common Tern (*Sterna hirundo*)

To 1 foot long and ¾ pound; wingspan of 2.5 feet. Common and widespread. Breeding adult is pale gray below, with black cap. Orangish-red bill has black tip. Tail forked; relatively short streamers do not extend beyond wing tips at rest. Typically feeds close to shore but may flock offshore to target fish schools. Dives from air to capture mummichogs, menhaden, herring, mole crabs, insects, and squid. Strongly migratory. Nests on islands, barrier beaches, and in salt marshes; present in Bay approximately April–October. Populations decimated by millinery trade in the late 1800s and challenged today by habitat loss. In 1886 ornithologist Frank Chapman counted the feathers of twenty-one common terns atop women's hats during two afternoon strolls through New York City. Some hats displayed the entire bird.

Least Tern (*Sternula antillarum*)

Smallest North American tern (to 9 inches long and 1.5 ounces; wingspan of 20 inches). Bay's summer breeding birds have white forehead set off by black crown and nape. Body is gray above and white below, with slender pale wings and forked tail. Legs and bill yellow. Black edge of outer wing obvious in flight. Feeds mostly nearshore, in bays, creek mouths, and tidal marshes. Eats a variety of small fishes (including menhaden and mummichogs), as well as shrimp and other invertebrates. Predators include great blue herons, raccoons, and foxes. Nests in colonies on sandy beaches and islands kept free of vegetation by tides or river flow. Once threatened by the millinery trade, now challenged by development and recreational use of breeding habitat. Classified as "threatened" in many parts of its range.

Royal Tern (*Thalasseus maximus*)

To 20 inches long and 1 pound; wingspan of 3.5 feet. Black, crested cap and large orange-red bill of breeding birds are distinctive. Develops white forehead in winter. Legs and feet are black; tail forked. Favors open salt water along sandy beaches; also seen in marshes. Eats mostly fish and shrimp, but diet varies with season, weather, and location. Usually forages singly or in small groups, but may flock above fish schools. Forms dense breeding colonies at sites free from predators such as foxes and raccoons. South Island, built near the mouth of the James River during construction of the Hampton Roads Bridge-Tunnel (HRBT), provided breeding habitat for 98 percent of the Virginia population. Paving of the island in 2020 due to expansion of the HRBT led to concerns regarding the bird's continued breeding success in Bay waters. In response, conservationists and state agencies quickly transformed a nearby island (Fort Wool) to provide suitable habitat—an action that seems to have succeeded.

Black Skimmer
(*Rynchops niger*)

Average 15–20 inches long and 9–12 ounces; wingspan of 1 foot. Males larger than females. Red, black-tipped bill is distinctive, with an obvious "underbite" in which lower mandible extends about an inch farther than upper. Black above and white below, with bright orange feet. Hunts fish in shallow nearshore habitats by flying just above the surface, with open bill skimming the water; snaps bill shut when it encounters prey. Eats mummichogs, herring, pipefish, and crabs. Naturalist R. C. Murphy described these birds as "aerial beagles hot on the scent of aerial rabbits," perhaps influenced by their doglike yips. Summer migrant to Bay; populations declining here and elsewhere, mainly due to development and recreational use of beach nesting habitat. Classified as "threatened" in Maryland.

Hand of Man

BULKHEADS

Bulkheads line many miles of Chesapeake Bay shoreline—a 1990 study mapped 71 miles in Virginia alone. Often built of wood, they are essentially vertical retaining walls whose main purpose is to keep soil or fill from eroding or slumping into the water. Bulkheads offer little protection from waves and are therefore typically used in sheltered locations such as marinas, channels, and tributary reaches with a limited fetch.

Widely employed from the 1950s to 1970s to defend shorelines during the post–World War II boom in bayside vacation cottages, bulkheads have fallen out of favor due to their relatively short lifespan (about 20 years), propensity to hasten their own demise due to scour from reflected waves, and similar erosive effect on adjacent marsh plants and seagrasses. Bulkheads also tend to sever the connection between land and water by blocking animal passage. Today, property owners who would have traditionally built a bulkhead or need to replace one that's failing are increasingly turning to living shorelines. In the early 2000s, these were legally recognized as the preferred method of shoreline protection in both Maryland and Virginia.

SEAWALLS

As the name attests, these are linear, vertical barriers—often concrete—built to protect seaside infrastructure from large waves. Because of their high cost and complex engineering requirements, seawalls are typically reserved for use in large-scale civic or military applications, such as along a municipal promenade, seaport, or naval base. They suffer from many of the same drawbacks as other "hardened" shoreline defenses, particularly in their propensity to hasten their own demise due to scour from reflected waves, but continue to be used to defend populous waterfronts exposed to big waves.

(Scour can be minimized through engineered solutions such as basal reinforcement and curved parapets.) Seawalls have also been proposed as a bastion against rising seas, but at great cost—$27 billion in Maryland alone according to a 2019 study (see the last chapter, "The Once and Future Bay").

PIERS AND WHARVES

Though they can both be used as mooring sites for watercraft, piers and wharves differ in their orientation to the shoreline. Wharves run parallel to the shore, and are therefore built in areas with deeper nearshore waters. A pier is an elevated structure that extends perpendicularly seaward into waters deep enough for berthing deep-draft vessels. Given the pervasive shallowness of its nearshore waters, the Bay features several prodigiously long piers. Some of the most remarkable are the thirteen at Naval Station Norfolk. The longest of these reach more than 0.3 mile (1,700 feet) into the Bay. If laid end to end, the baker's dozen would stretch 18,443 feet (3.5 miles). To learn about the Bay's many fishing piers, see the "Boating and Fishing on the Bay" chapter.

DRY DOCKS

A dry dock is a basin or pontoon that can be flooded to allow a ship to enter, then pumped dry to provide ready access for maintenance and repair of the vessel's normally submerged portions, including the hull and propeller(s). Chesapeake Bay is home to a number of notable dry docks. At 2,172 feet long, 249 feet wide, and 32 feet deep, Dry Dock 12 at Newport News Shipbuilding on the James River is the largest in the United States and sixth largest in the world. Not coincidentally, that's big enough to fit an aircraft carrier. Not far away, at Norfolk Naval Shipyard in Portsmouth, Virginia, is Drydock Number One, the oldest operational dry dock in the United States and now a National Historic Landmark. Completed in 1834, it was used during the Civil War to transform the USS *Merrimack* into the Confederate Navy ironclad CSS *Virginia*. The largest of the eight dry docks

in Portsmouth is 1,010 feet long, 144 feet wide, and 44 feet deep. Across the Elizabeth River at NASSCO-Norfolk, General Dynamics operates a floating dry dock that is 750 feet long and 126 feet wide, with the capacity to lift a vessel of 44,800 tons.

SHIPPING CHANNELS AND DREDGE SPOILS

The Chesapeake is remarkably shallow (see the introduction). Transit of deep-draft vessels is therefore restricted to river channels carved during the last ice age when sea level was much lower, to channels that are manually deepened, or both. Dredging of channels is an ongoing activity in the Bay, as they regularly accumulate sediment brought in by tributaries or churned-up by storms. Dredging is done by ships outfitted with what are essentially giant vacuum cleaners, some equipped with rotating heads to dig into the bay floor. Unlike many other East Coast waterways, which are floored by bedrock, the Chesapeake is underlain by thick layers of sediment. This is a natural blessing for the future of Bay commerce, as it allows relatively inexpensive dredging of channels to depths sufficient to handle "Post-Panamax" container vessels, which have drafts as deep as 60 feet. When current dredging projects are complete, the channels leading to Baltimore will bottom out at 51 feet and those leading to the Port of Virginia at 55 feet, making the latter the deepest port on the US East Coast. Of course, all the sediments dredged from shipping channels must be disposed of elsewhere. Now that both Maryland and Virginia have largely banned disposal of dredge "spoils" into open Bay waters due to concerns with contamination and habitat destruction, dredged materials are increasingly used to nourish beaches or "reclaim" low-lying coastal lands. A notable example is Craney Island near the Bay mouth, which is being expanded via spoils dredged from the new Post-Panamax channel into a facility for the porting of— Post-Panamax vessels!

BARGES

These shallow, flat-bottomed vessels are the pickup trucks of the Bay, hauling bulk loads of heavy, low-value commodities such as stone or timber in their often-rusty, dinged-up hold. A typical Bay barge measures 195 by 35 feet and can carry up to about 1,400 tons of cargo. Many Bay barges are "dumb," meaning they have no engines and must be towed or pushed by tugs. They provide one of the most inexpensive means of transporting heavy materials around the Bay region. From the late 1700s to the mid-1800s (until supplanted by railroads), mule-towed river barges were commonly employed to move cargo along canals dug parallel to Bay tributaries. Evidence of this activity is apparent with a visit to the C&O Canal along the north bank of the Potomac River, the James River and Kanawha Canal in Richmond, and the Chesapeake and Delaware Canal that connects the two bays across eastern Maryland.

CONTAINER VESSELS

At first glance, the name might seem redundant, like a head chef. But "container" here has a precise meaning: a corrugated metal crate designed to transfer cargo. These containers are also known as "TEUs"—twenty-foot equivalents—in reference to their dimensions: 20 feet long by 8 feet wide and 4¼–9½ feet tall. (Though nothing is ever simple: US shipping containers are typically 40 feet long, and thus equal to two TEUs.) "Containerization" of a ship's cargo came on scene in the 1950s and is now standard practice due to huge savings in time and cost compared to previous piece-by-piece lading/unlading, and the capacity for intermodal transport of TEUs from ship to rail or truck and back again. Container ships now carry more than 90 percent of global non-bulk goods. Because bigger vessels are more hydrodynamic and fuel efficient, container ships grow ever larger, as do the canals and ports needed to fit these leviathans. To date, the largest container ship to visit Chesapeake Bay is the *Evergreen Triton*, which at 1,210 feet long can hold 15,313 TEUs. Laid end to end, these would stretch more than 58 miles. One good place to view these behemoths is from Preservation Virginia's Cape Henry Lighthouse near the Bay mouth. Watch for vessels that look like they are carrying a raft of multicolored Lego blocks.

BULK CARRIERS

If container vessels are the fastidious packers of the shipping world, with a place for everything and everything in its place, bulk carriers are the last-minute travelers who simply dump loose materials into their open suitcase (well, they do carefully distribute their loads to prevent shifting). Bay "bulkers" typically move coal ("colliers"), grains, gravel, and other dry goods. They feature from one to as many as nine cargo holds, accessed by hatches nearly as wide as the ship. Bulkers come in two main types: geared and gearless. Geared bulkers carry their own conveyor belts or deck-top cranes, allowing them to lade at ports lacking that equipment. Gearless bulkers are restricted to ports with the machinery needed to fill or empty their holds. Good spots for watching Bay colliers are at spots near the Norfolk Southern coal terminal at Lambert's Point in Norfolk, the Dominion Terminal in nearby Newport News, and the CNX Marine Terminal in Baltimore.

PETROLEUM TANKERS

Tankers carrying crude oil once supplied a pair of bayside refineries—one near the York River mouth and the other in Baltimore Harbor. Though no longer refineries, these facilities continue to serve as transit points for petroleum products—crude oil, refined gasoline, and asphalt—and still handle traffic from tankers and oil barges. The nexus of tanker traffic in today's Bay is Dominion's Cove Point Terminal. Originally built to handle gas imports, then the domestic market, the terminal in 2018 completed a $4.4 billion, multiyear overhaul as an export facility for natural gas recovered by fracking of shale deposits in Appalachia. Piped from Pennsylvania and other states, this shale gas is cooled (to approximately -260°F!), condensing it to 1/600th the volume for more efficient shipboard transport as liquified natural gas (LNG). Scores of 1,000-foot-plus LNG tankers now ply the Bay each year, recognizable by the domes or trapezoids rising from their deck. These insulated holds, plus a profusion of deck-mounted pipes and valves, serve to keep the super-chilled gas a liquid during its long voyage to Japan and other overseas markets. To the dismay of at least some local residents, good spots to view these leviathans include Calvert Cliffs State Park in Maryland and nearby Cove Point Beach—neither a place (if there is one) anyone would ever want to suffer a spill. The LNG tankers dock more than a mile offshore, at a half-mile-long wharf supplied by an underwater pipeline.

HARBOR CRANES

Big boats and big loads require really big cranes. These gigantic "birds of quay" pierce the Chesapeake Bay skyline in both Hampton Roads and the Port of Baltimore. Harbor cranes come in two main flavors: gantry and tower. Gantry cranes feature a bridge-like horizontal structure supported by a vertical leg at either end. The largest gantry crane in the Bay, and the Western Hemisphere, rises above Newport News Shipbuilding. Known as "Big Blue," this 233-foot-tall behemoth has a 540-foot span and the capacity to lift 1,050 metric tons—as much as twenty Boeing 737s. Big Blue has helped build every American aircraft carrier since the USS *Theodore Roosevelt* in 1984. Hampton Roads also holds the Bay's largest tower cranes, which feature a

single mast and right-angle boom. Norfolk International Terminals operates 8 "Suez-class" cranes, so named because they can handle ships built to the width of that canal. These are twenty-seven stories tall and, with a 235-foot reach, can unpack ships that

are twenty-six containers wide. Baltimore installed four giant tower cranes in 2013—each fourteen stories tall and capable of lifting 187,300 pounds—in preparation for the 2016 widening of the Panama Canal. In 2019 the Virginia International Gateway erected a quartet of seventeen-story cranes to handle the new Post-Panamax vessels; these are the largest ship-to-shore cranes on the East Coast. Expect further increases in both ship and crane size as canals and ports continue competing for global maritime traffic in the coming decades.

SHIPWRECKS

Where there are ships, there will be wrecks, and the Chesapeake has more than its fair share—at least 1,800 at last count. Bay vessels have been sunk by everything from ice to hurricanes, nor'easters, grounding, cannonballs, accidental collisions, and purposeful scuttling. During the age of wooden sailing ships, fire was one of the gravest threats. In addition to the scores of shipwrecks that litter its commercial harbors, the Bay holds two particularly notable naval graveyards: Mallows Bay on the Potomac just downstream from Washington, DC, and just offshore of Yorktown near the mouth of the York River.

Mallows Bay holds more than 100 scuttled vessels.

With 118 vessels, Mallows Bay inters one of the largest concentrations of shipwrecks in North America. These coal-fired wooden steamships were hurriedly built to guard against German U-boats in the lead-up to World War I, but made obsolete by the advent of diesel power almost before they could be launched.

Outdated and unwanted, they were salvaged, scuttled, and left to the elements shortly after the war ended. Recognizing the historic value of this "Ghost Fleet" and adjacent cultural resources, in 2019 Congress and NOAA preserved the area as the Mallows Bay–Potomac River National Marine Sanctuary. Access for kayaks and other small watercraft can be had from the nearby Mallows Bay Boat Ramp.

At Yorktown, the remains of Lord Cornwallis's Revolutionary War fleet lie just yards off the popular swimming beach. The British—under siege by the land forces of Washington and Lafayette—first set several of their own ships ablaze and adrift in a vain attempt to set fire to French warships recently arrived from their Battle of the Capes victory. The British then scuttled their remaining vessels to deter a French landing. Historians estimate there were around fifty vessels in the British fleet. To date, marine archaeologists have found eleven of these, including the HMS *Charon*, *Shipwright*, and *Betsy*; the *Betsy* gave up more than 5,000 artifacts, some of which are on display in the nearby American Revolution Museum. The scuttled fleet was the National Register of Historic Places' first underwater listing (Yorktown Shipwrecks National Register District); there's currently a move afoot to nominate the site as a National Marine Sanctuary.

TUGBOATS

With pug nose, burly stature, and *toot-toot* demeanor, there is just something endearing about a tugboat. As they do in ports and bathtubs worldwide, tugboats in Chesapeake Bay play a vital role by helping move often immense seagoing vessels into narrow channels and unfamiliar harbors. With small crews and scant need for cargo space, tugs have been called floating engines. They've also been called dancers, handmaidens, lunch-box boats,

mighty-mites, sheep dogs, Sumo wrestlers, and workhorses. Bay tugs are no slouches, with some boasting engines exceeding 4,000 horsepower. Steerable propellers and a hull designed to help the prop dig into the water allow tugs to push, pull, and nudge vessels a hundred times their tonnage into even the tightest berths. Tugs also feature powerful winches to draw in their hawser lines when towing. Tugs are typically festooned with purpose-built fenders or used tires to protect the larger vessel, a feature that contributes to their roly-poly look. In addition to shepherding other self-propelled vessels, tugs are sometimes used to tow or push "dumb" barges with no engines of their own. Some tugs also pull double duty as fireboats. Of course, tugboats would be nothing without tugboaters and pilots—men and women with unmatched knowledge of a port's tides, currents, channels, shoals, and docking facilities.

AIRCRAFT CARRIERS

These immense, flat-topped vessels "allow for the mobile projection of Naval Air Power across the globe." They are "floating cities" in more ways than one. First, they hold the population of a small town, with a crew of 4,500–5,000 sailors. They also offer many urban amenities, including a barber shop; chapel; medical and dental offices; high-speed elevators; a fire station; a twenty-four-hour diner; gyms for weight lifting, cardio exercises, and boxing; a vacuum-powered septic system; and a general store. Each ship also has its own nuclear power plant and, of course, airport. Carriers also resemble a city in their legal status—each is a sovereign piece of US territory, but one that can steam anywhere within international waters at speeds exceeding 30 knots. US carriers are built at Newport News Shipbuilding, and seven are homeported at nearby Norfolk Naval Air Station: the USS *Abraham Lincoln, Dwight D. Eisenhower, George H. W. Bush, George Washington, Gerald R. Ford, John C. Stennis,* and *Harry S. Truman.* The *Ford* is the first in the newest generation of US carriers. Ships in this class are 1,092 feet long, with a flight deck that's 256 feet wide. They can carry and launch more than seventy-five aircraft, including Hornet, Super Hornet, and Growler fighter jets; Hawkeye "command and control" turboprops; Sea Hawk helicopters; and Greyhound cargo planes. The homecoming of a carrier strike group—and the reunion of family members separated during deployments lasting up to eight months—is always big news in the communities surrounding lower Chesapeake Bay.

AMPHIBIOUS VESSELS

These vessels bridge the boundary between water, land, and air. They first appeared during World War I and World War II as barge-like landing craft with a flat bow that could hinge open to deploy ground forces and combat vehicles in remote and hostile locations where conventional docking was impossible. During World War II, the US Navy established its Naval Amphibious Training Base near Solomons Island, Maryland, where Bay beaches provided training sites for mock invasion landings. Amphibious vessels have now diversified into myriad shapes, sizes, and capabilities that allow access to 75 percent of the world's beaches. Amphibious assault ships—which each carry around 1,600 marines and 1,000 sailors—can put troops on enemy shores via both water and air. The largest can transport and deploy two conventional landing craft and three air-powered hovercraft. Their air contingent includes helicopters, Harrier vertical-takeoff jets, and Osprey tilt-rotor aircraft. Homeported in Norfolk are the USS *Bataan, Iwo Jima, Kearsarge,* and *Wasp.* Landing craft can also be carried by dock landing ships, which can partially submerge to ease deployment from ship to shore. Homeported in Norfolk are the USS *Arlington, Mesa Verde,* and *San Antonio.* In addition to their combat role, amphibious vessels are used to support humanitarian operations.

CRUISERS AND DESTROYERS

Though both are "multi-mission warships," cruisers (5,000–27,000 tons displacement) tend to be bigger than destroyers (4,000–10,000 tons). Today's navy cruisers have the armaments needed to target surface ships, aircraft, submarines, and land-based assets. Some are equipped with Tomahawk cruise missiles for additional long-range capability. Cruisers homeported in Norfolk are the USS *Anzio, Gettysburg, Leyte Gulf, Monterey, Normandy,*

San Jacinto, Vella Gulf, and *Vicksburg.* Destroyers—aka "Greyhounds of the Sea"—were developed in the late 1800s as ships fast and maneuverable enough to counter the threat posed by the advent of torpedo boats and submarines. They still serve that role today but, like cruisers, have added guided missiles and advanced artillery, allowing them to destroy air and land targets as well. Destroyers homeported in Norfolk are the USS *Arleigh Burke, Bainbridge, Barry, Bulkeley, Cole, Donald Cook, Forrest Sherman, Gonzalez, Gravely, James E. Williams, Jason Dunham, Laboon, Mahan, Mason, McFaul, Mitscher, Nitze, Oscar Austin, Porter, Ramage, Ross, Stout, Truxtun,* and *Winston S. Churchill.* The newest, Zumwalt-class destroyers are unmistakable, with a wave-piercing bow and angular, radar-shedding outline. Gone are the deck-mounted turrets that gave traditional destroyers their characteristic bristling silhouette; these have been replaced with vertical-launch missile batteries and a gun system so advanced that it has yet to be finalized despite $505 million in research and development. The USS *Zumwalt* was commissioned in Baltimore in 2016.

SUBMARINES

The Bay's shallow waters have ironically played a key role in the development of US Navy submarines, boats that now regularly dive to depths greater than 800 feet. The first attempt to use a combat sub in the Chesapeake was made by Union forces during the Civil War. Built in 1862, the 47-foot *Alligator* was designed to counter the Confederate ironclad *Virginia*. Towed to Hampton Roads, the boat first attempted to clear obstructions from the James River and destroy a bridge across the Appomattox, but in both cases the water proved too shallow for full submergence, scuttling Union plans. The *Alligator* was then towed to the Washington Navy Yard on the Potomac, where workers replaced its sixteen oars with a hand-cranked propeller and President Lincoln watched a demonstration of the retrofitted vessel. The *Alligator* was lost in a storm off Cape Hatteras while being towed to Charleston for its first action. The Confederates also used the Bay as a submarine test bed. In 1861 at Richmond's Tredegar Iron Works on the James River, inventor William Cheney built a submarine that had a primitive airlock to allow a diver to exit beneath an enemy vessel. This submersible never saw combat.

In 1895 Columbian Iron Works in Baltimore won the first US Navy contract to build a submarine, the *Plunger*. Its steam engines proved impractical in a closed vessel; focus then shifted to the gas- and electric-powered USS *Holland*, the Navy's first commissioned, operational sub. Completed in New Jersey in 1897, the *Holland* was towed to the US Naval Academy in Annapolis, where it was used to train midshipmen with runs down the Chesapeake. In the same year, Columbian Iron Works built the *Argonaut*, a 36-foot "salvage chamber" that rolled along the bottom on three wheels, and from which a diver could exit and reenter. It was the first submersible to salvage items from the seafloor, prompting a congratulatory telegram from Jules Verne. Shortly before the United States entered World War I, a German U-boat with a cargo of much-desired dyes and rubber arrived in Baltimore Harbor after evading the British high-seas blockade.

It received a warm public welcome, with front-page stories and feting of the merchantmen. But as the U-boats' toll on American shipping continued to escalate, the United States joined Britain and its allies to fight the Germans, with the US Navy erecting a torpedo factory just down the bay in Alexandria, Virginia. (Today the closed facility enjoys a second life as the Torpedo Factory Art Center.) Also during World War II, the Navy strung steel submarine nets across the mouth of the James River to protect naval and civilian infrastructure. When needed, tugboats would open a floating gate to allow entry to the waters of Hampton Roads.

Today's submarines are a far cry from their early progenitors. Nuclear powered, they have almost unlimited energy, as well as air that's free from the potentially toxic by-products of internal combustion engines. They can survive months underwater, moving at speeds exceeding 25 knots. Two of the three classes of modern US attack submarines are built at Newport News Shipbuilding and include boats homeported in the Chesapeake. Los Angeles–class boats—built from 1972 to 1996 during the height of the Cold War—were designed with acoustic stealth and high speed to counter Soviet Union subs in the open ocean. At 360 feet long and 33 feet wide, they hold a crew of 16 officers and 127 enlisted, plus armaments that include Mark 48 torpedoes and Tomahawk cruise missiles. Norfolk-based LA-class boats include the USS *Albany*, *Boise*, *Helena*, *Montpelier*, *Newport News*, and *San Francisco*. The USS *Virginia* is the exemplar of America's next-generation attack submarine. Although close in size and speed to LA-class boats, Virginia-class submarines are designed to operate in nearshore waters, with sensors and systems to gather intelligence, find and neutralize mines, and support special forces. Automation aboard these boats gives them a smaller crew (15 officers, 117 enlisted). Norfolk-based Virginia-class subs include the USS *John Warner* and *Washington*. None of the Navy's ballistic missile submarines—designed to deliver nuclear warheads—are homeported in the Chesapeake.

A DEEPER DIVE

Andrews, J. D. "Fouling Organisms of Chesapeake Bay." Inshore Survey Program (Baltimore, MD: Chesapeake Bay Institute, The Johns Hopkins University, 1953).

Burke, M. "Thanks to Migratory Bird Act, Laughing Gulls Making a Comeback—No Joke." *Bay Journal* (Seven Valleys, PA: Bay Journal Media, 2018).

Burke, M. "For Ring-billed Gulls, Color of Feathers Is Often 'So Last Year.'" *Bay Journal* (Seven Valleys, PA: Bay Journal Media, 2018).

Burnett, J. W., G. J. Calton, and R. J. Morgan. "Dermatitis Due to Stinging Sponges." *CUTIS*, 39(476) (1987).

Dickon, C. *Images of America: Chesapeake Bay Steamers* (Charleston, SC: Arcadia Publishing, 2006).

Elston, D. M. "Aquatic Antagonists: Sponge Dermatitis." *CUTIS*, 80 (2007).

Full, R. J., C. F. Herreid, and J. A. Assad. "Energetics of the Exercising Wharf Crab (Sesarma cinereum)." *Physiological Zoology*, 58(5) (1985).

Goodall, J. L. H. *Pirates of the Chesapeake Bay: From the Colonial Era to the Oyster Wars* (Charleston, SC: The History Press, 2020).

Haug, J. "Wings—Breasts—Birds: The Use of Bird Feathers as a Fashion Ornament on Women's Hats and Accessories." *Victoriana* (2014).

Hicks, B. *Then & Now: Maryland Workboats* (Charleston, SC: Arcadia Publishing, 2009).

Quarenstein, J. V., and D. Mroczkowski. *Fort Monroe: The Key to the South*. The Civil War History Series (Charleston, SC: Arcadia Publishing, 2000).

Rago, G. "Virginia Paved Over Its Largest Seabird Nesting Site during the Hampton Roads Bridge-Tunnel Expansion." *Virginian-Pilot* (Norfolk, VA: Tribune Publishing Co., 2020).

US Navy. "Naval History and Heritage Command" (2020). www.history.navy.mil/content/history/nhhc.html.

Van Soest, R. W. M., et al. "World Porifera Database" (2020); www.marinespecies.org/porifera; 10.14284/359.

Watts, B. D. "Breeding Birds of Virginia." *Virginia Journal of Science*, 66(3) (2015).

Winkler, D. W., S. M. Billerman, and I. J. Lovette. "Gulls, Terns, and Skimmers (Laridae)." Birds of the World 2020. https://doi.org/10.2173/bow.larida1.01.

Yeatman, H. C. "Copepods from Chesapeake Bay Sponges including Aster-ocheres jeanyeatmanae n. sp." *Transactions of the American Microscopical Society*, 89(1) (1970). 10.2307/3224612.

Hunting FOR Fossils

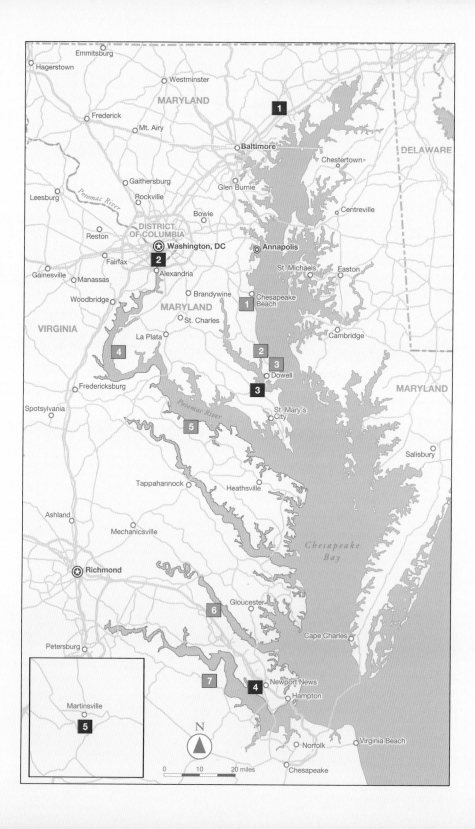

Ancient Life

Spanning 64,000 square miles from the Bay's tidal shoreline to the ridges of the Appalachians and Alleghenies, the Chesapeake watershed encompasses great geologic diversity. This includes thick layers of sedimentary rock with traces of ancient life reaching back more than 500 million years. A full accounting of this rich fossil record—ammonites, brachiopods, crinoids, dinosaurs, eurypterids, fishes, graptolites, etc.—is well beyond the scope of this book. Here we highlight a few of the younger and more familiar fossils found along Bay shores. We focus on the Pliocene fossils of the Yorktown Formation in Virginia (approximately 3–5 million years ago, or mya) and Miocene fossils of the Calvert, Choptank, and St. Marys Formations in Maryland (8–18 mya). Outcrops of these geologic units offer fruitful opportunities for amateur fossil collectors, most notably at selected state parks in Maryland and Virginia. To help conserve the precious scientific resource that fossils represent, always check with park personnel and private property owners before hunting or removing fossils. Several excellent paleontology museums also display collections of Bay fossils. SP = State Park, WMA = Wildlife Management Area

FOSSIL HUNTING SITES

1. Bayfront Park (Brownie's Beach)
2. Matoaka Cottages
3. Calvert Cliffs SP
4. Nanjemoy WMA
5. Westmoreland SP
6. York River SP
7. Chippokes Plantation SP

PALEONTOLOGY MUSEUMS

1. Natural History Society of Maryland
2. National Museum of Natural History
3. Calvert Marine Museum
4. Virginia Living Museum
5. Virginia Museum of Natural History (inset)

YORKTOWN FORMATION (VIRGINIA)

The Yorktown Formation comprises a layer of about 100 feet of sands and clays exposed in shoreline banks around the lower Chesapeake. These rocks contain large numbers of fossil bivalves and other prehistoric marine creatures from 3 to 5 million years ago, when shallow subtropical seas covered the region.

Scallops (*Chesapecten jeffersonius*)

To 6 inches or more. Almost circular, often heavy shell with two equal valves. Each has nine to twelve prominent radial ribs and finer radial lines, with two "wings" along the hinge. State fossil of Virginia and first North American fossil to be illustrated in scientific literature, in 1687.

 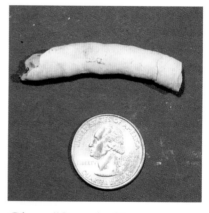

Barnacles (*Chesaconcavus* spp.)

Related to shrimp, these crustaceans are often found in life position, attached to the surface of other fossils such as scallops; may also break off as a discrete shell resembling a large tooth with a central cavity.

Clam "Snorkel"

These chalky white, hollow tubes were formed by the burrowing clam *Teredina fistula* to protect its fleshy feeding tube, or siphon, which extended up to the seafloor to filter food from the water.

Trace Fossils

These include burrows and other evidence of ancient activity. A trace fossil common to Yorktown clamshells is a countersunk hole, drilled by a predatory moon snail (two modern shells at top) using its barbed tongue and then secreting acid to reach the soft tissues within. What a way to go.

Corals
(*Septastrea marylandica*)

Commonly encrusts mollusks and other marine life, leaving behind a skeleton with polygonal cups that each held an anemone-like polyp in life. Here the skeleton covers a broken scallop, except where interrupted by a scar left by a once-attached slipper shell.

Bivalves

The Yorktown Formation is rich in fossil bivalves or clams, with more than 250 species. Here are just a handful, with brief tips to help identify them. Common traits for bivalve identification include the number and position of "teeth" in the hinge between the two shells, as well as shell ornamentation, including radial ribs and concentric growth lines.

Oysters
(*Ostrea compressirostra*)

Extinct relative of the Bay's most beloved modern bivalve, the eastern oyster. Lower shell is deeply cupped with a flaky outer surface like a croissant; upper is almost flat with concentric growth lines.

Costaglycymeris

Sturdy, symmetrical shell with fine radial lines and arched hinge bearing V-shaped teeth. Relative of modern bittersweet clams.

Mercenaria

The Yorktown Formation holds several extinct species of the modern hard clam. Today these "quahogs" are a favorite in the kitchen, sold by size as chowder clams, cherrystones, and littlenecks.

CHESAPEAKE GROUP (MARYLAND)

This geologic unit includes the Calvert, Choptank, and St. Marys Formations—layers of sand and mud that accumulated in a shallow coastal embayment from approximately 18 to 8 million years ago. They hold one of the longest-studied and best-known fossil assemblages on Earth, including a wealth of invertebrate and vertebrate remains. The latter includes groups as diverse as bony fishes, chimeras, crocodiles, marine mammals, rays, seabirds, sharks, and turtles.

Snails (*Ecphora quadricostata*)

Named for the four jutting ribs that encircle the main axis of the shell (*ekphora* means "protruding" in Greek). Preyed on other mollusks by drilling through their shells with its rasping tongue. State fossil of Maryland and one of the first North American fossils to be illustrated in scientific literature, in 1770.

Coprolites

There's no polite way to say it: "Coprolite" is Greek for fossilized poop. Of value to paleontologists, as these trace fossils can provide information about the diet of now-extinct animals.

Marine Mammal Bones

The Chesapeake Group holds one of Earth's most important collections of fossil marine mammals, spanning their rapid evolution from terrestrial forebears into modern forms. This includes sea cows and some of the world's oldest known true seals. In total, the deposits have revealed more than thirty species of cetaceans, including both baleen and toothed whales. The latter include sperm whales and early dolphins.

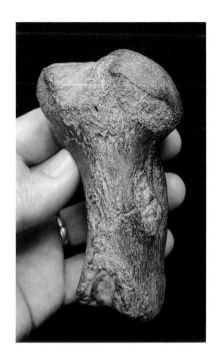

Shark Teeth

Highly sought after by everyone from Native Americans—who used them for tools and decoration—to modern amateur fossil collectors. Durable, given their intended use for slashing and tearing, and numerous, as sharks continually shed teeth during their lifetime. These may be locally abundant, particularly on beaches near coastal cliffs following storms. The fossil shark teeth of the Chesapeake Group represent species closely related to living progeny, including angel, bull, hammerhead, mako, sand tiger, thresher, tiger, and whale sharks. The largest shark in this fauna is the extinct megalodon (*Carcharocles megalodon*), whose teeth may be more than 5 inches wide. The shark itself grew to a fearsome length of almost 60 feet.

A DEEPER DIVE

Burns, J. *Fossil Collecting in the Mid-Atlantic States* (Baltimore and London: The Johns Hopkins University Press, 1991).

Campbell, L. D. *Pliocene Molluscs from the Yorktown and Chowan River Formations in Virginia*. Virginia Department of Mines, Minerals, and Energy (ed.) (Charlottesville, VA: Virginia Division of Mineral Resources, 1993).

Conkwright, R. D. "Maryland's Official State Fossil Shell" (1998). www.mgs .md.gov/geology/fossils/maryland_state_fossil_shell_fs.html.

Conkwright, R. D. "Fossil Collecting Sites at Calvert Cliffs" (2008). www.mgs .md.gov/geology/fossils/fossil_collecting.html.

Fraser, N. "Scavengers and Predators of Ancient Seas." *Virginia Explorer* (Martinsville, VA: Virginia Museum of Natural History, 1998).

Godfrey, S. J. (ed). *The Geology and Vertebrate Paleontology of Calvert Cliffs, Maryland, USA*. Smithsonian Contributions to Paleobiology, vol. 100 (Washington, DC: Smithsonian Institution Scholarly Press, 2018).

Hendricks, J. R., A. L. Stigall, and B. S. Lieberman. "Neogene Atlas of Ancient Life Southeastern United States." *Palaeontologia Electronica* (2020). https:// neogeneatlas.net.

Maryland Geological Survey. "Fossils" (2020). www.mgs.md.gov/geology/ fossils/index.html.

Petuch, E. J., and M. Drolshagen. *Molluscan Paleontology of the Chesapeake Miocene* (Boca Raton, FL: CRC Press, 2010).

Ray, C. E. (ed). *Geology and Paleontology of the Lee Creek Mine, North Carolina, III*, vol. 61 (Washington, DC: Smithsonian Contributions to Paleobiology, 1987).

Strain, D. "The Chesapeake's Excellent Fossils." *Chesapeake Quarterly* (College Park, MD: Maryland Sea Grant College Program, 2013).

Ward, L. "Virginia's Prehistoric Sea Creatures." *Virginia Explorer* (Martinsville, VA: Virginia Museum of Natural History, 1998).

People OF THE Chesapeake

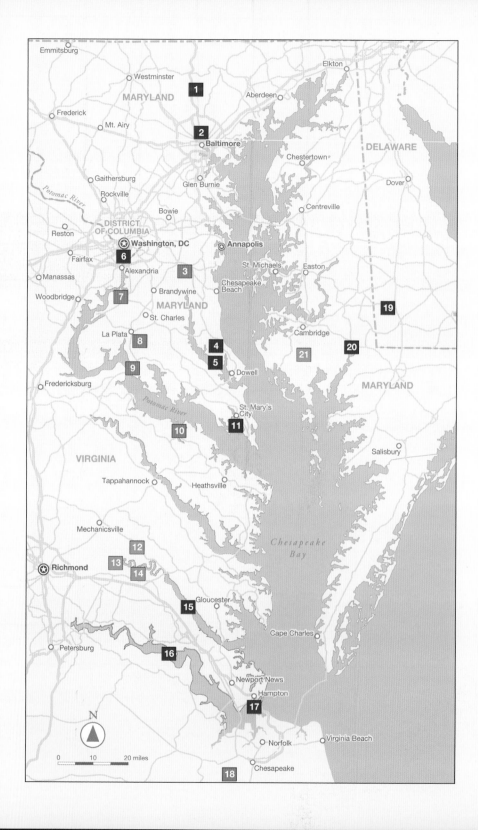

Native Americans

Museums and living history sites are in blue. Archaeological sites are in orange. Sites offered by Native tribes are in green. Search online for directions and current access information.

1. National Lacrosse Museum
2. Baltimore American Indian Center & Heritage Museum
3. Mount Calvert Archaeological Park
4. Maryland Archaeological Conservation Lab
5. Woodland Village (Jefferson Patterson Park & Museum)
6. National Museum of the American Indian
7. Accokeek Creek
8. Zekiah Swamp
9. Pope's Creek Shell Midden
10. White Oak Point Shell Midden
11. Woodland Village (Historic St. Mary's City)
12. Mattaponi Indian Heritage Museum
13. Pamunkey Indian Museum
14. Pamunkey Fish Hatchery
15. Werowocomoco
16. Powhatan Village (Jamestown)
17. Hampton University Museum
18. Great Dismal Swamp
19. Seaford Museum
20. Handsell Historic Site
21. Nause-Waiwash Band Longhouse

NATIVE AMERICANS HAVE INHABITED THE Chesapeake region since before the Bay was a bay. Devastated by the "guns, germs, and steel" of European contact, Native peoples and culture persevere today, with eleven tribes in Virginia, eight in Maryland, and one in Delaware. Their names adorn the *Chesapoic* itself—the "Great Shellfish Bay"—as well as many of the tributaries that provided their sustenance and transportation: the Mattaponi, Nansemond, Nottoway, Pamunkey, Patawomeck (Potomac), Piscataway, Rappahannock, and Susquehannock. These names reflect a landscape understood and named from the vantage of a dugout canoe, emphasizing the water's edge, wild plants, and wetland settings.

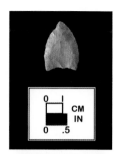

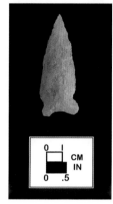

Archaeology shows that small bands of Paleo-Indians occupied the mid-Atlantic as early as 12,000 years ago, chasing big game through the spruce and fir that dominated the cold, wet, ice-age landscape. Though often depicted as hunters of woolly mammoth and mastodon, they more likely focused on elk, caribou, and white-tailed deer; the white-tailed deer was a cultural staple for the ensuing twelve millennia. With sea level 325 feet lower than present, they roamed what is now the bay floor and gazed out on the deep valleys of today's tidal rivers.

Around 10,000 years ago, meltwater from the waning ice sheets began to flood the Bay. During the subsequent Archaic period, Native Americans became increasingly reliant on aquatic and estuarine resources. They began to harvest arrow arum from freshwater marshes and initiated the earliest shell

Top: The Clovis Point was one type of arrowhead used by Paleo-Indians.
Bottom: This "Otter Creek" arrowhead is associated with Indians of the Archaic period.

middens about 4,500 years ago. One, at White Oak Point in Maryland, is now a 26-foot thick paella of soft-shell clams, ribbed mussels, and oysters. Today, most evidence of Paleo-Indian habitation lies beneath Bay waters (watermen have recovered arrowheads from the bay floor). Our understanding of local Archaic peoples is based largely on artifacts from a few key archaeological sites (see map entries in orange).

The appearance of pottery about 3,000 years ago marks the next stage in indigenous Bay history. Clayware and other signs show that what we now call "Woodland" Indians grew more sedentary and shifted their focus from inland and freshwater environments toward Bay resources such as oysters, herring, shad, striped bass, and sturgeon. The concentration of these resources in static locations—oyster reefs and spawning grounds—encouraged fixed seasonal habitations, as did increased

The appearance of pottery marks the beginning of the Bay's "Woodland" Indian stage.

This 1590 engraving by Theodor de Bry shows that Bay Indians used a wooden frame to cook their fish over a fire.

cultivation of corns, beans, and squash. This in turn led to increased political consolidation of previously roaming bands into the delineated chiefdoms present at European contact in the late 1500s and early 1600s.

Werowocomoco, soon to open as a National Park unit, was the seat of Powhatan's chiefdom.

Most of what we know of historic indigenous cultures is based on accounts by English colonists. A number of living history sites, museums, and events help expand and interpret this story, most focusing on interactions between Native and colonial populations. These include re-created native settlements at the Jamestown Settlement Museum in Virginia and in Maryland's Historic St. Mary's City, Jefferson Patterson Park and Museum, and Handsell Historic Site.

Native American groups also offer a number of cultural attractions. Museums located on the Pamunkey and Mattaponi reservations in Virginia focus on the history and living legacy of the Powhatan Confederacy. A favorite Mattaponi artifact is a necklace worn by Pocahontas. In Maryland, the Nause-Waiwash Band offer visits to a reconstructed longhouse. Particularly notable is the recent inclusion of Werowocomoco, the seat of the Powhatan chiefdom, into the National Park Service. Park staff are currently collaborating with Virginia's tribes and other partners to plan the exact nature of the park experience at this place of deep Native history.

Those interested in live events can visit powwows.com for a current listing of Bay-area powwows. Another must-see is Virginia's annual tribute ceremony. Based on the 1677 Treaty of Middle Plantation, it requires "every Indian King and Queen in the Month of March" to pay "the accustomed Tribute of Twenty Beaver Skins" to the governor as a sign of peace and mutual protection with England's King Charles II. Now celebrated near Thanksgiving, and with deer rather than beaver, it provides living proof of the continued resiliency of Bay tribes.

A DEEPER DIVE

Chesapeake Bay Program. "Indigenous Peoples of the Chesapeake" (2020). www.chesapeakebay.net/discover/history/archaeology_and_native_americans.

Diamond, J. M. *Guns, Germs, and Steel: The Fates of Human Societies* (New York: W.W. Norton, 1997).

Egloff, K., and D. Woodward. *First People: The Early Indians of Virginia* (Charlottesville, VA: University of Virginia Press, 2006).

Gowder, P. "Powwows" (2020). www.powwows.com.

Helm, J. "A Thanksgiving Ritual: Two Virginia Tribes Present Deer to Governor as Tribute." *Washington Post* (Washington, DC, 2015).

Jansen, A. "Shell Middens and Human Technologies as a Historical Baseline for the Chesapeake Bay, USA." *North American Archaeologist*, 39(1) (2018). 10.1177/0197693117753333.

Jenkins, J. A., and M. D. Gallivan. "Shell on Earth: Oyster Harvesting, Consumption, and Deposition Practices in the Powhatan Chesapeake." *The Journal of Island and Coastal Archaeology* (2019). 10.1080/15564894.2019.1643430.

Lubosky, E. "In the Chesapeake Bay, Shell Mounds Show a Long History of Sustainable Oyster Harvests." *Hakai* (2018).

Miller, H. M. "Living along the 'Great Shellfish Bay': The Relationship Between Pre-historic Peoples and the Chesapeake." *Discovering the Chesapeake: The History of an Ecosystem.* P. D. Curtin, G. S. Brush, and G. W. Fisher (eds.) (Baltimore: The Johns Hopkins University Press, 2001).

Rick, T., and G. Waselkov. "Shellfish Gathering and Shell Midden Archaeology Revisited: Chronology and Taphonomy at White Oak Point, Potomac River Estuary, Virginia." *The Journal of Island and Coastal Archaeology*, 10 (2015). 10.1080/15564894.2014.967896.

Rountree, H. *The Powhatan Indians of Virginia: Their Traditional Culture.* The Civilization of the American Indian Series (Norman, OK: University of Oklahoma Press, 1989).

Rountree, H. C., W. E. Clark, and K. Mountford. *John Smith's Chesapeake Voyages, 1607–1609* (Charlottesville and London: The University of Virginia Press, 2007).

Smith, J. *The Generall Historie of Virginia, 1624* (London: Printed by I. D. and I. H. for Michael Sparkes).

Smolek, M., et al. "Projectile Points. Diagnostic Artifacts in Maryland 2002." https://apps.jefpat.maryland.gov/diagnostic/ProjectilePoints/index-projectile points.html.

Sperling, S. T. "The Middle Woodland Period in Central Maryland: A Fresh Look at Old Questions." *Maryland Archaeology*, 44(1) (2008).

Stewart, R. M. "The Status of Woodland Prehistory in the Middle Atlantic Region." *Archaeology of Eastern North America*, 23 (1995).

The Pamunkey Indian Tribe. Official Tribal Website (2020). http://pamunkey .org.

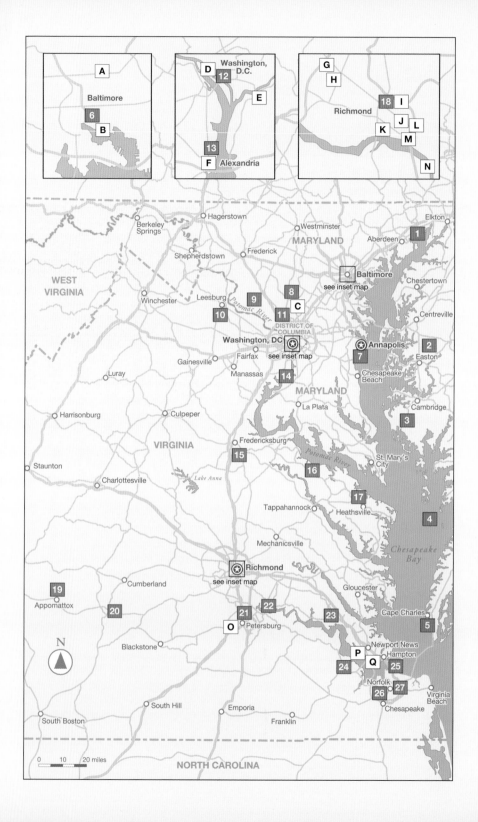

African-American History

No book that touches on the history of the Chesapeake would be complete without mentioning the trials and tribulations of its African-American population, or the triumph of their many achievements in the face of slavery and ongoing racism. Here we highlight some of the Bay's many Black-themed historic sites and museums.

1. Havre de Grace Maritime Museum (Underground Railroad Exhibit)
2. Frederick Douglass Park on the Tuckahoe
3. Harriet Tubman Underground Railroad National Historical Park
4. Tangier History Museum
5. Cape Charles Rosenwald School
6. Reginald F. Lewis Museum
   A. Frederick Douglass-Isaac Myers Maritime Park
   B. The National Great Blacks in Wax Museum
7. Banneker-Douglass Museum
8. Oakley Cabin African American Museum & Park
9. Button Farm Living History Center
10. Thomas Balch Library
11. Josiah Henson Museum & Park
   C. Matthew Henson State Park
12. National Museum of African American History and Culture
   D. Lincoln Memorial
   E. Frederick Douglass National Historic Site
13. Alexandria Black History Museum
   F. Contrabands and Freedmen Cemetery
14. George Washington's Mount Vernon
15. Historic Moncure Conway House
16. Stratford Hall Visitor Center
17. Holley Graded School
18. Black History Museum and Cultural Center of Virginia
   G. Arthur Ashe Monument
   H. Virginia Museum of History & Culture
   I. Maggie L Walker National Historic Site
   J. Virginia Civil Rights Monument
   K. American Civil War Museum— Historic Tredegar
   L. Lumpkin's Slave Jail
   M. Box Brown Plaza
   N. Richmond Slave Trail
19. Appomattox Court House National Historical Park
20. Robert Russa Moton Museum
21. Pocahontas Island Black History Museum
   O. Petersburg City Hall
22. Berkeley Plantation
23. Colonial Williamsburg Historic Area
24. The Schoolhouse Museum
25. Fort Monroe National Monument (Old Point Comfort)
   P. Emancipation Oak
   Q. Hampton History Museum
26. Portsmouth Community Library Museum
27. Attucks Theatre

The slave ship *Diligente*.

THE CHESAPEAKE BOOKENDS AMERICAN SLAVERY in both time and space. In August 1619, the first enslaved Africans arrived at Point Comfort, a sandy spit where the James River enters the Bay. On April 9, 1865, the Army of Northern Virginia surrendered to Union forces just 2 miles from the headwaters of a James tributary, the Appomattox River. For 246 years the streams of the Bay watershed bore witness to the unpaid labor that helped build a nation, carrying the sweat and tears of the enslaved back down to the very spot where all their heartbreak—and resiliency—began.

The northern end of the Bay, where the Susquehanna River enters at Havre de Grace, was a key stop on the Underground Railroad. Here, slaves escaping from western Maryland and Virginia could ferry across the river to reach the free state of Pennsylvania. Nearby, Harriet Tubman led small groups to freedom in Philadelphia, journeying from the marshlands of the Bayside Eastern Shore, across the Chesapeake & Delaware Canal, and along the backroads that bisect the narrow isthmus between the two bays.

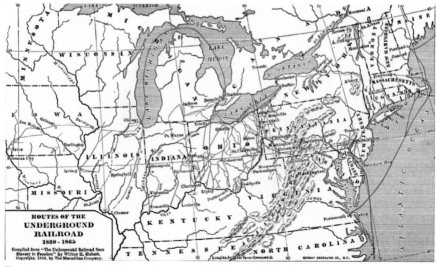

The northern end of Chesapeake Bay was a key stop on the Underground Railroad.

Harriet Tubman (left) led enslaved people to freedom along the eastern shore of Chesapeake Bay.

Frederick Douglass, here with his grandson, lived on a bluff above the Anacostia River near Washington, DC.

A number of historical sites offer visitors an opportunity to reflect on slavery and the experiences of enslaved Americans. What is now Old Point Comfort lies within Fort Monroe National Monument, which offers Black Cultural Tours along with views of Jefferson Davis's prison cell and quarters occupied by Abraham Lincoln in 1862. At Appomattox Court House National Historical Park, interpreters discuss the last days of the Civil War. The Harriet Tubman Underground Railroad Visitor Center on Maryland's Eastern Shore commemorates her life's incredible journey. It is part of a 125-mile self-guided driving tour of thirty-six significant sites. Virginia likewise offers a self-guided African American Historic Sites Trail.

Of course, the racism at the heart of slavery did not end in 1865. The Bay's farm fields, woodlots, working waterfronts, and fishing grounds have also borne witness to the promise of Reconstruction, the resurgence of the slaveholder mentality via the "Lost Cause" and "Jim Crow," and the achievements of the civil rights era. The Lincoln Memorial, site of Martin Luther King's famous "I Have a Dream" speech, rises just yards from the Potomac River, with views of the Tidal Basin and Washington Channel, both reclaimed from Bay marshland. The home of freedman and abolitionist Frederick Douglass—now a National Historic Site—sits on a nearby bluff above the Anacostia River. During the oyster boom of the 1880s, Blacks accounted for eight of every ten York River watermen, and dominated other Bay fisheries as well. The Northern Neck Chantey Singers continue to perform their work songs—a tradition of the preindustrial menhaden fishery—around the Bay and nation.

African Americans played a large role in the early menhaden fishery.

An African-American oyster tonger sells his catch to a Chesapeake Bay buyboat.

Today the Bay region remains a focal point for the struggle of Black Americans to be fully and fairly included in the American fabric. As this book goes to print, monuments to Confederate leaders fall before cheering crowds in Richmond, while peaceful protesters chant "Black Lives Matter" along the shores of the Potomac in Washington, DC. Author Clint Smith describes our current moment as "filled with rage, reckoning, and possibility." Visits to the Bay's many African-American milestones—sites of both historical reckoning and future possibility—afford unique opportunities to better understand this moment and to push it forward in a better direction.

The map on page 338 shows other historical sites with artifacts and programs relating to the history of slavery and the African-American experience.

A DEEPER DIVE

Chesapeake Bay Program. "African Americans in the Chesapeake" (2020). www.chesapeakebay.net/discover/history/african_americans_in_the _chesapeake_region.

Erickson, M. S. J. "Gateway to Freedom: Black Watermen Chart Course for Success on Hampton Roads Waterways." *Daily Press* (Newport News, VA: Tribune Publishing Co., 2018).

Isaac, R. *Landon Carter's Uneasy Kingdom: Revolution and Rebellion on a Virginia Plantation* (Oxford University Press, 2004).

Maryland Office of Tourism. "Discover Maryland's African-American History (2020). www.visitmaryland.org/list/discover-marylands-african-american -history.

McClure, J. "Underground Railroad on the Susquehanna: From Havre de Grace, Md., to Cooperstown, N.Y." *York Daily Record* (York, PA: USA Today Network, 2014).

Smith, C. "Looking for Frederick Douglass." *The Atlantic* (New York, 2020).

Stodghill, R. "Harriet Tubman's Path to Freedom." *New York Times* (2017).

Thompson, K. A. "A Brief History of Black People and the Chesapeake Bay." *Ocean Currents* (Washington, DC: Ocean Conservancy, 2019).

Virginia Folklife Program. "Northern Neck Chantey Singers and Lewis R. Blackwell Jr." (2011). https://virginiafolklife.org/sights-sounds/ northern-neck-chantey-singers-and-lewis-r-blackwell-jr.

Virginia Tourism Corporation. "African American Historic Sites Trail" (2020). www.virginia.org/blackhistoryattractions.

Visit Baltimore. "Baltimore's African American Culture" (2020). https://baltimore.org/guides/guide-to-baltimores-african-american-culture.

Vlach, J. M. "Boatbuilding." *The Afro-American Tradition in Decorative Arts*. Cleveland Museum of Art (ed.) (Athens, GA: University of Georgia Press, 1990).

Whitley, D. "Virginia, USA: Presidential Plantations with a Dark Past." *Traveller* (Sydney, Australia, 2015).

The Once AND
Future Bay

> There is but one entrance by Sea into this Country, and that is at the mouth of a very goodly Bay . . . heaven & earth never agreed better to frame a place for man's habitation.
>
> —*Capt. John Smith, 1624*

ON AUGUST 12, 1975, *The Progress-Index* of Petersburg, Virginia, broke a story describing how five workers at a chemical plant in nearby Hopewell had been hospitalized due to exposure to an ant and roach poison known as Kepone. Later that year, Governor Mills Godwin banned fishing in 100 miles of the James River between Richmond and the Chesapeake Bay, after officials discovered the plant's owner, Allied Chemical, was dumping the pesticide into the water, where it was building up in the meat of fish and oysters. Some parts of the ban lasted more than a decade, devastating the region's commercial and recreational fisheries.

On the nearby Elizabeth River, and at the other end of the Bay in Baltimore Harbor, two companies had for decades been preserving wood pilings with creosote and then leaving them on docks to drip-dry into the water. The resulting contamination was so severe that more than half the mummichogs at the Virginia site developed liver cancer. Restrictions on harvesting oysters or consuming striped bass from these waters remain today.

THE GOOD NEWS

Incidents like these were repeated at factories, military bases, landfills, and other sites across the Bay watershed, United States, and world throughout the nineteenth and twentieth centuries. They were widely accepted as "the price of progress" during the Industrial Revolution, until the scope of their impacts began to permeate public consciousness in the 1960s and 1970s. That concern ultimately led Congress to pass a string of landmark environmental laws, including the Clean Water Act of 1972, the Endangered Species Act of 1973, and the CERCLA "Superfund" law of 1980.

Today these laws continue to protect the Bay and its wildlife. The specter of a waste pipe spewing pollutants directly into a local waterway is largely a past concern. New construction requires an Environmental Impact Statement to gauge impacts on any endangered or threatened species. Severely polluted Superfund sites within the Bay watershed—thirty-four in Virginia, twenty-five in Maryland, twenty-four in Pennsylvania, nine in New York, and one each in Delaware and Washington, DC—are slowly being restored.

The Chesapeake Bay Program—a unique partnership among the Bay states, the US Environmental Protection Agency, academic institutions, and private organizations—works to implement the Chesapeake Bay Agreement of 1983, which has been amended and strengthened in 1987, 2000, 2010, and again in 2014. Its goal is to use a

Renee Dallman of Williamsburg, Virginia, plants oyster spat as part of a volunteer restoration program organized by the Chesapeake Bay Foundation.

"cooperative approach" to "address the extent, complexity, and sources of pollutants" in order to reverse "an historical decline in the living resources of the Chesapeake Bay."

Private organizations have also jumped in, with staff and volunteers working tirelessly to monitor, clean, and restore all manner of Bay-scapes, from beaches and tidal creeks to farm fields and working waterfronts. There are now voluntary "Clean Marina" programs in all Bay states; nineteen "Riverkeeper" groups in the Bay watershed with 18,000 volunteer supporters; and numerous "Clean-Up Days" that remove tons of trash and plastic each year. The nonprofit Chesapeake Bay Foundation, with 300,000 members, is a major voice for Bay health and restoration.

RUNNING IN PLACE

Yet despite all these efforts, the Chesapeake Bay Watershed Report Card—a barometer of Bay health issued annually by the University of Maryland Center for Environmental Science—remains mired in the D to C range, grades you wouldn't crow about at home to Mom and Dad.

Two intertwined concepts—one literary, one scientific—help explain this paradox. The first is based on a quote from the Red Queen in Lewis Carroll's *Through the Looking-Glass*, who tells Alice that in her new dreamscape, "it takes all the running you can do, just to keep in the same place." The second is the notion of a shifting baseline, which we'll discuss in a moment.

First to our Red Queen. All the grueling "running" we've done to improve Bay health—the hard-won legislation, court battles, and on-the-ground clean-up and

restoration—is barely enough to keep pace with the ever-growing sprawl of people and asphalt across the Chesapeake watershed. Indeed, in many ways, our efforts to cut "point-source pollution" was the easy part. Reducing contamination from the Kepone plant in Hopewell, the Mid-Atlantic Wood Preservers facility in Baltimore, the Little Creek Naval Base in Norfolk, or the Blue Plains Wastewater Treatment Plant in Washington, DC, may have cost decades of effort and billions of dollars, but they were discrete challenges of limited geographic scope. Our challenge now is nothing less than redirecting the American Dream of economic freedom and unfettered mobility into a less-malignant cancer on the Bay landscape.

One way to grasp the magnitude of this challenge is to read "The evolution of urban sprawl: Evidence of spatial heterogeneity and increasing land fragmentation" in the *Proceedings of the National Academy of Sciences*. Or you could simply drive south on MD 2 from Annapolis to Solomons, Maryland. Either way, you'll quickly discover the inescapable reality that the state's population grew by 39 percent between 1973 and 2000, and continues apace. Even more troubling for Bay health is that the acreage of "developed" land in Maryland multiplied more than three times faster, by 154 percent, as "McMansions" and hobby farms fragmented the forest into ever smaller bits. A drive from Newport News to Richmond in Virginia shows this isn't just a Maryland issue.

SHIFTING BASELINES: LOOKING BACK

Equally troubling is that for those involved, each freshly cleared lot and newly constructed rancher truly seems a piece of paradise: their own delicious taste of the Bay watershed, with a raccoon in the back yard and a great blue heron in the nearby marsh. But here is where the baseline shifts. Like a shopper who enjoys the taste of a store-bought tomato because they've never savored the glory of one just plucked from the garden, most of today's residents have little idea that what they consider a healthy, teeming

Bay is but a pale shadow of its former glory. Victor Kennedy of the Chesapeake Biological Laboratory has written an entire book chronicling this "generational amnesia."

Consider just a few of his then-and-now comparisons. In 1775 Reverend Andrew Burnaby noted that "some gentleman in canoes" caught more than 600 sturgeon in a single day in the Potomac River. Today, Chesapeake sturgeon are listed as an endangered species. In 1896 the Bay's annual harvest of river herring was 30 million pounds. In 1980, it was 1 million, and in 2005 these fishes were listed as "depleted." The inland fishery for the closely related American shad—a species abundant enough to feed the Continental Army at Valley Forge during the winter of 1777–78—was closed in 1994 due to low shad stocks and remains so today.

In the late 1880s, the Bay's oyster harvest peaked at 8-10 million bushels per year. Today it's a few hundred thousand. In the early 1800s, blue crabs were so abundant there was no market for them; watermen would cast Jimmies and sooks onshore to die

In the 1880s, the Bay's annual oyster harvest would fill an NFL stadium to the brim.

when they fouled their fishing nets. In 2008 the United States declared the Bay's blue crab fishery a disaster based on a decade-long decline in population and harvest, and the winter fishery remains closed.

In 1676 surgeon Thomas Glover reported "so many wild fowl as in winter time they do in some places cover the water for two miles," and Dutchman Jasper Danckaerts complained of losing sleep to the "screeching of the wild geese." In 1722 Robert Beverly marveled at the multitudes of swans, geese, canvasback ducks, and other waterfowl, boasting, "I am but a small sportsman, yet with a fowling piece I have killed above 20 of them at a shot."

In the mid-1800s, diamondback terrapins were so abundant that John Clayton, secretary of state for President Zachary Taylor, would buy an oxcart load for "one or two dollars," then shovel them alive into his cellar for later eating. In 1890 harvest of these "Baltimore Terrapins," as described on hotel menus across the region, peaked at 220,000 pounds. In 2007 Maryland banned the terrapin harvest due to low numbers. Virginia also has a harvest ban, and considers the Commonwealth's population as "near threatened."

In an 1859 novel, James Hungerford described the waters of Maryland's Patuxent River as "so transparent . . . that far out from the shore you may see, in the openings of the sea-weed forest on its bottom the flashing sides of the finny tribes as they glide over the pearly sands." In Gilbert Klingel's classic 1951 book *The Bay*, he reports visibility of 6 feet or more during several trips beneath the Chesapeake's waters in a diving bell and homemade "Bentharium." Today, Bay water is typically so clouded by sediment and algae that visibility is measured in inches.

The point of these rather dispiriting comparisons is not to dishearten but to provide context for the wonder we all feel when gazing out on a beautiful Bay-scape, encountering a drove of fiddler crabs, or savoring a plate of half-shell oysters. Only by recognizing that the Bay was once far more bounteous can we aspire to restore it to at least some semblance of its former glory.

An example of restoration efforts and their challenges comes from the world of seagrass. Historical accounts suggest the prehistoric Bay held at least 600,000 acres of submerged aquatic vegetation, or SAV. Careful study of aerial photos from the mid-1900s suggests SAV coverage had by then decreased to slightly more than 200,000 acres. The low point for Bay SAV likely occurred in 1978, at approximately 40,000 acres. The current restoration goal is 185,000 acres, in recognition that Bay water is now too cloudy to allow sunlight to penetrate deeper than 3 feet. Recent clean-up efforts have aided a resurgence to around 100,000 acres—a real success, but only half the Bay's already conservative restoration goal.

SHIFTING BASELINES: LOOKING FORWARD

Perhaps even more troubling than the historical decline in Bay health is the growing realization that population growth, sprawl, and climate change are likely to shift Bay baselines even further as we move into the future.

Robert McConnell, an ecologist at the University of Mary Washington, calculates that the Bay's human-carrying capacity is 8 million. That's the number of people it can support at current levels of consumption without irreversible degradation. Unfortunately, the human population of the Bay watershed is already at 18.2 million, and is predicted to reach 21 million by 2040. That's an increase of 15 percent in less than 20 years, on top of a doubling in the watershed's population between 1950 and 2017. And as we've seen, unless housing patterns change, this growth will clear and fragment an even greater percentage of what is now green space. As parking lots and fertilized lawns replace forests and meadows, runoff of sediments and excess nutrients will further cloud Bay waters.

These changes will play out against the backdrop of a rapidly warming planet. A 2010 synopsis of climate-change impacts to the Bay region paints a troubling picture. Air temperatures are forecast to increase an additional 3.5–9 degrees Fahrenheit by 2070, while sea level is projected to rise an extra 1.7 feet by 2050 and 5.2 feet by 2100. Bay water temperatures, which rose by about 2 degrees Fahrenheit between the 1960s and 1990s, will continue warming in the coming decades. Precipitation and runoff are expected to become more episodic, with harder rains and more intense storms punctuating deeper droughts. Low-oxygen "dead zones" are likely to increase in size, intensity, and duration, while Bay waters grow more acidic.

There may be some "winners" as the Bay warms, as subtropical species such as white shrimp, spadefish, and drums expand their range or seasonality northward. Unfortunately, these "winners" might also include new or supercharged parasites and diseases—including the oyster pathogens MSX (multinuclear sphere X) and Dermo (*Perkinsus marinus*), which are known to flourish in warmer waters.

For most Bay species, climate change will be yet another stressor. Eelgrass and soft clams are already near their upper temperature limit in the Bay and will likely disappear if summer water temperatures remain near 90°F for prolonged periods, while temperate fishes such as yellow and white perch, black sea bass, tautog, flounder, and scup will be severely stressed. Striped bass and Atlantic sturgeon will face a "squeeze"— too much warmth in summer's surface waters and not enough oxygen in the deeper, cooler water where they would normally take refuge or feed.

These stresses will be particularly troublesome for the many species that use the Bay as a seasonal nursery. There is growing evidence that some hungry migrants are arriving in the Bay after their planktonic prey have already bloomed due to an earlier, warmer spring, whereas fish and shellfish larvae are known to be more sensitive to ocean acidity than their parents. The growing season in the Bay region has increased by more than a month during the last century.

BETTER MANAGEMENT PRACTICES

What can we do to help the Bay avoid this dismal future? The websites of the Chesapeake Bay Program and Chesapeake Bay Foundation are two excellent sources for

Auto exhaust is a major source of Bay pollution.

the many meaningful steps we can each take to enhance Bay health. Here I focus on just a few instances where the link between our collective actions and Bay health may not be as obvious.

Nutrient pollution is the biggest problem facing the Bay. Using less fertilizer on our yards and farms, applying it more carefully to minimize runoff, and replacing grass with native vegetation are three clear ways to reduce the Bay's nitrogen load. A less obvious solution is to reduce our driving. Scientists estimate that more than a third of the Bay's nitrogen pollution comes from the air, with a large part of that from vehicle exhaust. By biking, carpooling, and reducing trips, we can each help the Bay keep to its "pollution diet."

Another option is to become involved in local government, either by speaking up at meetings or running for office. While federal legislation such as the Clean Water Act is imperative for restoring Bay health, where the rubber really meets the road is in the day-to-day land-use decisions made by county boards, city councils, and other local offices. Threats to Bay health have been compared to "death by a thousand paper cuts," in reference to the enormous cumulative impacts of seemingly minor individual actions—a bulkhead built here, a tree cut there. But this can work in the other direction as well: One hour spent arguing against a rezoning motion at your county's Board of Supervisor's meeting can have a huge impact when multiplied by similar citizen action across the countless jurisdictions that control land use within the Bay watershed.

A final, perhaps quixotic suggestion is to pay closer attention to the language used to discuss Bay issues. I earlier put quotations around land "development." When "developers" "develop" a 500-acre "parcel," it implies the land was previously undeveloped. I'm sure that would be news to a wise old owl as it watches chain saws fell centuries-old oaks and tuliptrees, while bulldozers scrape redbuds, ferns, mosses, and the living soil itself from the forest floor, forcing squirrels, raccoons, turtles, beetles, and myriad other creatures away from an intricate dance that had developed over countless millennia.

And last to "BMP." You are sure to encounter this term when speaking with traffic engineers, county administrators, and others involved in land-use planning. Short for "best management practice," it refers to retention ponds, constructed wetlands, and other mechanisms designed to minimize human destruction of natural habitats. This term is a misnomer. It should be "*better* management practice," as the *best* management practice isn't to build an artificial pond to slow runoff from a new eight-lane

freeway, but to refrain from widening the road in the first place. A retention pond or constructed wetland is indeed better for Bay health than a concrete spillway, but it will never provide the ecosystem services that forests and meadows offer up for free.

The hard truth is that we can employ all the BMPs we want, but unless we fundamentally change our behaviors by consuming less and limiting suburban sprawl, it will all be for naught. As Pogo famously said, "We have met the enemy, and he is us." Let us not be our own enemies.

CHESAPEAKE BAY, JANUARY 1, 2050

You have woken early and stepped to your kitchen window to look out on the world at the dawn of a new year. What will you see? And how will it make you feel? It all depends on how we treat the Chesapeake and its watershed today and for all its tomorrows.

Australian Glenn Albrecht has coined the term "solastalgia" to describe the "existential melancholia experienced with the desolation of a loved home environment" (in his case, due to coal mining). He distinguished this from "nostalgia," a "homesick" emotion felt when one has left an area; and "topophilia," coined by geographer Yi-Fu Tuan to describe the love of place and landscape.

By working together, we can ensure that the Chesapeake Bay will still be a place to inspire not solastalgia but topophilia in 2050.

A DEEPER DIVE

Albrecht, G. (2012). "The Age of Solastalgia." *The Conversation.*
https://theconversation.com/the-age-of-solastalgia-8337.

Brush, G. S., and W. B. Hilgartner. "Paleoecology of Submerged Macrophytes in the Upper Chesapeake Bay." *Ecological Monographs* 70(4), 2000: 645–67.

England, E. "Toxic Blood Levels Hospitalize 5 Plant Employees." *The Progress-Index.* Petersburg, VA, The Progress-Index, 1975: 1.

Hungerford, J. E. (1859). *The Old Plantation and What I Gathered There in an Autumn Month.* New York, Harper & Brothers, 1859.

Integration & Application Network. "Chesapeake Bay Report Card." https://ecoreportcard.org/report-cards/chesapeake-bay.

Irwin, E. G., and N. E. Bockstael. "The Evolution of Urban Sprawl: Evidence of Spatial Heterogeneity and Increasing Land Fragmentation." *Proceedings of the National Academy of Sciences* 104(52), 2007: 20672.

Kennedy, V. S. *Shifting Baselines in the Chesapeake Bay: An Environmental History.* Baltimore: Johns Hopkins University Press, 2018.

Klingel, G. *The Bay.* Baltimore and London: The Johns Hopkins University Press, 1951.

McConnell, R. L. "The Human Population Carrying Capacity of the Chesapeake Bay Watershed: A Preliminary Analysis." *Population and Environment* 16(4), 1995: 335–51.

Moore, K. A., D. J. Wilcox, B. Anderson, T. A. Parham, and M. D. Naylor. *Analysis of Submerged Aquatic Vegetation (SAV) in the Potomac River and Analysis of Bay-wide SAV Data to Establish a New Acreage Goal.* Annapolis, MD: Chesapeake Bay Program, 2004. Final Report: CB983627-01: 25.

Najjar, R. G. et al. "Potential Climate-Change Impacts on the Chesapeake Bay." *Estuarine, Coastal and Shelf Science* 86, 2010: 1–20.

Singer, B., L. Gibbs, J. Kuiphoff and M. Yu. (2014). "ToxicSites: Superfund." www.toxicsites.us/index.php.

Waterkeeper Alliance. "Chesapeake Bay." https://waterkeeper.org/waterkeeper/?region=chesapeake.

Wilson, I., and T. Tuberville. *Virginia's Precious Heritage: A Report on the Status of Virginia's Natural Communities, Plants, and Animals, and a Plan for Preserving Virginia's Natural Heritage Resources*. Richmond, VA: Virginia Department of Conservation and Recreation Division of Natural Heritage, 2003: 82.

Wojdylo, J., W. K. Vogelbein, L. Bain, and C. Rice (2016). "AHR-Related Activities in a Creosote-Adapted Population of Adult Atlantic Killifish, Fundulus heteroclitus, Two Decades Post–EPA Superfund Status at the Atlantic Wood Site, Portsmouth, VA USA." *Aquatic Toxicology* 177: 74–85.

INDEX

PHOTO CREDITS

All uncredited photos were taken by the author.

p. X Smithsonian National Museum of Natural History; **p. XI** Chesapeake Bay Foundation; **p. XV** (bottom) Donglai Gong/Virginia Institute of Marine Science; **p. XVII** Angie Wei/Chesapeake Bay Program; **p. 4** Library of Congress Prints and Photographs Division; **p. 7** (top) Library of Congress, Geography and Map Division; (bottom) Library of Congress; **p. 8** (bottom) Library of Congress from a print in *Harper's Weekly*; **p. 10** Virginia Institute of Marine Science; **p. 11** (top) Library of Congress; **p. 12** (top) Library of Congress; (bottom) Library of Congress, Geography and Map Division; **p. 13** (top) Library of Congress, Geography and Map Division; **p. 15** (top) Jeffery Goldman; **p. 16** Summer M. Anderson/US Navy; **p. 24** Library of Congress; **p. 25** Jamestown-Yorktown Foundation; **p. 29** (top) Ken Moore/ Virginia Institute of Marine Science; (bottom) Peter Bergstrom/NOAA; **p. 30** (top left) Ryan Hagerty/USFWS; (top right) Ken Moore/Virginia Institute of Marine Science; (middle) Christian Fischer; (bottom) Smithsonian National Museum of Natural History; **p. 31** Susan Maples; **p. 32** Donglai Gong/Virginia Institute of Marine Science; **p. 33** (all photos) Multispecies Research Group/Virginia Institute of Marine Science; **p. 34** (top) Stephanie Wilson/Virginia Institute of Marine Science; (bottom) Deborah Steinberg/VIMS; **p. 35** (middle) Multispecies Research Group/ Virginia Institute of Marine Science; (bottom) Robert Fisher/VIMS; **p. 36** (Atlantic Croaker, Black Drum, Red Drum, Northern Kingfish, Spot) Rob Aguilar/Smithsonian Environmental Research Center; (Weakfish) Alex Roukis; **p. 37** (top) NOAA Fisheries; (middle) Northeast Fisheries Science Center/NOAA; (bottom) Multispecies Research Group/Virginia Institute of Marine Science; **p. 38** (left) Multispecies Research Group/Virginia Institute of Marine Science; **p. 40** (bottom left) Kristen Sharpe/ Virginia Institute of Marine Science; **p. 41** (top) Aimee Halvorson/Virginia Institute of Marine Science; (bottom) Juvenile Fish and Blue Crab Survey/VIMS; **p. 42** (top) Brett Billings/US Fish and Wildlife Service; (bottom) Eric Hilton/Virginia Institute of Marine Science; **p. 43** (bottom) Virginia Institute of Marine Science; **p. 44** Ryan Hagerty/US Fish and Wildlife Service; **p. 46-48** all shark illustrations by Marc Dando; **p. 49** (top) Robert J. Varnon; **p. 50-51** (all photos) Lissa Fahlman; **p. 52-53** Danielle Jones/US Navy; **p. 54** (all photos) US Fish and Wildlife Service; **p. 55** (top left) US Fish and Wildlife Service; **p. 56** (all photos) David Rabon, US Fish and Wildlife Service; **p. 57** (bottom) Amanda Bromilow/Virginia Institute of Marine Science; **p. 58** (top) Laura Beauregard/US Fish and Wildlife Service; (bottom) Philippe Bourjon; **p. 67–77** all vessel illustrations by Claire McCracken; **p. 76** (bottom) courtesy of the Virginia Institute of Marine Science; **p. 78** Acroterion/Wikimedia Commons; **p. 81** Taylor Made; **p. 82** Virginia Institute of Marine Science; **p. 85** (left) Wikimedia Commons; **p. 88** (top) Nate Littlejohn/US Coast Guard; (bottom) A. Pasek, Chesapeake Chapter,

US Lighthouse Society; **p. 89** (top) Library of Congress Prints and Photographs Division; (bottom) US Environmental Protection Agency; **p. 90** A. Pasek, Chesapeake Chapter, US Lighthouse Society; **p. 91** A. Pasek, Chesapeake Chapter, US Lighthouse Society; **p. 105** (top) Chris Katella/Virginia Institute of Marine Science; **p. 109** (left) Scott Clark; (right) US National Herbarium; **p. 113** (bottom) Reba Turner/Virginia Institute of Marine Science; **p. 118** (middle) Smithsonian National Museum of Natural History; (bottom) Hans Hillewaert. **p. 121** (bottom right) Max Malmquist; **p. 123** (bottom right) Michael Malmquist; **p. 124** (both photos) Patrick Bloodgood/ US Army Corps of Engineers; **p. 125** (top) Scott Hardaway/Virginia Institute of Marine Science; **p. 129** Raeanna Morgan /US Naval Research Laboratory; **p. 137** April Bahen/CBNERRVA; **p. 141** Serina Whittyngham/Virginia Institute of Marine Science; **p. 159** (both photos) Center for Coastal Resources Management/Virginia Institute of Marine Science; **p. 173** (bottom left) painting by Mary Vaux Walcott courtesy of Smithsonian American Art Museum; **p. 174** (top) Troy Tuckey/Virginia Institute of Marine Science; (middle) illustration by Duane Raver courtesy of US Fish and Wildlife Service; **p. 175** all illustrations by Duane Raver courtesy of US Fish and Wildlife Service; **p. 176** Library of Congress; **p. 196** (top) Michael Malmquist; **p. 198** (top) Skip Brown/Smithsonian's National Zoo; **p. 200** (top) Jessie Cohen/ Smithsonian's National Zoo; **p. 203** (both photos) Smithsonian American Art Museum; **p. 213** Library of Congress; **p. 214** (top) Forest History Society, Durham, N.C; **p. 218** (top) Library of Congress; (bottom) Forest History Society, Durham, NC; **p. 219** (top) painting by Mary Vaux Walcott courtesy of Smithsonian American Art Museum; (bottom) Forest History Society, Durham, NC; **p. 229** (all photos) Mark Strong/Smithsonian National Museum of Natural History; **p. 250** (bottom photos) Michael Malmquist; **p. 274** Library of Congress; **p. 276** Virginia Port Authority; **p. 278** Library of Congress, Geography and Map Division; **p. 279** (top) Library of Congress; (bottom) Smithsonian American Art Museum; **p. 280** Christopher B. Stoltz/US Navy; **p. 281** Library of Congress Rare Book and Special Collections; **p. 290** Lisa Kellogg/Virginia Institute of Marine Science; **p. 296** (top) Amanda Boyd/ US Fish and Wildlife Service; **p. 298** (both photos) Lissa Fahlman; **p. 302** Christopher B. Stoltz/US Navy; **p. 303** (bottom) National Park Service; **p. 304** US Army Corps of Engineers; **p. 305** (top) Virginia Port Authority; **p. 309** (both photos) John Whalen/ Huntington Ingalls Industries; **p. 310** Virginia Port Authority; **p. 311** (both photos) Donald Grady Shomette/NOAA; **p. 313** Summer M. Anderson/US Navy; **p. 314** (top) Charles A. Ordoqui/US Navy; (bottom) Will Tonacchio/US Navy; **p. 316** Lt. Patrick Evans/US Navy; **p. 317** (top) Don S. Montgomery/US Navy; (bottom) Lt. Patrick Evans/US Navy; **p. 327** (both photos) Stephen Godfrey, Calvert Marine Museum; **p. 328** (both photos) Stephen Godfrey, Calvert Marine Museum; **p. 330-331** Scurlock Studio Records, Archives Center, National Museum of American History, Smithsonian Institution; **p. 334** (all photos) Maryland Archaeological Conservation Laboratory, Jefferson Patterson Park and Museum; **p. 335** (top) Library of Congress;

ACKNOWLEDGMENTS

Thanks to Carl Hershner, David Johnson, Rowan Lockwood, Lauri Malmquist, Mike Malmquist, and Sheldon Steinberg for their early reviews. Any remaining errors are the responsibility of the author. Special thanks to illustrator Claire McCracken for generously sharing her lovely ship illustrations and to Susan Stein for her figure preparations. Thanks also to those who assisted me in sourcing images: Maria Alvarez (Chesapeake Chapter, US Lighthouse Society); Hilary Cooley (Bruton Parish Church); Carol Coughlin (Hargis Library, Virginia Institute of Marine Science); Mark Howell and Tracy Perkins (Jamestown-Yorktown Foundation); Eben Lehman (Forest History Society); Kristen Minogue (Smithsonian Environmental Research Center); Eden Orelove (Smithsonian Office of the CIO), Kay Peterson (National Museum of American History), and Shaune Thomas and Carla Welsh (Virginia Port Authority). Other image contributors are acknowledged in the photo credits. My final thanks are to Sarah Parke, Meredith Dias, Melissa Evarts, and others at Globe Pequot for their help in design and publication. I dedicate this book to all those working to conserve and restore the Chesapeake Bay ecosystem.

ABOUT THE AUTHOR

DR. DAVID MALMQUIST is the Director of News & Media Services at William & Mary's Virginia Institute of Marine Science, where he has spent the past 20 years reporting on research activities in and around the Chesapeake Bay and developing Bay-related web tools. He earned his PhD in Earth Science from the University of California, Santa Cruz. His career in science writing began with a mass-media fellowship at the *Dallas Morning News* through the American Association for the Advancement of Science, and continued as the Science Communications Manager for a partnership between climate scientists and insurers at the Bermuda Institute of Ocean Sciences. Malmquist, an award-winning photographer, lives near the shoreline of Chesapeake Bay in Williamsburg, Virginia, with his spouse, Deborah; sons, Sam and Ben; and black Lab, Oliver.